Waiting for
Rain

This book is dedicated to the memory of

Mindy Schachter Greenberg z"l
1963-2006

*Our beloved daughter-in-law, wife and
soul-mate of David, extraordinary mother of
Sacha, Keren, Itai, Yael, and Noam.
Mindy loved life and treasured her family above
all else. She lived her days to the fullest, with style,
beauty, class, and humor. Steeped in her Judaism, she
felt its full joy. Mindy remained deeply anchored to her
faith, never gave up hope and never stopped praying.
With her life, she inspired her family and friends forever.*

Blu and Yitz Greenberg

Bryna Jocheved Levy

Waiting for
Rain

Reflections at the
Turning of the Year

2008 • 5768
The Jewish Publication Society
Philadelphia

JPS is a nonprofit educational association and the oldest and foremost publisher of Judaica in English in North America. The mission of JPS is to enhance Jewish culture by promoting the dissemination of religious and secular works, in the United States and abroad, to all individuals and institutions interested in past and contemporary Jewish life.

The Jewish Publication Society
2100 Arch Street, 2nd floor
Philadelphia, PA 19103

Design and Composition by Pageworks

Manufactured in the United States of America

Library of Congress Cataloging-in-Publication Data

Levy, Bryna Jocheved.
    Waiting for rain : reflections at the turning of the year / Bryna Jocheved Levy.
    p. cm.
    Includes bibliographical references.
    ISBN-13: 978-0-8276-0841-2
    1. High Holidays—Meditations.   2. Hoshana Rabba—Meditations   3. Shemini Atzeret—Meditations   4. Simhat Torah—Meditations.   I. Title.
    BM693.H5L48 2008
    296.4'31—dc22
                                        2007043967

To Daniel,
with whom I waited for rain

Contents

Sunbeams

Waiting for Rain has been, and I aver to say that it will probably always be, a lifelong endeavor. The actual writing was undertaken over the course of the last five years, and so the multitude of students, teachers, family, and friends to whom I owe thanks is beyond accounting.

The mission of articulating my gratitude in words is impossible, and even the challenge of *ve-eleh shemot* ("these are the names"), that is, simply listing them, is easier said than done. At the great risk of leaving out many a blessed soul (please forgive me), I venture to mention a cherished few whose contribution to my life has been immeasurable.

But first I must thank the Jewish Publication Society for taking on the task of publishing my book. The technical nuts and bolts were not simple, given the ocean that separates Jerusalem from Philadelphia. The human predicament also presented a formidable challenge. So I thank Ellen Frankel, Rena Potok, Carol Hupping, and Janet Liss for their insight, editorial know-how, forbearance, and kindness. I also acknowledge the *Torah shel Hesed* of my esteemed colleagues who gave generously of their time and expertise to discuss or review ideas developed here: Professors Elie Assis, David Weiss HaLivni, Shnayer Z. Leiman, Pinchas Mandel, Yeshayahu Maori, and Daniel Schwartz, Rabbis Eliezer Schwartz and Schubert Spero, and Dr. Noam Zion.

Waiting for Rain would never have happened without Susan Handelman. Susie listened to the first *Hoshana Rabbah* lecture and insisted that the oral Torah be transposed into the written. As a precious and devoted sister, she encouraged me, with tremendous affection and authenticity, to undertake the project. Susie believes and promotes *torat nashim* (women's Torah), as she learned to do from her Rebbe, Rabbi Menachem Mendel Schneerson. Susie's very essence is *hen ve-sekhel tov b'einei Elohim ve-adam*—grace and good sense in the eyes of God and man. These gifts impel her, with a sublime measure of finesse, again and again, *le-hagdil Torah u-le-ha'adirah*—to amplify Torah and glorify her.

Susie shared with me a conversation she had with the Rebbe, when he inspired her to help others give birth to books that, otherwise unwritten, would be like children unborn. Susie, my blessing, which I extend to you with outstretched arms, is from the Book of Books: "Naomi took the child and held it to her bosom . . . And the women neighbors gave him a name saying, 'A son is born to Naomi!' " (Ruth 4:16–17).

As students, teachers, and *yedidot nefesh*, who played an active role in the writing of the book, Netta Shapira, Osnat Reinman, and Anne Gordon deserve honorable mention, one by one, verse by verse.

It is one thing to plant a garden; it is another to have someone else tend it. "God planted a garden in Eden and placed the one whom He had formed to till it and tend it there." I thank Netta Shapira for her role in cultivating my Torah garden at Matan.

"Jacob was left alone. And a man wrestled with him until the break of dawn" (Gen. 32:25). Osnat of Beit El: You have been my counterpoint to the tower of Babel. May you take hold of identity and destiny, and achieve harmony and reconciliation. As you ascend God's ladder with dancing angels, may you be granted vision like that of Jacob the dreamer of Beit El. May you see the incursion of the sacred into the profane. I pray that you and I will continue our existential stroll together. In the words of Rabbi Yehoshua ben Levi, "He wrestled with him like a man who embraces his friend"—or a woman who embraces hers.

"There is no end to the writing of books," however, at some point, there must be a *sof davar*—the last word. Without it, we would all still be waiting for rain. I thank my dear friend and *morat derekh*— pathfinder—Anne Gordon for her invaluable assistance. Anne, this verse is for you:

B'et tirtzeh le-deah ohavakh
B'libo ve-asher kizev ve-kihesh
She-al et libkha ki hu yehiyeh lakh
Kemo kosem u-vo nahesh tinahesh.

There is also no finish to the writing of symphonies, and mine would never have come to an end without a conductress. Anne, *La-minatzeah mizmor*, I thank you for your heart, with all my heart. *Ke-mayim ha-panim la-panim kein lev ha-adam le-adam.* "As face answers to face in water, so does one man's heart to another" (Prov. 27:19). *Mes remerciements* for reflecting with me at the turning of the year.

The gift of Matan is a treasure bestowed by the gift givers. Without them there is no beginning, and with them there is no end. The groundwork for *Waiting for Rain* was laid in Matan, the house of my midrash, and I soulfully wish to thank those whose lead I followed.

I thank my soul mates Suzanne and Michael Hochstein. Eleven years ago Suzy, Judy Kaufman-Hurwich (of blessed memory), and I sat over coffee and dreamed together of the future of women's Torah learning. Suzy and Mickey gave me the capacity to pave a wondrous path with colorful mosaics. They have not strayed from my side, despite the circuitous route.

My blessing to you is itself a mosaic, combining *Torah she-be-al peh* with *Torah she-bi-khetav*, voice with action, intention with intensity: "*Ve-khol banayikh limudei Ha-Shem ve-rav sh'lom banayikh. Al tikrei banayikh ela bonayikh. Shalom rav l'ohavei toratekha v'ein l'amo mikhshol. Yehi shalom be-helekh shalva be-arminotayikh.*"

One could make a good case that Joan and Shael Bellows have a *neshamah yeterah* not only on Shabbat, but every day of the week. I have been graced through them, with them, and by them. Ten years ago, had I been offered one wish, I'd hope I would have sought to "live in the house of the LORD all the days of my life, to gaze upon the beauty of the LORD, to frequent His sanctuary" (Ps. 27:4). Joan and Shael: as I sit daily in the *beit midrash*, and teach in the Biblical Studies program established in your honor, it becomes eminently clear that *sheli ve-shelahen shelakhem hi*—our Torah is yours. As your students who have been transformed into teachers, we love you and thank you for allowing us to become part of your beautiful family. May God, whose throne is the heaven and whose footstool the earth, bless you with new and ever-expanding vistas. *Ki ka'asher ha-Shamayim ha-hadashim ve-ha'aretz ha-hadashah omdim le-fanai ne'um Ha-Shem ken ya'amod zara'khem ve-shimkhem* (Isa. 66:22).

When George Blumenthal is called up to the Torah by his Hebrew name, they announce, "Arise, Naftali ben Menachem." What's in a name? Naftali, one of the tribes of Israel, receives the blessing of Moses: "Naftali is satisfied and full of the grace of God." George, you were called up to the Torah and have "cast your bread upon the waters." My blessing to you is from the Great Isaiah Scroll: "Listen to Me you who pursue justice, you who seek the LORD: Look to the rock you are hewn from, to the quarry you were dug from. . . . Truly the LORD has comforted Zion, comforted all her ruins. He has made her wilderness like Eden, her desert like the Garden of the LORD. Gladness and joy shall abide there, thanksgiving and the sound of music" (Isa. 51:1–3).

George, you have taken my visions and my voices, and those of so many others, and transposed them into music. You have lifted me from the lowest points to great new heights. Your compassion and passion and that of your beloved sister Deborah Marin have brought me to Mount Sinai and back to Jerusalem with grace and graciousness. To you both, I send boundless thanks and celestial music.

A woman of valor has been found. For most anyone else, it would be a cliché; for Fanya Gottesfeld Heller, it is revelatory. Fanya, you have taught me *Torat hayim v'ahavat hesed, u'tzedakah, u'vrakhah ve-rahamim ve-hayim ve-shalom*—the Torah of life, lovingkindness, charity, blessing, compassion, vitality, and shalom. It is from you that I learned about waiting for rain after long years of drought . . . about reawakening. Fanya—of *alle males*—who walked up my steps on a *yom tov*, and turned our sukkah into a *sukkat shalom*. To you, I sing *shirei ma'alot*—songs of ascents. Fanya tells a story and writes a book, and tells another story and is the book.

"Though I have fallen, I rise again; though I sit in darkness, the LORD is my light" (Micah 7:8). It is impossible to describe the camaraderie of Matan; it can only be experienced. Each of us at Matan with her own fate, her own lot, has been knocked down and we get up together. In the words of the book of Esther, "Consequently, these days are recalled and observed in every generation: by every family, every province, and every city. And the days of Purim shall never cease among the Jews, and the memory of them shall never perish among their descendants" (Esther 9:28). I reached out to help my friends, only to be knocked down myself. Matan reached out to me and held me up. Thank you for your gifts: Yardena Lev, Sarit Shalev, Naama Erez, Ashot Mkhitaryan, Tamar Stern, Gila Mayerson, Rammy and Siggy Ohev Zion, HaRav Ariel Holland, HaRav Binyamin Fisher, Yardena Cope-Yossef, Naava Cohen, Yafit Clymer, Rivka Yaakobov, Rivka Basch, Yael Schlossberg, Nili Samet, Oshra Koren, Medinah Korn, and the entire faculty and board of Matan.

Embedded on the pages of this book are dear friends whose lives were eclipsed by lightning bolts. Their absence is ever present: HaRav Dr. David Yaakov Halevi Applebaum and his daughter Naava Halevi Applebaum, Joy-Jocheved Rochwarger-Balsam, Judy Kaufman-Hurwich, Rifka Rosenwein-Lichtenberg, Phyllis August-Rothman, and Shelly Seif-Seiff.

Ve-ha-kelaliut shel ha-Tov einah nimdedet be-midah shel zeman, ve-shel kol hagbalah, ki l'olam Hasdo. "And the totality of Goodness is not measured in time or with any limitation for His *hesed* is forever" (R. Abraham Isaac HaCohen Kook, *Seder Tefillah im perush Olat Raayah,* Vol. II:88 [Jerusalem, 1985]).

How blessed to be surrounded by circles of friends. Thank you *ahai ve-re'ay,* my sisters, brothers, and friends, for your warm embrace and for *pekuah nefesh*—the threefold blessing of saving my life, reawakening my life, and sustaining my life in the best and the worst of times.

I begin by singing the praises of my beloved sister Debbie Gross.

There are no words to describe the care, love, and ceaseless devotion you have shown me. No expression could be as powerful as Deborah's song—a song you have made your own—"Till you arose, O Deborah, Arose, O mother, in Israel." I continue with love and gratitude to: Miriam and Rabbi Aharon Adler; Judy and Rabbi Nahum Amsel; Shira and Josh Daniel; Dr. Karen Djemal; Dr. LeeOna Fisher Feld; Rachel, Shalom and Sivan Fishheimer; Martha and Joel Fredman; Debbie and Yossi Gvir; Judy and Jay Kalish; Debbie Krim; Danielle Lax; Debbie Margolis; Goldie and Izzy Marins; Naomi, Andrew, and Abi Newman; Sarah Newman; Deena and Rabbi Jonathan Porath; Tammy and Gary Quinn; Wendy and Rick Schottenstein; Susan Silks, Cheryl and Yossi Singer; Esti and Akiva Tekuziner; Sarah and Rabbi Aryeh Weil; Kayla and Howard and Ilana Weisband; Leah and Ozer Zelver—all of my wonderful friends and neighbors in *Kehilat Neve Orot*.

Additional thanks to friends here and abroad: to Elyssa Ben Refael; Vicky and Rabbi Meyer Berglas; Rooki and Rabbi Heshie Billet; Marion Blumenthal; Itai Boeing; Edna Cohen; Shelly, Harvey, Adam, and Binny Dachs; Rena Fredman Friedlander; Anne and Bernie Hoenig; Marcie Lenk; Ronit Oz; Chana Ringel; Lionel, Natalie, and Shlomit Rosenfeld; Roz Schwegold; Yaffa Shamam; Yehudit and Moshe Halevi Spero; Jillian and Stan Sved; Terez and Moshe Turgeman; Dr. Julian Ungar; Steven Zerobnick.

My brothers and sisters deserve a special place: David and Rhonda Seidman, Eli and Terri Seidman, Shari and Judah Seidman. Shari, your *hesed* has surpassed them all. A special note of thanks to my step-father, Rabbi Moshe Weiss, for years of devotion and care.

Comfort, strength, and hope inhere in the eternal words of Isaiah, the prophet of consolation, and I utter them as a blessing and a tribute to you all: "Arise, shine, for your light has dawned . . . upon you the LORD will shine, and His Presence be seen over you. . . . Raise your eyes and look about: they have all gathered and come to you. Your sons shall be brought from afar, your daughters like babes on shoulders. . . . No longer shall you need the sun for light by day, nor the shining of the moon for radiance [by night]; for the LORD shall be your light everlasting, your God shall be your glory. . . . *Ve-amekh kulam tzadikim*—And Your people, all of them righteous, shall possess the land for all time (Isa. 60:1–4, 19–21). *Barkhenu avinu kulanu ke-ehad b'ohr panekha*—Bless us Our Father all as one with the light of Your Countenance.

Acknowledgments

Moving beyond the all-encompassing embrace of thankfulness to a more familial note, I confront the unfathomable challenge of *hakarat ha-tov*, the recognition of goodness. How does one begin to express gratitude for such a magnitude of blessing? As a student of Bible, I venture to write a *sefer tehillim*—a book of psalms.

I begin as a daughter thanking my parents. I thank my mother, Shyrle Seidman Weiss, who has taught me to read the book of knowledge. She nobly weathered many a storm of her own, and stood by me in the worst of times. She is a role model of courage, wisdom, defiance, and compassion. Above all, my mother instructed me as to the value of truth. May Mom be inscribed in the Book of Life, Health, and Contentment. I thank my father, *adoni avi mori ve-rabbi* (my master, my father, my teacher, my rebbe), Rabbi Aaron Bear Seidman, who wrote:

> Man seeks
> His Master always
> In words and deeds
> In movements;
> And finds
> The search
> More beautiful
> At each point in time
> In every space
> Where man
> And His universe
> Coincide.
>
> "In Search," *Numbered Days* (March 7, 1972), 39.

xviii ❧ Acknowledgments

In this poem, my father charted our course in life. As his daughter, this devotional map helped me navigate while writing *Waiting for Rain*. His ceaseless dedication as a father, teacher, and Jew serve as an everlasting example to me, as well as an infinite source of inspiration. My father never ceased to view the world with wonder, taking nothing for granted. He strove to deepen and broaden his understanding in all areas of intellectual exploration. He was constantly fascinated by the deep truths of nature and continuously investigated the possibilities of language. For him, a word was a world, and a flower was the promise of eternity. These were treasures to be shared with family, friends, and students. He taught us to observe, reflect, and give concrete expression to all intellectual and emotional experiences: to paint a picture, to plant a tree. It was Dad who showed us how to share a story . . . to write a poem . . . an essay . . . a book. Writing *Waiting for Rain* made this ideal a reality. In the words of *Tehillim*, Psalm 90: "*Ve-yehi no'am Ha-Shem Eloheinu alenu u-maasei yedeinu konena alenu u-maaseh yadenu konenehu.* May the favor of the LORD, our God, be upon us; let the work of our hands prosper. . . !" (Ps. 90:17).

Waves of gratitude emanate from me as a daughter inspired by my mother and father and flow from me as a mother inspired by my daughters and sons. Shira Leah, Aharon Dov Mordechai, Naftali Zvi, Elisheva Yehudit, Leora Malka, and Ayelet Eliana: you are my song, my soul, my grace, my ardor, my light, and my joy. Your kindness, devotion, compassion, perspicacity, belief, and integrity during these years have been unwavering. It all defies words, as does my limitless and eternal love for each of you and for all of you.

May you be blessed, *benei tziyyon ha-yikarim ha-mesula'im be-paz*—children of Zion, valued in gold—with enthusiasm, from the Greek *en-theos*, meaning "having God within." *Ki Hu amar ve-yehi Hu tzivah va-yaamod . . . Atzat Ha-Shem l'olam taamod mahshevot libo l'dor va-dor.* "For He spoke and it was; He commanded and it endured . . . What the LORD plans endures forever" (Ps. 33:9,11). *Ki Hu tzivah va-yehi—*

Praise the LORD; for He is good,
His steadfast love is eternal.
Praise the God of gods,
His steadfast love is eternal.
Praise the God of heaven,
His steadfast love is eternal. (Ps. 136:1–2,26)

BRYNA JOCHEVED LEVY
Jerusalem 5767

Preface

Surveying the parched earth at the end of a long, dry summer, the farmer waits for rain, as did his predecessors, who tilled the same fields before him. The cisterns are empty and the springs have ceased to flow; throats are dry and voices are muted. The season is replete with expectancy and yearning, with the hope for rain that is the hope for life. It is a time of reflecting on the past harvest gathered in, and anticipating harvests that may come. It is a moment poised on the edge of eternity.

When the clouds finally burst and the first drops grace the ground, nature sighs with relief. The earth absorbs and ardently guards every drop, mysteriously transforming heavenly moisture into the power of life and sustenance. Plants begin to sprout, buds appear on trees, and flowers bloom. Man lifts up his voice in song, his prayers having been answered from on high. Rain is where heaven and earth meet.

> For as the rain and the snow fall from heaven
> And return not there,
> But soak the earth
> And make it bring forth vegetation,
> Yielding seed for the sower
> And bread for the eater.
> So is the word that issues from My mouth.
> It does not come back to Me unfulfilled,
> But performs what I purpose,
> Achieves what I sent it to do. (Isa. 55:10–11)
> [author's translation]

The poignant words of the prophet Isaiah highlight the parallel between rain and the word of God, which quenches our existential thirst and revitalizes our desiccated souls. The metaphor captures our need for deliverance. Our souls are broken fields plowed by pain. We long for refreshment, for a renewal of faith in a world in which our beliefs have withered. We hope to recapture our sense of amazement and to rebuild our trust in ourselves, in others, and in our responses to life. We pray that truth—shadowed by death, despair, and vulnerability—will once again come to light.

As the month of Tishrei draws to a close, the sun's fierceness begins to abate. Cooler breezes at eventide promise respite from the summer's scorching days. The afternoon shadows now offer a modicum of relief. Eyes turn heavenward looking for a wisp of cloud, for any clement harbinger of the first rains of autumn. But there is no surcease, no life-giving moisture to slake the thirst of the people and their flocks, or to revive the earth.

As lonely wanderers in the great desert of life, we make our way across trackless wastes of meaninglessness, searching for oases of cooling drafts of spiritual refreshment, where we may imbibe deeply of the waters of the living God. The prayer for rain is an appeal for the revival of our souls.

King David gives expression to the spirit of man, parched and yearning for God:

> My soul thirsts for You,
> My body yearns for You,
> In a sere and weary land that has no water.
> I shall behold You in the sanctuary And see Your might and
>   glory. (Ps. 63:2–3) [author's translation]

This transition is paralleled by the mystical transformation of the Days of Awe. Rosh Hashanah becomes Hoshana Rabbah as, at the end of the day, the *aravot* fall to the ground and the white *kittel* is folded and put away for another year. The *etrog* is consigned to citron jelly and the *lulav* to fuel for burning the Passover *hametz*. Yom Kippur glides into Shemini Atzeret, which is characterized in talmudic law by a single practice: the insertion into our prayers of the simple declaration, *Mashiv ha-ruah u-Morid ha-geshem*—God causes the wind to blow and the rain to fall.

This, our first reflection at the turning of the year, is, in essence, the final prayer of the penitential season. And so our eyes seek the Master of the Universe, longing for Him to restore our spirits, just as He causes the rain to fall.

Introduction

Waiting for Rain: Reflections at the Turning of the Year, a collection
of meditations on the Jewish High Holiday season, began as
"The Hoshana Rabbah Lectures," delivered annually at Matan—The
Sadie Rennert Women's Institute for Torah Studies in Jerusalem.
Matan served as the venue for these lectures and impacted greatly
upon them. It is from the unique Torah that I learned and taught at
Matan that these meditations emerged, carefully crafted.

Matan spearheaded the revolution in women's Torah learning
today. As a *yeshivah gevohah* (a Torah academy), Matan affords women
of all ages and walks of life the opportunity to engage actively in
Torah study, participate in spiritual dialogue, and find their own
voices. Through learning, women discover the emotional and intellectual themes that animate texts of Torah and resonate deeply within their own lives. Their perceptions, sensitized to human emotion
through years of nurturing and caregiving, allow for an understanding
of psychological subtleties and are reflected in new meaning revealed
in familiar texts.

Although *Waiting for Rain* began as the "Hoshana Rabbah Lectures," in the course of time, it developed to include the entire spec-
trum of holidays from Rosh Hashanah through Simchat Torah. The
essays in this volume explore the interface between Bible and biblical
interpretation, and the dynamic meshing of text and life. They also
represent the points of contact between the Bible and the holidays.
The method of interpretation that characterizes the essays in this volume is an integrative one, in which insights from contemporary biblical scholarship and literary studies are conjoined with fresh readings
of traditional medieval and Rabbinic interpretation. The power and
passion of Scripture are revealed in a new light and enable an evolv-
ing modern Jewish theology.

The volume is divided into two parts. "On the Threshold of

Majesty" focuses on themes related to Rosh Hashanah, the 10 Days of Repentance, and Yom Kippur, and "Waiting for Rain" deals with Hoshana Rabbah, Shemini Atzeret, and Simchat Torah. Some of the biblical selections dealt with in the context of a given holiday are well known to readers, insofar as they play a central role in the liturgy, the Torah readings, or the haftarah readings. The connections of other scriptural passages to the holiday cycle are less well known. The story of Noah after the Flood and its link to Rosh Hashanah becomes a test case of a man judged and found wanting in his humanity. David's last psalm recorded in 1 Chronicles 29 is transformed into the template for prayer during the 10 Days of Repentance. Joseph and his brothers provide the basis for understanding Yom Kippur, and the saga of Samuel at Mizpah serves to explain the customs associated with Hoshana Rabbah.

Waiting for Rain is far more than a collection of meditations; it is a *korban todah*—an offering of gratitude to the people of the Book. For me, the people of the Book are first and foremost the biblical characters who are the key players in *Waiting for Rain*. These heroes and heroines emerge from the incandescent light of the ancient Bible. They are endowed with both spiritual grandeur and profoundly human qualities. Although they lived thousands of years ago, they play an active role in my life. For many readers of the Bible, these are the men and women whose inspired lives are compelling and demanding of investigation. But for me, as a student and teacher of Bible, their closeness guides me through enchanted pathways in life and allows me to call upon them for guidance. *Waiting for Rain* is a collection of memoirs of the people whom I most love and respect.

It therefore gives me great pleasure to thank Noah for teaching me about hope, Abraham for teaching me about faith, and Isaac for teaching me about defiance. My heart goes out to Rachel who taught me about love, to Ezra who taught me about joy, and David who taught me the significance of prayer. Moses, our teacher, taught me about compassion, and Joseph gave me the ability to dream. From Samuel I learned about leadership, from Elijah, courage, and from Jeremiah the prophet of doom, eternal optimism. It is Micah who defined humility, and Joshua who gave new meaning to the word devotion.

In *Waiting for Rain*, I have embraced the well-known stories of these characters and engaged in explication de texte. The analysis of the biblical passages has allowed me to mine Scripture again and again, searching and discovering the many gems still waiting to be unearthed. Each figure explored in the book stands for an epoch—its aspirations and conflicts. And yet their lives span the generations and reflect the eternal qualities of the human condition. They permit us to accompany them to the depths of religious history, while inviting us to embark upon our own spiritual voyages.

There are, however, additional people of the Book whom you will meet in this volume. They are the great Jewish thinkers who interpreted the Bible (*parshanim*). Their activity began the minute biblical characters appeared on center stage and invited readers to view them through the 70-faceted prism of interpretation. These commentators understood the Bible as the template for life, and its characters as representatives not only of their times, but as teachers and guides, showing us how to apply and integrate their experiences with our own.

In this regard, I have been inspired by my teacher and mentor, Professor Nehama Leibowitz, whose classic works are collectively titled *Iyunim be-Sefer Bereshit-Devarim be-'Ikvot Parshanenu ha-Rishonim ve-ha-Ahronim (Studies in the Books of Genesis-Deuteronomy: In the Footsteps of Our Sages Throughout the Centuries)*. Nehama not only studied the texts by following in the footsteps of intellectual and spiritual giants of Jewish thought, she delved into biblical commentaries, known and obscure, bringing their genius to light. Nehama highlighted their brilliance in biblical interpretation, as well as their ability to demonstrate the interface between the Bible and the reality in which they lived. She shared these outstanding thinkers with the world and introduced books, which might have remained unopened by thousands, to become popular and beloved.

Moreover, Nehama's forays into Holy Writ are not only "in the footsteps" of these commentators; she continued their journey, leaving footprints of her own. Nehama Leibowitz blazed new trails in the world of biblical interpretation. She approached Torah as a tree of life and a tree of wisdom, allowing words of truth to inform all of us and the modern world in which we live.

In this volume, I have tried to remain loyal to her technique, and so I thank Professor Nehama Leibowitz—*Morah*—the teacher of Israel, and all of her colleagues. This delegation of the people of the Book includes everyone from the Rabbis of the Talmud to Rashi, and from Rabbi Abraham Sabba to Rabbi Joseph ibn Caspi—biblical commentators, known and obscure, whom you will meet on the pages of this book.

There is another great woman of Israel I would like to thank: Rabbanit Malke Bina, the founder and *Rosh Yeshivah* of Matan. In the words of Proverbs: "She epitomizes wisdom, her voice gives rise to understanding. She takes her stand on the topmost heights, by the wayside at the crossroads" (Prov. 8:1–2) [author's translation]. Blazing uncharted trails, *derakheha darkhei noam ve-khol netivoteha shalom* (3:17). Her path is one of gentility.

Malke's vision created Matan and continues to make it flourish. Her *emunah shlemah*—her innate belief and her belief in women and Talmud Torah—has provided a milieu for spiritual and intellectual growth for thousands upon thousands of women in Israel and throughout the world. Her unabiding love of Torah, of *am Yisra'el*, her ingenuity and genuineness, her lovingkindness and generosity of spirit are unsurpassed. According to *hahamenu zikhronam l'vrakhah* (our sages of blessed memory), *takhlit hokhmah teshuvah u-maasim tovim* (B. Ber. 17a), the objective of wisdom is *teshuvah* and good deeds. Malke is a *talmidat hakhamim*, an apprentice to the Sages, in every sense of the term.

I am blessed to have Malke as my *yedidat nefesh*, a kindred soul. She has given me a place *bein yoshvei beit ha-midrash*—in the study halls of Torah—to build a spiritual learning community, together. *Ra'uhah vanot va-ya'ashru'hah melakhot . . . ve-yehalleluhah* (Shir HaShirim 6:9)—the women of Zion come to Malke's royal chamber and acclaim her crown of Torah. Malke herself has shown me *ein sof shel hasadim*—infinite kindness. There is no ample degree of thankfulness to extend to Malke and her wonderful husband Ha-Rav Aharon Bina, and so I offer them a prayer, *b'ahavah u-v'ratzon:* May you continue together, with love and passion, to be *the* example to us all of: *hevei me-talmidav shel Aharon ohev shalom, v'rodef shalom, ohev et ha-beriot u-mekarvan la-Torah*—as protégés of Aaron, loving peace, pursuing peace, loving humanity and bringing them close to Torah (M. Avot 2:12).

The Rabbis of the Jerusalem Talmud note that in the merit of three things the rains fall: in the merit of the Land (*Eretz Yisra'el*), in the merit of lovingkindness, and in the merit of afflictions—and they are all mentioned in one verse (J. Ta'an. 14b). All three of these elements contributed to *Waiting for Rain.*

In the merit of the Land:

The book encapsulates *Torat Eretz Yisra'el*—the unique Torah of the Land of Israel. It derives from a rich and multifarious social, historical, and spiritual reality. In *Eretz Yisra'el* every word resounds with a truth all its own.

As a denizen of the Land for the last 27 years, I am filled with wonder as I contemplate my journey to Israel and my odyssey within it. I began writing the introduction to *Waiting for Rain* in a thunderstorm in Tzfat and witnessed there, with marvel, a rainbow sprawl over Mount Meron. Many a morning, I continued writing in my home, as the Jerusalem sky turned from *tehelet* to *karti*, from azure to aquamarine. I applied the final brushstrokes to this canvas, as the sun set over Caesarea.

Timelessness inspired my thoughts, my feelings, and my words. They are mere reflections of those experienced by the great and the simple women and men of every generation who lived, labored, and loved in this awesome Land. They fill the silence of rainless days and beat to the rhythm of the raindrops. They are firmly tethered by the Torah that comes forth from Zion and the Word of God that reverberates in Jerusalem.

In the merit of lovingkindness:

It would not have been possible to write *Waiting for Rain* without my magnificent children, family, friends, and students, who showered me with boundless love and support. In the words of the Zohar: "In the name of the God of Israel, on my right Michael, on my left Gabriel, in front of me Uriel, and behind me Rafael, and above my head the Divine Presence of God." *Be-shem Adonai Elohei Yisra'el, mi-yemini Mikhael, u-mi-semoli Gavriel, u-mi-lefanai Uriel ume-ahorai Refael, ve-'al roshi Shekhinat El.*

Children, family, friends, and students were the hosts of angels who enabled me to write this book. Through divine providence and design, they were instantly summoned like clouds that are blown and like doves [who soar] to their cotes (Isa. 60:8). At every juncture, they poured love upon me and saturated me with serenity.

And in the merit of afflictions:

Much personal and national catastrophe came to bear upon this book. The Sturm und Drang gave way to artistic endeavor. Painful inquiry inspired my wonder of wisdom and restored the buoyancy of life. Values that hold my passions decreased my sense of isolation, and sharing the written word allowed me visions of a world mended. The shadows that suffuse life were chased away while waiting for rain.

Bi-zekhut gimmel devarim ha-geshamim yordim: bi-zekhut ha-'aretz, bi-zekhut ha-hesed, bi-zekhut ha-yisurin; u-sheloshtan be-pasuk ehad: 'Im le-shevet, 'im le-'artzo, 'im le-hesed yamtzi'ehu.

In the merit of three things the rains fall, and all three are woven into one book—*Waiting for Rain.*

Part I

✢

On the Threshold of Majesty

Rosh Hashanah

On the Threshold of Majesty, etching by Elisheva Yehudit Levy

Two women standing in front of the ocean of being. Mother and child, child and mother draw strength from each other and from the sea of infinity. Gently holding her daughter's hand, the mother guides the girl by showing her life, beauty, and love. She passes on to her child the truth of God's presence in this world and the unwavering belief that there is no artist like God.

For He spoke and it was—*Elu ha-banim*—these are *my* children"
(B.Shab. 152a).

At the heart of memory lie mystery and infinity. They move me to
surrender to the miraculous scope of divine magnanimity. It is there
that I listen to the echo of the biblical Job, who whispered, "Therefore, I recant and relent, being but dust and ashes" (Job 42:6). Dare I
say that he too waited for rain? After Job's experience of borderless
despair and confusion, the Almighty replied out of the tempest, *min
ha-se'arah*, and asked:

> Who cut a channel for the torrents
> And a path for the thunderstorms,
> To rain down on uninhabited land,
> On the wilderness, where no man is
> To saturate the desolate wasteland,
> And make the crop of grass sprout forth?
> Does the rain have a father?
> Who begot the dewdrops? (Job 38:25–28)

The multifaceted prism of Rashi glistens. He explains the verse "And
the LORD replied to Job from out of the tempest" in contrasting ways.
First, from the storm from which you reproached Me, I appear
. . . And alternatively, through a storm, God smote Job and through
a storm, He restored him (Rashi, Job 35:1).

From the maelstrom of life, I have come to understand both of
Rashi's ineluctable truths. It is from amidst the very tempest that I was
placed into the gentle hands of the *Ribbono shel Olam*, Master of the
Universe. Moreover, through a storm, He smote me, and through a
storm, He drenched me with rain, cleansed me, and restored me.

*Hodu la-Shem ki tov ki l'olam hasdo; Hodu l'Elohei Elohim ki l'olam
hasdo . . . Hodu la-El ha-Shamayim ki l'olam hasdo.*

Chapter One

❧

Somewhere over the Rainbow

❧

The golden thread of memory is intricately woven into the fabric of Rosh Hashanah, the first Day of Awe. In the Bible, Rosh Hashanah is called Yom ha-Zikaron—the Day of Remembrance. All of our memories pass before us, impelling us to take stock of our merits and our inadequacies. The power of memory on this holiday involves a chastening assessment as well as a comforting reassurance.

But it is not only human beings who remember on Rosh Hashanah—it is God as well. In the second part of the *Musaf* service, known as *Zikhronot*, a series of scriptural verses describe God's recollections. He nostalgically reminisces about His beloved Ephraim in whom He delighted so. He remembers His covenant with His people Israel.

But the paradigmatic case of remembering in this section of the liturgy is the story of Noah: "God remembered Noah and all the beasts and all the cattle that were with him in the ark, and God caused a wind to blow across the earth, and the waters subsided" (Gen. 8:1). Why was Noah, of all people, chosen as the symbol of memory?

This choice is in keeping with the universality of Rosh Hashanah.

It is the day on which we acknowledge the sovereignty of the Almighty as king over all of humankind. Like Adam—the original man, Noah—father of the world reborn after the Flood—is an individual who represents all of humanity and is, therefore, singled out to give expression to the idea that just as God remembered him, we pray that He will remember all of His creations for life. Moreover, Noah symbolizes the power of one person to begin again. His story of renewal is singularly appropriate for Rosh Hashanah. Presumably, Noah is to serve as an inspiration for us all as we begin the new year.

Noah, however, is central to Rosh Hashanah—the Day of Judgment—for a different reason: he was a man judged and found wanting. The story of Noah and the Flood is a powerful statement about the individual's relationship to the community of others. As we shall see, God had great expectations for Noah and met with grave disappointment. Noah epitomizes God's memory of what was and what might have been. The liturgical reference to Noah, in the *Musaf* service, awakens in our minds the image of a man inundated by haunting memories about the world he left behind, and about his role as heir, witness, and survivor. As a case in point of how man lives with and by the judgment of God, let us now examine the life of Noah, son of Lemech. As we shall see, Lemech and his heritage provide us with a backdrop for the midrash on Noah's name—a name that is central to Noah's destiny, and to our understanding of it.

Lemech was the ninth-generation descendant of Adam. Day after day, he labored in the fields, as was decreed for all descendants of the first man. He had inherited the burden of the cursed earth, the legacy of Adam's fall. His wearisome toil was well-nigh unbearable; however, he had something to look forward to. His wife was expecting, and in those early days of "be fruitful and multiply," a birth was still a momentous occasion. Returning to his home one day, Lemech was greeted by the healthy cry of a newborn, piercing the silence of the sullen world into which he had emerged. Lemech's heart swelled with joy. He immediately knew what he would name the child. He proclaimed: "This one will provide us relief (*yenahamenu*) from our work and from the toil of our hands out of the very soil which the LORD placed under a curse" (Gen. 5:29).

What did Lemech have in mind by that statement? How would this child reverse man's struggle with the unyielding earth that brought forth thorns and thistles instead of produce? Perhaps it was the simple creative vigor of birth that highlighted life's immanent value and momentarily overshadowed the battle for survival. The 12th-century biblical commentator Rashbam notes that Noah was the first child born after the death of Adam, establishing a continuum between him and primordial man. Noah would be Adam redivivus, turning back the clock to a world that preceded original sin and punishment.

The Rabbis in *Bereshit Rabbah* offer us several intriguing interpretations of the comfort that Noah was to provide the world. One midrashic position states that Noah discovered the plow. Whereas the Bible explicitly informs us of inventors such as Jubal, who was "the ancestor of all who play the lyre and the pipe" (Gen. 4:21), and Tubal-cain, who "forged all implements of copper and iron" (4:22), the Rabbis imagine Noah as having made an equally significant contribution to material culture. Such an invention would indeed have been a comfort to the browbeaten and weary people of the time. Another comment plays on the name Noah, which means "ease," positing that with his appearance a sudden calm spread over the world. Nature, which until then had been recalcitrant, was suddenly compliant with man's efforts. Fields filled with grain, fruit appeared on trees, flowers turned heavenward, skies seemed to brighten, bluebirds sang, and the world radiated with color. So in both Lemech's declaration and in the Rabbinic amplifications of the account of his birth, Noah provided the world with a small measure of comfort and respite. However, storm clouds were gathering on the horizon. The harmony of human brotherhood had given way to discord. Arrogance and contempt prevailed among Noah's contemporaries. Bitterness and frustration turned people into despicable beings concerned only with their own welfare, with total disregard for all else.

> The LORD saw how great was man's wickedness on earth, and how every plan devised by his mind was nothing but evil all the time. And the LORD regretted that He had made man on earth, and His heart was saddened. The LORD said, "I will blot out from the earth the men whom I created—men together with beasts, creeping things, and birds of the sky; for I regret that I made them." But Noah found favor with the LORD. (Gen. 6:5–8)

Human wickedness spread malignantly until it undermined the very foundations of society. The pillars upon which the world rested tottered—and finally collapsed. God sadly acknowledged that the proclivity for evil was woven into the basic fabric of human nature. It is not clear when these trends began, but by Noah's time they had reached crisis proportions. The Lord had arrived at the limits of divine tolerance, and so with great sorrow, He resolved to call a halt to the world that He had created. But before He did, He opened His heart to Noah, the one man who had found favor in His eyes.

> God said to Noah, "I have decided to put an end to all flesh, for the earth is filled with lawlessness because of them: I am about to destroy them with the earth." (Gen. 6:13)

We who have read the Bible numerous times know what one so informed should do under such circumstances. With no prompting, we can think of two other biblical characters with whom God shared His plan for mass destruction. When the Lord informed Abraham that He planned to destroy Sodom, Abraham made an impassioned plea to save the city and its inhabitants; and when God informed Moses that He was about to erase the people of Israel and start again with him, Moses staunchly refused the offer and pleaded the case of his people. Both Abraham and Moses rose to the occasion with great courage and challenged God. Therefore, when God tells Noah that He is going to wipe out the universe, we are shocked that Noah offers no resistance.

Noah's behavior is dealt with in a fascinating work known as *Zeror ha-Mor*, by Rabbi Abraham ben Jacob Sabba of Zamora—a biblical commentary written, destroyed, and reconstructed during a period of mass destruction of the Jewish people.

In the year 1492, along with all of his brethren residing in the kingdoms of Castille and Aragon, R. Sabba was exiled from his land. Like many other Jews during the Inquisition, R. Sabba made his way to Portugal, only to find himself in the very same situation five years later. There, too, the Inquisitorial knell was heard, and the Jews of Portugal were commanded to bring all of their holy books to be burned in the main plaza of Lisbon. Noncompliance with the edict was punishable by death. Defiantly, R. Abraham Sabba took his three Torah compositions, his commentaries on the Pentateuch, *Avot*, and the Five *Megillot*, in which he had invested years of his life, and buried them under an olive tree outside of the city. He then joined 10,000 of his brethren in the public square, where they were forced to choose between the cross and the sword. At the end of the *auto da fé*, 40 Jews remained; the rest, including two of Sabba's sons, had chosen apostasy or death. Through a stroke of luck or divine providence—perhaps both—Rabbi Abraham's life was spared. He languished in prison for six months, after which time he was able to escape on a rickety vessel—a veritable ark of salvation—and make his way to Fez in Morocco, where he began rebuilding his life and reconstructing the Torah works he had left behind. Fortunately for us, he was able to rewrite his Torah commentary, in which he offers a startlingly profound and penetrating analysis of Noah, a fellow refugee and survivor:

It would have been appropriate when Noah realized that Satan stood before God [that he] plead their case and pray for them, or bring a sacrifice to assuage the anger of God at the world; to selflessly devote himself to his flock in the way that Moses did when he said, "Erase me" (Exod. 33:32). But he didn't. He simply inquired about his own needs and salvation, and when told by God: "I shall destroy the world," Noah asked: "and what shall I do?" to which God replied: "Go make yourself an ark of gopher wood for you to save yourself." (*Zeror ha-Mor*, Gen. 6:13)

Zeror ha-Mor's critique of Noah's indifference is arresting. Noah saved himself; where was his conscience? He was supposedly the pinnacle of antediluvian humanity. Did he not realize the responsibility this role carried? He, and only he, was privy to the murmurings of God's heart. Not for naught did God choose to share his disappointments and regrets with Noah. The Master of the Universe hoped Noah would bring Him comfort, pleading His cause and the cause of mankind. Noah missed the opportunity to engage in dialogue with the God who had called his name and thereby try to save not only himself, but the entire world.

But are we being fair to Noah? Not everyone is an Abraham or a Moses. Perhaps he was simply not equal to the daunting task of changing the course of history. *Zeror ha-Mor* picks up this gauntlet and asserts that we need not look only to such towering giants as Abraham and Moses as standards of comparison. Indeed, it is Gideon—a much humbler example of leadership in later biblical history—to whom *Zeror ha-Mor* compares Noah, to show that Noah had been put to the test and found wanting

Gideon was the judge who was appointed to save the people of Israel from Midianite oppression. The plight of the Israelites at that time is dramatically conveyed in the book of Judges, chapter 6. The people are described as hiding in dens and caves, like animals. Their produce was destroyed and their sheep, oxen, and donkeys carried off by Bedouin-like marauders. The Midianites are described as numerous and ruinous as a plague of locusts, and as having the tactical advantage of possessing camels without number. The wave of pillage and destruction they inflicted was unbearable. The text sums up the situation with the words: "Israel was reduced to utter misery by the Midianites" (Judg. 6:6).

Gideon was the man elected by God to save the day. God commissioned him while he was threshing wheat inside a winepress—to keep it safe from the Midianites. The encounter is described as follows:

> The angel of the LORD appeared to him and said to him, "The LORD is with you, valiant warrior!" Gideon said to him, "Please, my lord, if the LORD is with us, why has all this befallen us? Where are all His wondrous deeds about which our fathers told us, saying, 'Truly the LORD brought us up from Egypt'? Now the LORD has abandoned us and delivered us into the hands of Midian!" The LORD turned to him and said, "Go in this strength of yours and deliver Israel from the Midianites." (Judg. 6:12–14)

Zeror ha-Mor notes that Gideon himself was in dire straits. He might rightly have replied, "Spare me the platitudes—could you please help me with this wheat?" But putting aside his own troubles, he focused on the plight of Israel. Gideon's actions, according to R. Sabba, stand in direct contradistinction to Noah's:

> So Gideon who went out on a limb for Israel and rose to greatness while the righteous Noah neglected to consider the needs of society, and simply asked that his own needs be provided, saying, "What shall I do?" To which God replied: "Make yourself an ark of gopher wood." In *Midrash ha-Ne'elam*, it says: When Noah saw the world destroyed, he began to bewail and lament, and said, "Master of the Universe, You are called merciful and compassionate. How could You have behaved so cruelly with Your children?" This is implicit in His sending the raven, since it is merciless with its fledglings, as it says . . . "[who gives the beasts their food,] to the raven's brood what they cry for" (Ps. 147:9). God replied, "I did all of this since you did not pray prior to the Flood." When Noah realized that he had sinned, he began to offer sacrifices. In addition, it is for this reason that God bided time in the building of the ark and

the bringing of the animals and food, hoping that Noah would find it in his heart and awaken his spirit to pray before the Lord. (*Zeror ha-Mor*, Gen. 6:13)

Zeror ha-Mor's assertion is significant: one need not be on the level of Abraham or Moses to rise to the occasion and plead the case of one's fellow man in the face of divine wrath.

Noah missed his cue. He could have countered God, questioned His judgment, and thereby saved the world from perdition. Why did-n't he do so? Maybe he simply did not believe the Flood would really happen. Certainly God would not destroy the entire world because of fools (B. Avod. Zar. 54b)! Maybe Noah was humbled by the chal-lenge. Who was he to object to a divine plan? He himself lacked merit; how could he petition for others? And so he said nothing: "And Noah did just as the LORD commanded him" (Gen. 7:5). He simply followed directions. Noah's passivity is described by Sabba as unconscionable. His indictment of him suggests that one may sin through excessive modesty just as sorely as through overweening pride.

As the winds howled and sheets of rain began to fall, Noah entered the ark. And when God closed the door behind him (Gen. 7:16), Noah turned his back on the world that once had been. Day after day, he heard the torrents of rain beating down on his wave-tossed shelter, the earth outside gradually submerged by a tempest with no foretellable end. As he peered through the tiny window, he saw the sinister darkness of heaven; nothing more. He couldn't possi-bly fathom what was happening out there. In the storm that raged without, God was reversing the process of Creation. The deluge reunited the celestial and terrestrial waters, which had been divided in the Beginning. The separation between dry land and the waters of the sea had disappeared. Men who had been given dominion over the ani-mals were now together with them in the same boat.

And while God was undoing Creation, Noah was sustaining the only life that was left. The text supplies us with little information about what happened in the ark. That is the charming stuff of which children's books are made: Noah the zookeeper took great care of the animals that managed just fine, cooped up for 40 days and 40 nights. And when the birds gave Noah the high sign, he and the animals delightfully pranced out of the ark. He built an altar to God and offered sacrifices. God was pleased and resolved to accept the flaws in man, and not to curse the world again, but to restore the rhythms of life. He then blessed them to be fruitful and multiply, and established a covenant, brightening the empty world with the glistening colors of the rainbow. Finally, He handed over governance of the world to Noah and his family. Noah, now liberated from the responsibility of the ark, was able to start again in a world restored to its pristine lustre by the Flood.

But this is not quite the tone yielded by a close reading of the text. The exit from the ark begins with a little-noticed verse, a tableau that should not be missed:

Va-yasar Noah et mikhseh ha-tevah va-yaar ve-hineh harvu penei ha-adamah.

When Noah removed the covering of the ark, he saw that the surface of the ground was drying. (Gen. 8:13)

This standard translation of the verse renders the expression *ve-hineh harvu penei ha-adamah* as "he saw that the surface of the ground was drying." However, the word *harvu* in biblical parlance often connotes not just desiccation but desolation, and indeed such was the case with Noah.

When he removed the cover of the ark and surveyed the world, he saw devastation all around him. The text does not go into details—it leaves us to imagine the shock of it all. Noah, the survivor, beholds the spectacle of death, the vision of heaven having been heedless to man's agony. His ears were pierced by the endless silent scream of those who trod the earth no more. His sorrow and his guilt could not encompass the enormity of the events. How could he and his family ever really live again in the world of the dead? Noah's very existence was a testimony to his betrayal of humankind. As reality set in, Noah realized he had made the wrong choice before the Flood. But there was no one to whom he could explain it. There was no one to whom he could apologize, and no one with whom he could share his anguish. *Va-yisha'er akh Noah* (Gen. 7:23)—he was the lone survivor, fated to live out his days in infamy and isolation. And so the renascent world became a haunted, hollow, and horrifying place for Noah.

Noah's actions, which might have been considered a case of benign neglect, are scathingly condemned by *Zeror ha-Mor*:

> *Vayehal Noah*—In the beginning, he was called a righteous and flawless man, prepared for all goodness; but when he was indolent in requesting clemency for his generation he was described merely as righteous; and now that the world was destroyed, he is called neither righteous nor flawless but rather "a man of the earth," meaning the man because of whom the earth was destroyed. And the expression *vayehal* means he went from *kodesh* to *hol*; from being holy to being profane. (*Zeror ha-Mor*, Gen. 9:20)

Zeror ha-Mor's denunciation of Noah appears extreme and unfair. It can perhaps be understood both subjectively and objectively. On the one hand, it may reflect his personal experience as a survivor of the Inquisition, in Spain and Portugal. As a rabbinic leader unable to save his communities, he may be responding to his own survivor's guilt. On the other hand, as a biblical commentator his insight derives from the textual link of Noah's salvation followed by his drunken stupor. Sabba bases himself on the following perplexing vignette:

> And Noah who had become a man of the earth planted a vineyard [author translation]. He drank of the wine and became drunk, and he uncovered himself within his tent. (Gen. 9:20–21)

In order to gain insight into the rudderless Noah after the Flood, we do well to view him through a double lens. Biblical interpretation, from the Rabbinic period to the modern age, has tried to understand Noah's actions of planting a vineyard, getting drunk, and exposing his nakedness. Unwilling to explain the episode away as a simple case of escapism, the commentators creatively probed his conscience and subconscious. At the same time, casting Noah as the survivor of a holocaust opens up a contemporary window through which we may understand what he experienced, and consequently what motivated his actions. One parallel between classical commentary and modern research is revealed in Terrence Des Pres' magnum opus *The Survivor.* Des Pres documents testimonies of Holocaust survivors for whom the horror of the past inexorably blighted their present and their struggles to create a future. These perspectives on time, memory, reality, and morality serve to inform and clarify Noah's actions. Although the Holocaust is a sui generis experience of destruction and tragedy in the history of the Jewish people, there is a parallel that can be drawn between the destruction of the world in the time of Noah and the annihilation of the Shoah. Indeed, the history of biblical exegesis suggests that Noah's fate may be universalized to the experience of all survivors of catastrophe.

Terrence Des Pres asserts that time is among the many things destroyed for the survivor; with it, goes growth and purpose.

> Structured time, the blessing of a foundation for measure and purposive action, is one of civilization's great gifts. But in extremity the forms of time dissolve, the rhythms of change and motion are lost . . . The death of time destroys the sense of growth and purpose, and thereby undermines faith in the possibility that any good can come from merely staying alive. This too the survivor must face and withstand. (*Des Pres*, 12)

This contention may explain what Noah did after leaving the ark: "And Noah who had become a man of the earth planted a vineyard"

(Gen. 9:20) [author's translation]. Despite God's blessing to be fruit-ful and multiply, Noah did not father another child. He no doubt was gravely ambivalent about bringing life into such an austere and daunt-ing universe. As a livelihood, he didn't choose shepherding—he had had his fill of animals; they were too close to his trauma. They brought him back to the cold, damp darkness of the ship of death, his vehicle of self-preservation and the symbol of his guilt. Rather, Noah planted a vineyard. Working the land, he prayed for the rapid passage of time, the burden of which lay heavily upon him in the eerie stillness of an empty world. He yearned for rebirth and for purpose. He involved himself in planting, hoping to regain control of time and to be encour-aged by visible signs of renewal. Every day he gently tended and dressed his vines, trying to heal the soil ravaged by the torrents of the Flood.

But perhaps working the land was motivated by a desire to cling to the past. Des Pres explains:

> The self comes to feel grounded in its personal past, as indeed it is; and the more our lives are burdened by distress and uncer-tainty, the more we value what has already been lived. We cling to the past, sometimes in pride, more often in guilt and confusion, but cling all the same. And increasingly as we age we turn in memory to our particular past as to a world in reserve for rest and assurance. Novelists know this especially well. What they seek through their work is reclamation of the past which will proclaim the reality of human selfhood to its deepest foundations. (Des Pres, 183–184)

Maybe Noah planted because on some subconscious level, Noah, *ish ha-adamah*, a man of the earth, hoped to turn back the clock and retrieve his original destiny and innocence. Perhaps Noah want-ed no more than to restore the gladness and comfort that had met his invention of the plow. Then, young and naive, he had been able to alleviate the suffering caused by God's curse of the earth. Although he knew he could not reverse the devastation or silence the ghostly voices that pursued him in his dreams, maybe he could re-create his former psychic reality in the simple context of comfort, all seated "under their vine and their fig tree" (1 Kings 5:5). The early medieval midrash *Pirke de-Rabbi Eliezer* posits that grapes represented Noah's longing to celebrate. Grapes would bring forth wine and wine would bring with it gladness and rejoicing. Oh, how he missed that!

In kabbalistic literature, another approach is suggested. In the words of the 14th-century Italian kabbalist Rabbi Menachem Recanati, in his commentary to Genesis 9:20: "He planted a vineyard and went to explore and probe matters related to this vineyard, in an effort to discern between the good and evil within it." Recanati's comment deals with such a search for good and evil, attaching profound and symbol-laden mystical significance to Noah's search taking place in the vineyard. Wine, the product of fermentation, results from a process of decomposition. Something wondrous emerges from that which is rotten. Let it be, thought Noah, that the rotting cadavers that lie beneath the surface of the earth shall bring forth life. Let sadness sprout into joy; let me recover lucidity and once again discern good from bad. Let nature again clue me in to the fine-line distinctions of which I have lost sight amid the chaos, so that survival shall not be without value.

This notion dovetails well with Terrence Des Pres' analysis of the deep-seated need of the survivor to clarify his fundamental knowledge of good and evil:

> By virtue of the extraordinary demands made upon men and women in extremity, their struggle to live humanly involves a process of becoming more—essentially, firmly—human. Not the humanness of refinement and proliferation, of course, but

of the fundamental knowledge of good and evil, and of the will to stand by this knowledge, on which all else depends. (Des Pres, 21)

The biblical verse continues: "He drank of the wine and became drunk, and he uncovered himself within his tent" (Gen. 9:20). The Rabbis ask:

God said to Noah: Noah, shouldn't you have learned from Adam, who stumbled because of wine (since the forbidden fruit was that of the vine)? (B. Sanh. 70a)

The answer, of course, is that Noah deliberately followed Adam's lead and threw himself headlong into oblivion. In her article, "Drinking Wine to Inebriation in Biblical Times," Louba Ben-Noun lists alcohol-induced amnesia among the effects of inebriation. Noah drank to liberate himself from his painful memories. She adds:

Why did Noah and Lot drink? Each protagonist got drunk after narrowly escaping the end of the world. Were they trying to wash away survivor's guilt? To forget the emptiness of the new world? To escape the awesome responsibility of having to start the world anew? To feel the power of being the only people left in the world? Or did they turn to alcohol as a self-punitive means of reducing their conscious or unconscious stress? Is there a similarity between the apocalyptic experiences of Noah and Lot and that of all alcoholics whereby nothing exists in the world except the contents of the bottle? (Ben-Noun, 63)

It is safe to say that all of these elements play a part in Noah's drunken stupor. But the state of inebriation also represents an attempt to escape from a delirious state of nightmare waking that constitutes the survivor's ongoing struggle—as we see in Terrence Des Pres' observation about survivors of another historical nightmare:

> The concentration camps were in this world and yet not in this world, places where behavior was grossly exaggerated, without any apparent logic, yet fiercely hostile and encompassing. These are the components of nightmare, and if they join with the prisoner's psychic state—the confusion and stunned emotion, the dread and impotence, the split between a self that is victim and a self which, as through the wrong end of a telescope, merely watches—then the sense of nightmare is bound to prevail. (Des Pres, 83–84)

The Rabbis, using ingenious midrashic symbolism, describe Noah's experience as an expression of these very ideas:

> He planted a vineyard and was disgraced by the wine. The Rabbis contend that on the very same day he planted the vine, it produced fruit, he harvested the grapes, pressed them, drank and became drunk, and exposed his shame. They explain that when he was about to plant the vineyard, Satan came and stood before him and asked: "What are you planting?" He answered, "A vineyard." "Tell me about it." "It has sweet fruit, both fresh and dried, and you can make wine out of it which gladdens hearts, as it says: 'And wine gladdens the hearts of man' " (Psalms 104:15). Satan said, "Let's be partners in this vineyard," to which Noah said, "*L'hayim!*" [to life!] What did Satan do? He brought a ewe, killed it, and placed it under the vine; then he killed a lion, then a pig, then a monkey, and sprinkled their blood underneath the vineyard—to imply that when man drinks, he is first tame as a silent lamb and a sheep before shearing, then he becomes as confident as a lion, then like a pig who filthies itself, and then like a monkey who

stands, dancing and frolicking profanely. All of this, Noah experienced. If this was the case with Noah, whom God praised so highly, for all the rest of us, how much more so! (*Midrash Tanhuma, Noah* 13)

On a simple level this midrash describes the perils of drinking. Through inebriation, man is revealed in his worst light, wallowing like a filthy pig and cavorting like a stupid monkey.

On a deeper level, however, this passage contains artful echoes of the Garden of Eden story. The dizzying pace with which man acts, stumbles, and experiences the repercussions of his actions is reminiscent of the Rabbinic portrait of Adam's sin. Satan, generally the symbol of life's demonic undertow, here becomes the reincarnation of the snake, man's alter ego, who encourages him to sin in the Garden. The striking parallel between Noah's vine and Adam's Tree of Knowledge is compelling.

Let us consider, furthermore, the role of the animals in each of these biblical narratives. Adam named them, Noah saved them, but in this passage they are slaughtered. Their blood becomes the wine that Noah drinks. Noah rewrites Adam's narrative, casting it in frighteningly ominous shadows. Noah's psychotic acts of derangement move him radically from passivity to frenetic activity. He wants to defy God, to eat of the forbidden fruit, to wrong his rights, and to fail miserably. He wants to kill rather than save, drink blood rather than abstain from it (Gen. 9:4). All barriers between man and beast, between blood and wine, have collapsed. Noah wants to undo Creation, bringing about dissolution of himself and of the world. There is no other way he can absolve himself of his awesome and unbearable responsibility. He seeks total abandon until he reaches a point of ultimate futility, *u-motar ha-adam min ha-beheimah ain ki ha-kol havel*, "Man has no superiority over beast, since both amount to nothing" (Eccles. 3:19). The midrash grippingly depicts the unendurable guilt of the survivor, nihilistically acting out his infernal torment and profound awareness of his worthlessness. Noah seeks to redeem life through negating it.

His death wish is so strong that he longs to return to the dark side of Eden, to the commission of sin as an assertion of existence: I sin, therefore I am.

Noah plants a vineyard because he desperately wants to get back to the Garden. But it is not only the dark side of Eden that awakens his longing for paradise lost. After the Flood, Noah's fires of desire have been quenched. His days are *yamim asher ein ba-hem hefetz*—"days in which there is no desire" (Eccles. 12:1) [author's translation]. He passionately yearns to reengage the world and looks to the fruit of the vine to enable him to feel longing once again.

The yearning for Eden is echoed in a comment of Rabbi Moshe Sofer, about what happens to Noah next.

> He became drunk and uncovered himself in his tent (Gen. 9:20): He thought that the world had reverted to the state before original sin, "they were naked and not ashamed" (2:25); he was therefore not concerned about revealing himself naked in his tent. (*Hatam Sofer*, Gen. 9:20)

No sooner had he become inebriated than Noah revealed a hope hidden deep within his heart: that cleansed by the Flood, the world could once again return to the innocence of Eden, when Adam and Eve wandered in the Garden unclothed and "yet they felt no shame" (Gen. 2:25). With the present too horrible to bear, the immediate past unthinkable, the drunken Noah projects himself back to the unadorned innocence of the world as it was originally meant to be.

Furthermore, by psychologically returning to Paradise, Noah hoped not only to become like Adam—he hoped to become like God. Noah's vineyard is the second act of planting mentioned in the Bible. The first planting was done by the Almighty Himself: "The LORD God planted a garden in Eden, in the east, and placed there the man whom He had formed" (Gen. 2:8). After the Flood, Noah chose to engage in the divine act of planting. He closed his eyes and flashed back to the darkness that came before the light; the eternity that preceded the

beginning of time. He pictured God creating from the void. He imagined the Master of Universe, all alone, breaking ground and sowing
seeds. God had planted a garden for man and placed him therein. He
had invited Adam to partake of all of its delectable fruit, but far more
important, He had charged him to tend His divine garden. Now Noah
planted, and prayed that God would come into his garden, blessing it
with gentle nourishing rain. Although he knew full well that only
God could plant a Tree of Life or a Tree of Knowledge, he hoped that
he and God could be partners in all other growing things, re-creating
a world in which man could thrive. After a night of despair, Noah
chose to awaken and embrace life again through imitatio Dei.

The act of planting was indeed a step forward for Noah. Sadly, he
immediately took two steps back, by getting drunk and exposing himself. He is seen in his nakedness by his son, Ham, whom he curses,
while blessing Shem and Japhet who had covered him respectfully.
Devora Steinmetz explains the significance of these acts in her article,
"Vineyard, Farm, and Garden: The Drunkenness of Noah in the
Context of Primeval History:"

> For the first time the one who pronounces the punishment
> and who utters the curse is a human being. . . . Noah here
> takes the place of God; it is Noah against whom Ham sins and
> it is Noah who stands in judgment. Noah, not God, utters the
> blessings and the curse which conclude this first moment in
> the postdiluvian world and which shape the rest of biblical
> history. . . . While for Adam the attainment of knowledge
> threatened a dangerous breach of the boundary between
> human being and God, Noah's task is to become more God-
> like. (Steinmetz, 207)

This interpretation of the story of Noah's vineyard moves man to
a new phase vis-à-vis his fellow man. The world will be a better place
because of man's moral initiative. Noah has come full circle. He

actively has taken the reins of justice, thereby compensating for what he did not do before the Flood.

And so Noah, in his new role in a re-created world, takes his first faltering and imperfect steps, like a drunken sailor early in the morning. It is no wonder that he stumbled. He stood isolated on a lonely planet, whose past had been erased forever. From where was Noah to draw the emotional strength and inspiration to carry on without being crushed by hopelessness? Mankind had failed the world and the world had failed mankind. And so, when he emerged from the ark, Noah received from God a gift not of this world, a most precious thing: the gift of hope. From the very clouds that brought the Flood, a rainbow appeared.

What was the meaning of this spectacular and enigmatic symbol? For centuries, commentators have struggled to decipher it. Ostensibly, the rainbow is an assurance that man will never again suffer the ultimate slings and arrows of outrageous fortune; the rainbow is the unforgettable sign of the covenant. But is it merely a symbol?

Before the Flood we are told that "Noah walked with God" (Gen. 6:9); now, after the trauma of the Flood, Noah was left bereft of spirituality. When he reached his lowest point, Noah was given the emblem of hopeful reawakening. *Après le déluge*, the rainbow allowed him to reconnect with the divine, for the secret of the rainbow is in the power of color, the catharsis of beauty, and in the healing experience of the aesthetic. These awaken in our souls the transcendental yearning for what lies somewhere over the rainbow. This we have been taught by Rabbi Joseph B. Soloveitchik in his essay "Exaltation of God and Redeeming the Aesthetic":

> The apprehension of beauty elevates the mind, cleanses the spirit, and at least for a moment, ennobles the heart. A man feels overcome by the impact of beauty. However, he is not crushed by it; on the contrary, he recovers a sense of worthiness and dignity. . . . Only through coming in contact with the

beautiful and exalted may one apprehend God instead of com-
prehending Him, feel the embrace of the Creator, and the
warm breath of infinity hovering over finite creation.
(Soloveitchik, 55, 59)

The startling beauty of the rainbow ennobled Noah's heart,
enabling him to apprehend God. It would always serve to remind him
of the new, immutable covenant. And yet, interestingly, the biblical
text relates the experience to God's memory as well:

When I bring clouds over the earth, and the bow appears in
the clouds, *I will remember My covenant* [italics added] between
Me and you and every living creature among all flesh, so that
the waters shall never again become a flood to destroy all flesh.
(Gen. 9:14–15)

The verses imply that in addition to remembering His covenant,
God also remembers that He had destroyed all flesh. This recollection
holds within it what Edith Wyschograd has termed the "double disclosiveness of memory."

To remember is to grasp occurrences in the manner of hold-
ing-in-front-of-oneself not only that which was but that which
could have been. It is this double disclosiveness of memory, its
inclusion of paths not taken, that place possibility within the
conspectus of the past. (Wyschograd, 24)

The Omniscient One could have sustained no greater disappointment than being compelled to destroy all that He had created, knowing as only He could have known the full range of possibilities of all
those paths not taken.

On Rosh Hashanah, the day of *Zikhron Teruah*, of resounding memories (Lev. 23:24), we too recall what was and what might have been.
This painful realization fills us with guilt and disappointment. We

shield ourselves with liturgical allusions to our illustrious ancestors, hoping to focus upon them and deflect attention from our inadequacies. Yet in the *Zikhronot*, pride of place is given to Noah: "God remembered Noah and all the beasts and all the cattle that were with him in the ark, and God caused a wind to blow across the earth, and the waters subsided" (Gen. 8:1). God compassionately remembered His creatures for life. If love and mercy undergird His memory, then we can be hopeful that we may be graced with a fresh start.

The significance of the story of Noah as a message of hope for renewal was clear to another generation of survivors, millennia ago. The prophet Isaiah, formulating his prophecy of consolation for survivors of the destruction of Jerusalem, placed before them the memory of God's promise to Noah as a model of how their own hopes and dreams for a new life might come to fruition:

> For a little while I forsook you,
> But with vast love I will bring you back.
> In slight anger, for a moment,
> I hid My face from you;
> But with kindness everlasting
> I will take you back in love.
> said the LORD your Redeemer.
> For this to Me is like the waters of Noah:
> As I swore that the waters of Noah
> Nevermore would flood the earth,
> So I swear that I will not
> Be angry with you or rebuke you.
> For the mountains may move
> And the hills be shaken,
> But my loyalty shall never move from you.
> Nor My covenant of friendship be shaken
> said the LORD, who takes you back in love.
> (Isa. 54:7–10)

Perhaps as he spoke these immortal words of consolation, Isaiah was pointing to a rainbow over Jerusalem, a luminous symbol of God's everlasting love. The ancient sign of God's covenant with all mankind was given new meaning in that era of anticipation, as a mark of His love for Israel. A new facet of the covenant was revealed at that moment, but it was not to be the last word of hope. We are all descendants of Noah; we are all children of survivors. In every generation we look up into the heavens, searching the clouds for a sign that the hue and cry of our lives will be transformed into all of the colors of the rainbow, allowing us once again to begin anew.

Chapter Two

✂

Tears from Heaven

✂

Some time afterward, God put Abraham to the test. He said to him, "Abraham," and he answered, "Here I am." And He said, "Take your son, your favored one, Isaac, whom you love, and go to the land of Moriah, and offer him there as a burnt offering on one of the heights that I will point out to you." (Gen. 22:1–2)

The story of the *Akedah* (the Binding of Isaac) is the most compelling scriptural reading of the Days of Awe. Its soul-stirring testimony to faith, devotion, courage, and love is a powerful message for Rosh Hashanah. On that Day of Judgment we contemplate the trials and tribulations of the past year and wonder what awaits us in the year to come. How will we withstand the challenges of our fate? How will we maintain our belief in God, distanced from Him as we are by ordeals and tragedy that we are unable to understand? The story of our father Abraham's willingness to sacrifice his beloved son Isaac has been viewed, throughout Jewish history, as the greatest demonstration of unwavering belief that the world has ever known. For many, the magnitude of Abraham's trial overshadows their own challenges and doubts and offers a degree of perspective.

In his discussion of the purpose of the trial of the *Akedah*, the 13th-century Provençal biblical commentator Rabbi David Kimhi (Radak) grapples with the philosophical conundrum of an omniscient God testing Abraham. Kimhi dismisses the standard explanation that the trial was intended to sanctify God's holy name by making Abraham's spiritual achievement manifest to others. He points out that there was no one present to witness the supreme devotion of the "knight of faith." Furthermore, none would have believed Abraham had he later reported the event. Kimhi asserts instead that the biblical account is meant to serve as the paradigm of the love of God for all people, for all times.

> Today, the vast majority of the world accepts the Torah of Moses our teacher and its narratives, even if they disagree with us regarding the commandments and claim that they are allegorical. Since most people believe this great story, it is a supreme testimony to our father Abraham who loved God completely and extraordinarily; all should learn from him the way to love God. (Radak, Gen. 22:1)

The *Akedah* is an ordeal where love is put on trial. It is the story of an elderly father commanded to take his only son and offer him as a sacrifice. All of Abraham's dreams had focused on his beloved Isaac. Everything he had done in his life had been a spiritual investment, which he intended to hand over to his heir. Through Isaac, his legacy would live on. Given his unabating love and trust in the God he had made his own, one can only begin to imagine the pain and despair that Abraham must have experienced upon being told by the Almighty that his hopes were to be dashed upon the stones of Mount Moriah.

However, the *Akedah* is not the first trial Abraham confronted. Abraham's life was full of challenges. The Rabbis understood that they were not mere happenstance, but rather a battery of tests administered by God to forge Abraham's spiritual character and justify God's selection of Abraham as a theological innovator and leader.

Abraham our father, may he rest in peace, was put to ten trials and withstood them all, demonstrating how dearly beloved
Abraham was [by God]. (M. Avot 5:3)

What were these 10 trials? The Mishnah does not list them, leaving room for later interpreters to speculate about their identity. One
opinion seizes upon a tradition, not recorded in the Bible, which
describes Abraham's rejection of paganism preceding his election by
God as trial number one. In that midrashic tradition, Abraham, as a
young salesman in his father's idol shop, actively demonstrated the
futility of idolatry and was persecuted for his faith by King Nimrod.
Abraham was cast into a fiery furnace and miraculously saved. This
account serves to explain God's choice of Abraham as His chosen one,
based upon a decision that he himself had made. By proving his spiritual mettle, he demonstrated that it was appropriate that he be
appointed the herald of monotheism. Furthermore, the tradition
claims that Abraham was willing to give his own life for his faith,
which might be understood as a template of devotion, justifying his
later readiness to sacrifice Isaac.

Other commentators suggest that the first of Abraham's trials was
the divine command of *lekh lekha*—"Go forth." In that trial, Abraham
was both transported and transformed:

Go forth from your country, your birthplace and from your
father's house to the land that I will show you. (Gen. 12:1)
[author's translation]

Abraham, founding father of the Hebrew nation, was born in
Mesopotamia, the land between the Tigris and Euphrates rivers. He was
raised in the colorful culture of polytheism. It was a vibrant world in
which men fashioned idols in their own image to give concrete expression to the mystifying powers of nature. Monuments were erected to
deities and cultic trees marked their holy places. In Abraham's circles,
child sacrifice was not out of the ordinary; it represented the noblest

gesture of unmitigated devotion to one's ancestral gods. This was the heritage of Abraham's father, Terah, and would no doubt have been Abraham's legacy as well, had he not received the divine call, establishing a new phase in the bond between man and God.

Why was it necessary for Abraham to leave Mesopotamia—his country, his birthplace, and his father's house? Perhaps Abraham simply had to embark upon a journey. God did not tell Abraham to go to the Land of Canaan; he was to go "to the land that I will show you." Ostensibly, it was the *journey*, not the destination of the Holy Land, that carried with it deep significance:

> God's initial encounter with His chosen one takes place at the start of a journey. God and man meet as travelers on a road which moves away from the static, familiar confines of the past towards the unknown and uncertain horizon of the future. . . . Man's journey with God is predicated upon an act of separation: removing oneself from the natural bonds of the past, from the kindred and parental ties which bind one to a specific place, a home. Separation from the static, human past is the necessary prerequisite for moving on to the dynamic, God-given future. (Och, 166)

But why was Abraham, a scion of an idolatrous society, selected to be the progenitor of a people chosen by God? Again the text is silent. However, a vital message is heard through that resounding silence:

> The patriarch bursts upon the scene of history with astounding suddenness. The first seventy-five years of his life are passed over in total silence. God's call comes in an instant, without forewarning or preparation. It is brief and compelling in its demands, and Abram's immediate response marks the true beginning of his life. The momentous events unfold with startling rapidity, and any introductory embellishment could only have a diminishing effect. The divine silence that persisted for

ten generations is shattered. The voice that first set Creation in motion and that, when last heard by man, brought a message of hope and blessing to the human race resounds once more. (Sarna, 88)

God's initial command launched Abraham on a spiritual trajectory, the exact course of which would be determined by his own actions. The trial of *lekh lekha* represented the first step in the covenant of the land that God made with Abraham, as well as the first of an unrelenting series of trials. After a long journey, Abraham returned home, to the land that God had promised him. He arrived in the Promised Land granted to him and his descendants for posterity. It is therefore startling that no sooner had he come than he was forced to leave (Gen. 12:10). This was Abraham's next trial. The first *oleh* (new immigrant) became the first *yored* (emigrant), as famine compelled Abraham and Sarah to pack their bags and head for Egypt in search of food. Imagine the cognitive dissonance Abraham must have experienced, arriving in the Land—to be immediately exiled! The cosmic significance of the event can only be appreciated when this trial is viewed as a test of faith. The Rabbis raised the experience to another plane, interpreting Abraham's descent to Egypt as the prefiguration of the path his descendants would follow two generations later. They too would be forced down to Egypt in the wake of famine. They too would weather the storm, and eventually return to the land of their forefathers.

Abraham's role as the recipient of God's promise of land and posterity is reflected in the Covenant of the Pieces, which God contracted with him as a reward for his unwavering faith and devotion. Abraham, who had been assured land, progeny, and blessing, was once again made aware of the intense dialectic with which his offspring would be forced to contend. They would spend generations enslaved in a foreign country. Only after insufferable years of slavery and devastation would they return to the Promised Land, regroup, and begin their national life.

All of the long-range blessings and promises were far from encouraging. Abraham was old and childless. Of what use were his claims to the land with no one to inherit him? Deeply troubled, Abraham exclaimed: "Since You have granted me no offspring, my steward will be my heir" (Gen. 15:3).

Reassuringly, God responded: " 'That one shall not be your heir; none but your very own issue shall be your heir.' He took him outside and said, 'Look toward heaven and count the stars, if you are able to count them.' And He added, 'So shall your offspring be' " (Gen. 15:4–5).

Every evening Abraham would gaze at the myriad stars and hear the fading reverberation of God's promise: "Look toward heaven and count the stars, if you are able to count them. . . . So shall your offspring be" (Gen. 15:5). Yet night after night, Sarah would cry herself to sleep, and each morning the couple would awake to the stillness of a home without children. The promise remained as nebulous as the galaxies; children, a mere gleam in their eyes. Abraham and Sarah painfully struggled with their barrenness for many long years.

For Abraham, blessing eased the pain at age 86, with the birth of his firstborn son, Ishmael. The child's mother was Sarah's handmaiden Hagar—not exactly what Abraham and Sarah had prayed for. Sarah's hopes were deferred, but at long last, Abraham was granted an heir apparent, a new beginning, ostensibly the key to the actualization of God's promises.

The years passed and Ishmael grew up. The child's development became the focus of daily life. A family dynamic was established in which Abraham, Sarah, Hagar, and Ishmael each assumed their respective roles. But one day, messengers arrived with the news that things were about to change. Abraham and Sarah were told that they too would be blessed with a child, hard as that was to believe, with Abraham being 100 years old and Sarah 90. But so it was. Miraculously, Isaac was born, bringing blessing and laughter into the lives of an elderly couple bound together by faith, love, and hope.

Abraham was overjoyed. When Isaac was weaned, Abraham threw a party. Life seemed perfect; two sons, two contented wives and one very proud father. Little did Abraham know that the occasion would precipitate his next difficult trial. Sarah had been watching Ishmael for years, and she didn't like what she saw. Something in his behavior was amiss. Now that she was a mother, she zealously guarded her im-pressionable young son Isaac from Ishmael's negative influence. She ordered Abraham to banish the handmaiden Hagar and her son, Ishmael. God concurred with Sarah's demand: Ishmael had to go. But how could Abraham cast out his son? He was crushed, overcome by anguish and confusion. What was to become of his hopes for the future, his belief in God's promises? This sore trial required that he set aside all of his feelings, exercise supreme faith, and obey the Lord's command. With a heavy heart, father Abraham rose to the occasion.

Ishmael was gone, leaving a gnawing emptiness, but Abraham's life became preoccupied with young Isaac. The boy was a source of comfort to his father and mother. Abraham focused on God's promise: "For it is through Isaac that offspring shall be continued for you" (Gen. 21:12). Isaac was now the key to all of Abraham's hopes. The past would be overshadowed by the glorious future, which was yet to unfold. And then the unthinkable happened. God presented Abraham with the ultimate test—He commanded him to sacrifice his beloved son.

> Some time afterward, God put Abraham to the test. He said to him, "Abraham," and he answered, "Here I am." And He said, "Take your son, your favored one, Isaac, whom you love, and *lekh lekha* [author's change] to the land of Moriah, and offer him there as a burnt offering on one of the heights that I will point out to you." (Gen. 22:1–2)

His last trial sent Abraham on a journey to end all journeys. Commanded to take his only son and sacrifice him, Abraham once again followed a path to an unknown destination. Traversing the rugged road to Mount Moriah, Abraham simultaneously underwent an inner journey toward faith and submission. He suspended both his rational faculties and his passionate feelings to reach exalted spiritual heights. In the end, Isaac was spared. Abraham the father was relieved, and as the father of the nation, his doubts and conflicts were again replaced by promises and blessing. He had yielded to the will of God, facing each of the ten trials with extraordinary belief and courage.

The *Akedah* is counted as the 10th and final trial. It was the culmination of all that had come before. How could anything be more difficult? Yet, there are those who note that the ultimate trial is actually described in an unlikely passage at the end of the story: an epilogue, which at first glance appears to be singularly anticlimactic.

> Some time later, Abraham was told, "Milcah too has borne children to your brother Nahor: Uz the first-born, and Buz his brother, and Kemuel the father of Aram; and Hesed, Hazo, Pildash, Jidlaph, and Bethuel"—Bethuel being the father of Rebekah. These eight Milcah bore to Nahor, Abraham's brother. And his concubine, whose name was Reumah, also bore children: Tebah, Gaham, Tahash, and Maacah. (Gen. 22:20–24)

The narrative of the *Akedah* ends with Abraham descending Mount Moriah, joining his servants, and returning to Beersheba. The Torah continues with a listing of the children born to Abraham's brother Nahor. What meaning is there in this registry of Abraham's nephews and nieces?

The classic explanation offered for this epilogue to the story of the *Akedah* focuses on what the list implies. Cognizant of the near miss of the *Akedah*, the text assures the reader that the future is secure. Bethuel is the father of Rebekah who will be Isaac's wife, a marriage that will guarantee the continuity of the family and the fulfillment of the divine promise.

Alternatively, it has been argued that embedded within this passage is yet another trial. We are told, at the end of the harrowing ordeal of the *Akedah*, that Abraham walked away with one son, by the skin of his teeth, as it were. In contrast, his brother Nahor, who had stayed home in Mesopotamia—Terah's son who did not hear the divine call of *lekh lekha*—merited 12 children. Twelve, of course, represents the biblical number of peoplehood, as in the 12 tribes. Abraham would not be thus blessed for two more generations. The final note of the story, therefore, leaves us wondering about the measure of justice in God's world, and suggests that the last trial of Abraham, the forefather of the Hebrew nation, was not the 10th but rather the 11th. His ultimate ordeal was a test of his long-range vision, of his ability to look beyond the contradictions and disappointments of the present moment. Such farsightedness was required of Abraham, and would be required of his descendants for Jewish survival throughout the ages.

Vision and blindness are central to the interpretation of the story of the *Akedah*. These elements reveal to us much that is left unsaid by Abraham and Isaac in the story. Recall that when God commanded Abraham to leave his home in Ur of the Chaldees, He told him to go "to the land which I will show you," and when He told him to bind Isaac, it was to be done "on one of the mountains which I will tell you." In both the first and the 10th trials, Abraham's destination was unknown. He blindly followed God's lead to uncharted territories, until the Almighty was prepared to put things into full focus for him. As he proceeded to the land of Moriah, the text informs us, "On the third day Abraham lifted his eyes and saw the place from afar" (Gen. 22:4) [author's translation]. The Rabbis embellished this verse:

Abraham asked Isaac: "Do you see what I see?" "I see a handsome, fine, cloud-capped mountain." At which point

Abraham turned to his servants and asked them the same. They replied, "No, we see nothing." (*Midrash Tanhuma B, Va-yera'* 46)

For Abraham the picture was clear; he would leave his benighted servants behind, while he and Isaac, who saw the destination clearly, would follow their vision and scale the spiritual heights.

Indeed, only the farsighted venture out on difficult spiritual journeys. A midrash (*Va-yikra Rabbah* 14:2) explains the beautiful custom of calling all converts to Judaism "son of Abraham," "daughter of Abraham" (as when they are called to the Torah). R. Nathan quotes a verse from the book of Job (36:3): "I shall proclaim my knowledge to those who come from a distance *(le-merahok)*" [author's translation]—and explains: "Those who have come near from afar are considered to be [the children] of Abraham, who came from afar." We then expect R. Nathan to make reference to Abraham's coming from Ur of the Chaldees, or the like. Instead, he quotes our verse: "He lifted his eyes and saw the place from afar." Clearly, the idea underlying this midrash is that both Abraham and those who have chosen to join his descendants through the ages possess a gift of clairvoyance that enables them to transcend the here and now, and focus on eternity. This idea is also echoed by Jeremiah, who proclaim: "The Lord revealed Himself to me from afar, with eternal love" (Jer. 31:3) [author's translation] —true revelation comes from afar, born of perspective and nurtured by love.

Notably, at the denouement of our story, Abraham again lifted his eyes:

Abraham lifted his eyes and they fell upon a ram, caught in the thicket by its horns. So Abraham went and took the ram and offered it up as a burnt offering in place of his son. (Gen. 22:13) [author's translation]

The simple meaning of the text is obvious: Abraham was spared having to sacrifice Isaac and offered an animal in his place. However, the Rabbis view this turn of events as being symbolic of the future in which Isaac's descendants would also be saved, their redemption heralded by the ram's horn, the shofar. This long-range vision—this prophecy—was vouchsafed to Abraham in merit of his unswerving obedience to the word of God. In the Jerusalem Talmud, the discovery of the ram caught in the thicket foreshadows Israel's tumultuous history, which eventually will bring about complete salvation:

> R. Huna said in the name of R. Haninah bar Yitzhak: All that day Abraham had seen the ram caught in a tree and released, caught in a bush and released, caught in a thicket and released. God said to Abraham: "So, too, your children are destined to be enmeshed in sin and entangled among the nations, from Babylonia to Media, from Media to Greece, and from Greece to Edom (Rome)." Abraham asked: "Will it be thus forever?" God replied: "In the end they will be redeemed through the horns of this ram," as it says (Zech 9:14): "My Lord God shall sound the ram's horn and advance in a stormy tempest." (J. Ta'an. 2:4)

Before turning home, Abraham named that terrible and holy place "The Lord will see"—a reference, perhaps, to his earlier statement to Isaac "God will see to the sheep for His burnt offering, my son" (Gen. 22:8). Abraham's vision will be rewarded with God seeing to all that will be required to fulfill the destiny that He has promised. And indeed, the Torah immediately tells us that in later days that place will be known as the mountain "where God will appear." According to tradition, the precedent of sacrifice that Abraham our father established determined the future location of the Temple, and the merit of the Akedah shields the Children of Israel in times of trouble forever.

So much for Abraham and his vision. What about Isaac? The ordeal of which we speak is not "the Binding of Abraham" but rather "the Binding of Isaac." Let us set out for Mount Moriah once again, this time viewing the odyssey through the eyes of Isaac.

> The journey is like a silent progress through the indeterminate and the contingent, a holding of the breath, a process which has no present, which is inserted, like a blank duration, between what has passed and what lies ahead. (Auerbach, 10)

We must remember that Isaac, who is of indeterminate age in this story, set out on the journey following his father without any fore-knowledge of what was to be expected of him. For him, it was simply a long and arduous trek, whose destination was unclear. But as an obe-dient son, he followed his taciturn father's lead and struggled to keep up. Day turned to night, and again to day. Perhaps during the long hours on the road the lad occupied his mind with visions of adventure and excitement, as boys are wont to do, dreaming of places at which he could arrive only in the farthest reaches of his mind. And then, on the third day, imagination gave way to confusion and fear. It was at just that juncture that he saw his father gaze off into the distance. He lifted his eyes, and his countenance seemed to change. He had arrived.

The text does not indicate that Abraham informed his son of what lay ahead. He turned to his servants and provided them with an excuse: "You stay here with the ass. The boy and I will go up there; we will worship and we will return to you" (Gen. 22:5). He then gathered up the necessary equipment, and, we are told, "Abraham took the wood for the burnt offering and put it on his son Isaac" (Gen. 22:6).

This detail, offered by the biblical text, seems straightforward enough. Abraham had chosen to leave his servants and the pack mule at the base of the mountain. He and Isaac would continue alone. No one else must know of the dreadful act that was to be performed. Abraham and his son would make the climb alone, Abraham carrying the firestone and the knife; the wood, however, was loaded onto Isaac's shoulders.

The Rabbis were not content to gloss over this detail, and sug-gested two possible interpretations. Under the view that this trial was Abraham's alone, Isaac's carrying the wood is a pathetic detail of the story—here is a child unknowingly bearing the instrument of his own holocaust, "like a man who carries his own cross on his shoulder" (*Bereshit Rabbah* 56:4). In other accounts, Isaac is portrayed as knowing full well what awaited him, and choosing to participate in the preparations for his fate. In these renditions, Isaac has been transformed from a passive child into an active, responsible adult. The object of the ultimate ordeal becomes its subject, and this terrible trial of Abraham is also a trial of his successor, Isaac.

It is at this point in the episode, and at this point alone, that the voice of Isaac is heard.

> Abraham took the wood for the burnt offering and put it on his son Isaac. He himself took the firestone and the knife; and the two walked off together. Then Isaac said to his father Abraham, "Father!" And he answered, "Yes, my son." And he said, "Here are the firestone and the wood; but where is the sheep for the burnt offering?" And Abraham said, "God will see to the sheep for His burnt offering, my son." And the two of them walked on together. (Gen. 22:6–8)

This is the only exchange between father and son on the three-day journey to Mount Moriah. Implicit in this simple conversation, though, is a heartrending dialogue of their inner voices. Isaac's first touching words, "my father!" are met by Abraham's stirring response, "my son." No words could be more powerful in intimating the ultimate questions that Isaac posed. Have you forgotten that I am your son, your only son, the one you love? I am the child for whom you waited a lifetime! I am the key to your future. Without me all hope is lost! Abraham need only whisper the words "my son" to make it clear that he is fully cognizant that his past, present, and future may be instantly obliterated through one fateful action. Yet he reassures Isaac and unequivocally asserts his faith that God will provide the lamb for slaughter.

Scripture has framed this dialogue by repeating the expression "And they walked together." Why does this description appear twice? Whereas initially it is simply a description of their perambulation, after their exchange, they have achieved a tacit understanding, and nothing more need be said. They are now together in spirit; as one, they submit to the will of God.

Knowing now the fate that might await him at the end of the road, Isaac walks beside his father. His fear of that outcome is held in check by his love for Abraham, and by his unwavering trust in his father's protective power. Atop Moriah, Abraham slowly but unflinchingly makes all the preparations for the dreadful deed that he has been commanded to do. As the altar rises and the fire leaps heavenward, Isaac is seized by fear and trembling. Where is the lamb that his father has promised that God will provide? He feels the cords with which his father silently binds him; then he sees the glint of the sacrificial knife. In those unbearable seconds of terror, Isaac's frightened eyes search frantically for compassion in his father's stern gaze. However, he sees only grim determination to fulfill the awful will of God. The utter tragedy of that moment is captured poignantly by Rembrandt in his 1635 painting *The Angel Prevents the Sacrifice of Isaac*, which now hangs in the Hermitage. The artist added one detail that does not appear in the biblical text: he portrays Abraham as covering Isaac's face. Dedicated as he was to carrying out God's command, Abraham knows that if he looks into his son's eyes at the moment of truth, he will simply not be able to perform the terrible act.

Just then, an unseen angel calls out to Abraham from the heavens and commands him to cease and desist. Abraham immediately raises his eyes, and behold! There is a ram caught in the thicket by its horns. Relieved, he offers it in place of his beloved son Isaac. He is then called a second time by the angel, who proclaims that his faith has been vindicated and will be rewarded throughout the generations.

Unlike Abraham, Isaac does not lift up his eyes. He cannot, because the world has gone dark for him. As the midrash puts it

(*Bereshit Rabbah* 65:10), when the knife cast its shadow on Isaac's face, tears fell from heaven. Isaac's eyes flickered like uncertain lights and became cold as gray agate. On that tragic day, Isaac went blind. Although Isaac's blindness is recorded much later in the biblical context, the Rabbis connect it to what happened on Moriah. As we shall see, they probed the reaches of the second patriarch's subconscious and concluded that the binding of Isaac led to the blinding of Isaac.

Isaac's weakness of vision is mentioned in the context of the story of the rivalry between his sons Jacob and Esau. We are told that Isaac's blindness was simply a function of aging: "When Isaac grew old, his eyes became dim" (Gen 27:1). Literarily, this loss of vision is essential to the narrative, since it allows Jacob to impersonate his brother. Figuratively, it may be implied that Isaac's choice of Esau as the favored son is a result of his clouded perception. The Rabbis take this reading much further and suggest that Isaac's infirmity was directly caused by Esau. Some say that just looking at Esau—whom they saw as evil incarnate—caused Isaac's blindness. Others accuse Esau of chicanery, causing Isaac's vision to be clouded by his flattery and bribery: "for bribes blind the eyes of the discerning..." (Deut. 16:19). He prefers Esau to Jacob, merely because Esau hunted for him, while Jacob remained at home. Another group of midrashim say that the cause was Esau's marriage to pagan women: either that the incense they burned to their idols affected his eyesight, or that God mercifully dimmed Isaac's vision to spare him the sight of that travesty in his house. In all of these midrashic passages, Esau is the central focus (*Midrash Tanhuma, Toledot* 8).

But there is a second group of midrashim—those that suggest that some suppressed past experience surfaced at that juncture in Isaac's life. That experience was, of course, the *Akedah*.

And his eyes became dim from seeing—From the intensity of that sight. When our father Abraham bound his son Isaac on the altar, the angels cried, as it says, "Hark, the Arielites cry aloud [outside]. The angels of peace weep bitterly. Highways are desolate, wayfarers have ceased. A covenant has been renounced, cities rejected, mortal man despised" (Isa. 33:7–8). Their tears fell in his eyes and were imprinted in them, so that when he became old his eyes grew dim. (*Bereshit Rabbah* 65:10)

The verses from the book of Isaiah quoted in this midrash refer in their biblical context to the devastating situation in Israel during the Assyrian period. The portrait is of destruction so extensive that even the hosts of heaven mourn. What the midrash fails to explain is why the angels cry in our context. Of what relevance are those tears of the angels to the stories of the *Akedah* and the blindness of Isaac?

An investigation of parallel midrashim supplies the answer. In one alternative version (*Bereshit Rabbah* 56:5), the statement "A covenant has been renounced, cities rejected, mortal man despised" is turned into a question: How could God scorn Jerusalem, and destroy the Temple that was to have been the inheritance of the descendants of Isaac? On the basis of that reading, the connection to the *Akedah* is clearer. The Midrash is portraying the angels asking how God could deny the destiny of Mount Moriah. Abraham's journey to Moriah was the paradigm of pilgrimage. It was he who offered the first and the ultimate of all sacrifices on the Temple Mount. What began with Abraham was supposed to reach a spiritual crescendo in the Temple in Jerusalem. Accordingly, the angels raise the same objection in both the last and the first chapters of the story. At the *Akedah*, the angels wonder: Will the dynasty of faith that Abraham had just begun be severed with one stroke of the slaughterer's knife, leaving the spiritual potential of both person and place unfulfilled for all times? The tearful protest of the angels is not so much about the travesty of Abraham being commanded to slaughter his beloved Isaac as it is about the repercussions of that action, over the dream that the descendants of Isaac will never see fulfilled.

Yet an alternate rendition of this midrash amplifies the outrage of the heavenly hosts and shifts its emphasis. It reads as follows:

When Abraham reached out to take the knife and slaughter
his son, the angels cried: "Hark, the Arielites cry *hutzah* [out-
side]. What is the meaning of the term *hutzah?* R. Azaria said:
Outrageous! It is outrageous that he should kill his son with
his own bare hands! What did they [the angels] say?
"Highways are desolate"—was it not Abraham who took in
wayfarers? . . ."A covenant has been renounced"—but He said
"I will uphold my covenant with Isaac!" . . . "Mortal man
despised"—has Abraham no merit? (*Bereshit Rabbah* 56:5)

The focus in this version of the midrash is on the inconceivabili-
ty of that which is about to take place. How could such bad things
happen to such good people? How could Abraham, the man of kindness, have ultimate cruelty foisted upon him? How could he have been
required to perform such a savage act with his own hands? How could
God renege on His promise? The celestial hosts weep bitterly as they
observe the inconsistency between the actions of the loyal servant of
God and the fate that had befallen him. Here the despair and pain of
the angels does not stem from the wasted potential of a master plan
that has been foiled. Rather, their eyes cloud with tears as they perceive moral deviance in the Almighty. They cry out of confusion and
lack of clarity. Those angelic tears fall into the eyes of Isaac and are
not washed away.

However, beyond the response of the celestial hosts to the moral
travesty of the *Akedah*, Rabbinic opinion posits that Isaac was blinded by what he himself saw, on Mount Moriah, at that very moment:

And his eyes became dim from seeing—From the intensity of the
vision which he beheld. When our father Abraham bound his
son Isaac on the altar, Isaac lifted his eyes heavenward and
gazed at the *Shekhinah* (the Divine Presence). . . . God said: If
I kill him now, I shall seal the fate of Abraham my beloved. I
therefore decree that his eyes will become dimmed. (*Bereshit
Rabbah* 65:9)

Lying upon the altar, Isaac's eyes were seared by the blinding light of the Divine Presence. In the biblical worldview, "Man may not see Me and live" (Exod. 33:20). However, in the merit of Abraham, Isaac was spared. Since in the talmudic worldview, "a blind man is considered as dead" (B. Ned. 64b), the compromise view is that Isaac lost his sight. By classifying Isaac as blind, the Rabbis imply that from the moment of the *Akedah* onward, Isaac was no longer an active player in the world of the living.

Note that the logic of the first part of the midrash is unclear. The angels cry, their tears fall into Isaac's eyes, but his blindness does not set in until he is aged and preparing to bless his sons before his death. Why should this be so? Seemingly, the Rabbis have chosen to make a statement about Isaac's religious myopia—his inability to look into the spiritual future. At the end of his life, when the time comes to hand over the reins of covenantal destiny to his sons, Isaac needs to address issues of character and morality. However, precisely at that point, memories long repressed and suppressed come to the surface, preventing Isaac from seeing beyond the here-and-now. This view is succinctly expressed by a midrash in *Bereshit Rabbah* (67:2): " 'And Isaac trembled a great trembling'—Twice did Isaac tremble, once upon the altar and once now." With the shocking realization that Jacob had obtained his blessing deceitfully, Isaac had a flashback to a past moment when a father-son relationship of his had been radically disrupted. In both cases, the precipitating cause was the destiny of what would become the nation of Israel. Both times, Isaac proved unequal to the task of seeing things through a spiritual lens.

The extent of Isaac's blindness becomes crystal clear when we compare this episode with Jacob's blessing of Joseph's sons. There too we are told: "Now Israel's eyes were dim with age; he could not see" (Gen. 48:10). When Joseph brings his sons to Jacob, he gives the younger one precedence and the greater blessing. Joseph objects, thinking that his father simply was unable to see clearly and therefore mistook the younger for the elder. Jacob replies: " 'I know my son, I know. He too shall become a people, and he too shall be great. Yet his younger brother shall be greater than he, and his offspring shall be plentiful enough for nations.' So he blessed them that day, saying, 'By you shall Israel invoke blessings, saying: God make you like Ephraim and Manasseh.' Thus he put Ephraim before Manasseh' " (Gen. 48:19–20). Though visually impaired, Jacob was clairvoyant; his father, Isaac, was not. Isaac couldn't even distinguish between his two sons when they stood before him. He wailed to Esau: " 'Who was it then . . . that hunted game and brought it to me? Moreover, I ate of it before you came, and I blessed him; now he must remain blessed!' " (Gen. 27:33). Why such disproportionate despair about what had transpired? Why did Isaac focus on the food he had eaten? Why couldn't Isaac see beyond the present, as Jacob later would?

A solution to the riddle of Isaac's personality emerges if we join together the two midrashim cited above. Isaac was doubly blinded, both by the angelic tears of moral outrage and by the searing vision of God at what he believed to be the penultimate moment of his life. Traumatized by the incomprehensibility and numinosity of God, Isaac averted his gaze from the future and remained fixed in the material present to the end of his days.

In his enlightening essay "Isaac: The Forgotten Patriarch," Dov Elbaum points out that Isaac was the only patriarch who did not have his named changed by God. He was the only one who did not carry on a dialogue with the Almighty. Even when he prayed for a child, the Torah did not record his words. Thundering silence resounds in his life. It is as if Isaac was not interested in a relationship with the Almighty; he turned a blind eye to Him. Or perhaps Isaac felt that God had turned away from him and was less interested in a relationship with him than with his father and his son. Could that realization have contributed to Isaac's sense of desolation and abandonment? Did these ruminations lead Isaac to conclude that the covenant his father made with God was not for him? He would forge a different kind of covenant with Esau, a bond of flesh expressed in the hunted game his son would bring him. Isaac rejected a grand view of his life because the skies had opened up for him at the place that Abraham renamed

"*Adonai-yireh*," "the mountain where God will appear" (Gen. 22:14). There Isaac had witnessed the enormity of love his father had for the Master of the Universe, but he also perceived evil that he could not explain. What, if not evil, could allow a father to raise the knife against his beloved child? What, if not evil, could have caused the ultimate Father to demand that action of his most loyal vassal Abraham? Isaac looked up and saw the black holes in the divine cosmos.

Recall that in the last verse of the *Akedah* story, we are told that Abraham rejoins his servants, and they return to Beersheba. Someone is missing here, and his absence fairly cries out to us from the text. It is as if Isaac never, ever came down from Mount Moriah; the trauma never left him. Eventually, he would marry and carry on a domestic life. He would raise his family and work his fields, but he could not see beyond his next meal. His field of vision did not include the expansive vistas of covenant, blessing, and redemption. What had been a spiritually electrifying experience for Abraham left Isaac speechless, blind, and inert.

So it might have remained, had it not been for a person of long-range vision who entered the story—the mother of Jacob and Esau, the Matriarch Rebekah. It was she who played the pivotal role in that chapter of salvation history. It was not Isaac but Rebekah who was the crucial link between Abraham and Jacob. She was the one who responded to the divine call, and left her land, her birthplace, and her father's home to follow her vocation.

Seder Eliyahu Rabbah 25:7 highlights Rebekah's virtues alongside those of the other Matriarchs. It was the Matriarchs who were responsible for the turn of events that liberated the Children of Israel from Egypt and transformed them into a nation. This midrashic passage mentions all four Matriarchs. Three of them—Sarah, Rachel, and Leah—are given credit for having made the same concession. Each allowed her husband to take additional wives in order to bear them sons, thereby literally building the nation of Israel. Not so Rebekah. While living in Mesopotamia, she was visited by Abraham's servant, who came to take her to Canaan to be Isaac's wife. Resistance to her immediate departure was posed by her father and brother. In a daring step, the servant suggested that Rebekah herself be consulted: " 'Let us call the girl and ask for her reply.' They called Rebekah and said to her, 'Will you go with this man?' And she said, 'I will go' " (Gen. 24:57–58) [author's translation]. In the merit of her unequivocal response "I will"—an expression of her total trust in God—she was chosen to be among the favored few who built the Jewish nation.

Like Abraham's, Rebekah's life was riddled with trials. She began with the ordeal of *lekh lekha*. Thereafter, she contended with twenty years of barrenness, physical and emotional turmoil during pregnancy, choosing between sons, losing one, then losing both. Notably, when the twins struggled within her, it was she and not Isaac who "went to inquire of the LORD" (Gen. 25:22), and was granted a revelation regarding the nations that were to spring from her womb. Sustained by that proclamation of her destiny, Rebekah remained steadfast throughout all her tribulations. She displayed spiritual fortitude in awaiting the unfolding of the covenant, viewing it from a distance like that cloud-capped mountain.

How appropriate, therefore, that in response to her consent "I will go," the following blessing is bestowed upon her by her family:

O sister! May you grow
Into thousands of myriads;
May your offspring seize
The gates of their foes. (Gen. 24:60)

Don Isaac Abarbanel points out that "it appears as if these are the words of the Living God, as if He placed them in their mouths [Laban and Bethuel] since these are the very words spoken to Abraham at the *Akedah*, 'And your descendants shall seize the gates of their foes'" (Gen. 22:17). Rebekah's blessing was an echo of the blessing for Abraham's faith and dedication at the *Akedah*, for her actions indeed guaranteed the continuity of the Hebrew nation. Upon arriving in

Canaan, we are told "And Rebekah lifted her eyes, and saw Isaac" (Gen. 24:64) [author's translation] —her outlook allowed her to see the light where Isaac had retreated into tunnel vision.

In the end, the story of Isaac concludes with a hopeful note. In a fascinating passage, the first-century Jewish philosopher Philo of Alexandria asserts that immediately upon blessing Jacob, Isaac's sight was restored. The biblical text would seem to corroborate this point. For when all is said and done, Rebekah approaches her husband directly about sending Jacob to find a wife back in the old family homestead of Aram. Isaac not only agrees, but he says to his son: "May He grant you the blessing of Abraham to you and your offspring, that you may possess the land where you are sojourning, which God assigned to Abraham" (Gen. 28:4). At the very end of his days, Isaac's vision is restored—just in time for him to catch a glimpse of his descendants' path into eternity.

Chapter Three

✣

A Voice on High

✣

As is the case on Sabbath and holidays, the scriptural readings for Rosh Hashanah consist of Torah passages, followed by selections from the Prophets. In the Torah portion for the first day of Rosh Hashanah, we read of the birth of Isaac, and on the second day we read the story of *Akedat Yitzhak*—his near-death experience. These dramatic choices portray the inexplicable nature of God's judgment. As Master of the Universe, He grants a son to the elderly Sarah and Abraham, and then paradoxically threatens to take him away. Perhaps, the Rabbis chose these passages to give expression to our own lack of clarity regarding fate and destiny.

It is not readily apparent how the concomitant prophetic narratives, the *haftarot,* that we read on Rosh Hashanah relate to these stories of the perplexing judgment of Abraham and Sarah. In fact, an alternate tradition—reading chapter 2 of the book of Joel as the prophetic selection on Rosh Hashanah—places this question in stark relief.

The prophet Joel proclaims, "Blow a *shofar* in Zion, sound an alarm on My holy mount. For the day of the Lord has come, it is close" (Joel 2:1) [author's translation].

This chapter relates directly to repentance performed by the entire nation, from commoners to priests. Joel poignantly implores the people: "Rend your hearts rather than your garments, And turn back to the LORD your God . . ." (2:13).

Such a haftarah coalesces with the theme of Rosh Hashanah, expressed in the Pentateuchal passages. Rosh Hashanah is the awesome day of the Lord, on which we appeal to the Judge of all mankind to be merciful. In the words of Joel:

> For He is gracious and compassionate,
> Slow to anger, abounding in kindness,
> And renouncing punishment.
> Who knows but He may turn and relent,
> And leave a blessing behind . . . (Joel 2:13)

We pray that His mercy upon which we rely might be evoked in our case as well.

As a commentary on God's judgment and our dependence upon His compassion, the haftarah from the book of Joel builds upon themes found in the Torah portions. However, Joel, chapter 2, did not gain widespread popularity as the haftarah of the day. The Rabbis looked elsewhere for religious inspiration. The haftarah they chose for the first day of Rosh Hashanah was the story of the barrenness of Hannah and the long-awaited birth of Samuel. As for the haftarah of the second day, they chose Jeremiah's prophecy of consolation, which contains a poignant reference to the comfort Jeremiah offered to the Matriarch Rachel about the restoration of her children.

Why were these scriptural texts selected as the pivotal readings of Rosh Hashanah? Ostensibly, their inclusion emanated from the common fate of the three women involved. The following reason is found in the Talmud: "On Rosh Hashanah, God took account of Sarah, Rachel, and Hannah" by blessing them with children (B. Yev. 64b). This explanation of why we read what we read has become standard fare. However, it is nowhere mentioned in Scripture that these notable conceptions had any connection with the first day of Tishrei. This rather weakens the force of the Talmud's contention. In fact, it is tempting to suppose that the notion that these noble women were redeemed from barrenness on the same special day arose from these stories being read on Rosh Hashanah, rather than motivating their selection. What then was the substantive reason for the Rabbis preferring these passages to all others for the lectionary of the day? The simplest explanation is that the three stories about Sarah, Rachel, and Hannah are tales of birth, life and renewal. Rosh Hashanah is the day the world was born—*Ha-yom harat olam*, says the *mahzor*, and the day we are remembered for life. This vital theme reverberates throughout the liturgy. What could be more appropriate than to include the joyful stories of women who suffered childlessness for so many long years only to be rewarded for their faith and forbearing with the gift of life? The long road from barrenness to motherhood is truly a form of redemption, a reawakening of dreams long put to rest. These profound accounts of longing and fulfillment strike responsive chords in our own lives.

Moreover, Rosh Hashanah is the day we lift our voices in prayer. These stories are sterling examples of passionate pleas to God that were answered. Let us listen to the voices of these women, one by one. We begin with Sarah:

The LORD took note of Sarah as He had promised, and the LORD did for Sarah as He had spoken. Sarah conceived and bore a son to Abraham in his old age, at the set time of which God had spoken. Abraham gave his newborn son, whom Sarah had borne him, the name of Isaac. And when his son Isaac was eight days old, Abraham circumcised him, as God had commanded him. Now Abraham was a hundred years old when his son Isaac was born to him. Sarah said, "God has brought me laughter; everyone who hears will laugh with me." And she added,

"Who would have said to Abraham
That Sarah would suckle children!

Yet I have borne a son in his old age."
(Gen. 21:1–7)

Sarah's story is one of overwhelming joy. We may easily imagine her astonishment and excitement at becoming a mother for the first time at the age of ninety. She laughs like a young girl at her good fortune, gladdened and rejuvenated. Indeed, Sarah and Abraham have won their battle with despair; they will revel in the newfound serenity and pride of parenthood. However, as all parents know, raising children is far more difficult than bearing them. Isaac was Sarah's first child, but Abraham's second. Thirteen years earlier, Sarah had given her Egyptian handmaiden Hagar to Abraham as a concubine, hoping—in keeping with a belief quite widespread in biblical times—that this act would lead her to conceive as well. Hagar gave birth to Ishmael, but Sarah remained childless. Only God's subsequent blessing brought her fruit of the womb. With Isaac's birth, all of Sarah's maternal instincts, which long had lain dormant, surfaced and reshaped her perceptions of everything around her. Suddenly Ishmael's antics, which previously were seen as harmlessly amusing, became a threat, a looming detrimental influence on the apple of her eye. At the celebration of Isaac's weaning, Sarah decided that action had to be taken. She confronted Abraham with a harsh demand.

> Sarah saw the son whom Hagar the Egyptian had borne to Abraham playing. She said to Abraham, "Cast out that slave-woman and her son, for the son of that slave shall not share in the inheritance with my son Isaac." (Gen. 21:9–10)

To contemporary ears, this sounds like a cruel and heartless move. In an effort to soften its callousness, scholars have suggested that Sarah's request that Hagar and Ishmael be sent away was precipitated by a conflict over inheritance rights. In ancient Mesopotamia, freeing a maidservant disqualified any son she had borne to the master of the house from inheriting his estate. So when Sarah said: "for the son of that slave shall not share in the inheritance with my son Isaac," she was simply asking Abraham to carry out a legal procedure that would cause Ishmael to forfeit his right to inheritance.

We are also informed about Abraham's response to Sarah's request: "The matter distressed Abraham greatly, for it concerned a son of his" (Gen. 21:11). Rashi, the great medieval Northern French biblical commentator, explored Abraham's conscience. He explains that "the matter" that "distressed Abraham greatly" was that he heard that Ishmael had taken to degenerate ways. This suggestion is based on the midrashic exposition of the word "playing." The Rabbis take the matter to the extreme, proposing that Ishmael's sinister play indicated that he had homicidal, sexually objectionable, and idolatrous tendencies even at a young age. By suggesting cardinal infractions on the part of the boy, they thereby exonerate Sarah for her suggestion and Abraham for agreeing to his banishment, which otherwise might be viewed as morally reprehensible.

The simple meaning of the verse, however, is stark and moving. "The matter distressed Abraham greatly, for it concerned *his son*." Abraham was crestfallen. Even if Sarah's intuitions were correct, how could he banish his own firstborn child? The divergent feelings of the parents Sarah and Abraham might have led them to an impasse; however, the matter was immediately resolved by the Almighty. "But God said to Abraham, 'Do not be distressed over the boy or your slave; whatever Sarah tells you, do as she says, for it is through Isaac that offspring shall be continued for you" (Gen. 21:12). This verse encapsulates the essence of Rosh Hashanah as *Yom ha-Din*, the Day of Judgment. The fate of Isaac and Ishmael hung in the balance, and God rendered His verdict. He not only decided in favor of the prosecution, He offered an explanation of His decision. Sarah's voice won out. Her difficult decision ensured the continuity of the covenant. Her voice— a mother's voice, one of wisdom and vision, was heard and obeyed by Abraham and by the Almighty Himself.

The second woman's voice immortalized in the scriptural readings of Rosh Hashanah is that of Hannah. In the haftarah for the first day of the holiday, we are introduced to Hannah, a barren woman living in the town of Ramatayim Zofim (literally, the twofold outlook of Ramah). She is married to Elkanah, who was blessed with children from his second wife, Peninah. Hannah's unendurable pain and emptiness were underscored time and again during the family's annual pilgrimage to Shiloh. There, Elkanah and Peninah gathered their children around them, leaving Hannah engulfed by loneliness. Hannah's distress was augmented by the taunting of her rival, Peninah, who was jealous of Elkanah's greater love for Hannah. Initially Hannah was silent, her pain expressed only through tears. When we first hear her voice, it is in prayer, beseeching God *sotto voce* to see her pain, remember her, and grant her children. Hannah is confronted by Eli the High Priest. He accuses her of drunkenly profaning the sanctuary. This is a surprising allegation; why would Eli suspect Hannah, a woman praying, of being inebriated? The answer may lie in the observation of the Rabbis that Hannah was a revolutionary innovator in the world of prayer (B. Ber. 32a-b). They provide a long list of the liturgical precedents set by Hannah that serve as a model of *tefillah* for all generations, and many later sages and interpreters have amplified those observations. Let us focus, though, on one point that has not been well understood. Eli was a cultic functionary; in his eyes, prayer in the sanctuary was to be proclamational, composed of triumphant declarations of the sovereignty of God—examples being psalms that were clearly intended for ritual recitation. Of course, he knew that there were other forms of prayer; the Torah records Moses' personal petitions for Miriam's healing and for his own entry into the Promised Land. The book of Judges also tells of Samson's calling out to God, and being answered. However, what neither Eli nor the rest of Israel had seen before was the combination of the two—bringing personal petitional prayer into the House of the Lord. Motivated by her own deep maternal need and by a strong belief in God's mercy, Hannah initiated a paradigm shift that would reverberate through the ages. Hushed, sincere words of supplication—the service of the heart, *avodah she-ba-lev*—had not been heard in the Tabernacle precincts before Hannah drew courage to plead her case quietly, calmly, with a strength drawn from her innermost being. It was that unique prayer that merited God's response; the following year she was blessed with a child.

Hannah's story, though, does not end there. In the second section of the haftarah, she becomes fully voiced in buoyant song, praising the Almighty as the source of all blessing. Hannah extols Him and describes His incomparability. He alone has the power to transform and intervene on the part of the powerless. Hannah does not refer exclusively to her own reversal of fortune from barrenness to fertility. She expands the scope of her psalm to include the hungry who are sated, the poor who become rich, and the vanquished who reign victorious. As arbiter of life and death, God's cosmic power is mobilized for all those who are weak and hopeless.

It is therefore singularly appropriate that Hannah's voice is heard in the synagogue on Rosh Hashanah, the Day of Judgment. She champions the cause of people whose hopes have ebbed, and reassures them that God is capable of reversing their fortunes. Hers is a powerful testimony to the efficacy of petitionary prayer and a striking example of exultant praise of the God who inscribes us in the Book of Life.

And so, on the first Day of Awe, we read the story of Sarah, an elderly mother whose voice was heard. We continue with the story of Hannah, another mother answered; and we expect that on the second day of Rosh Hashanah, we will read the story of the third barren woman, Rachel, about whom we are explicitly told: "Now God remembered Rachel; God heeded her and opened her womb" (Gen. 30:22). Rachel's story, however, is not a straightforward account of answered prayers. Genesis 29–30, which describes Rachel's life with Jacob and yearning for children, is a sophisticated, crafted portrayal of a marriage in distress. We feel the strains and cracks in the love between Jacob and Rachel, which had been won at the cost of 14 years' hard labor. Rachel's agonizing childlessness has sapped her life of joy; in her despair, she lashed out at her husband as if he were at fault:

When Rachel saw that she had borne Jacob no children, she became envious of her sister; and Rachel said to Jacob, "Give me children, or I shall die." Jacob was incensed at Rachel, and said, "Can I take the place of God, who has denied you fruit of the womb?" (Gen. 30:1–2)

Indeed, Rachel did conceive of Jacob as being in the place of God, as the sole source of fulfillment in her life. In her unconditional and devoted love for him, which alienated her from her father and the rest of her family, Rachel had placed Jacob on a pedestal of perfection. When she turned to him to provide her deliverance, Jacob adamantly answered, "Can I take the place of God, who has denied you fruit of the womb?" His words at once reveal and conceal. Jacob may be giving expression to his deep-seated desire to live up to Rachel's expectations, and to provide her with what she desired most. Would that he were God-like, able to bestow life and redeem her once and for all from her living death! Yet perhaps in the deepest realm of his subconscious Jacob was distressed by Rachel's lack of comprehension. Jacob was the son of Isaac and the grandson of Abraham; he understood that Rachel's barrenness was not a matter of biological chance. His mother, Rebekah, did not conceive until Isaac facilitated it through intense prayer, and his grandmother Sarah had in her time given birth to Isaac only after God's direct miraculous intervention. The births of Jacob's children were an expression of the covenant that God had made with Abraham, a step along the road of national destiny. How God might decide to bring about that destiny was far beyond Jacob's ken, and he knew it; man cannot take the place of God. Rachel, born into a simple idolatrous family, just did not understand this. She believed in the efficacy of giving her concubine to her husband, of mandrake roots, and of the cultic fetishes—the *terafim* that she later smuggled out of her father's house—to force God's hand. One could only imagine Jacob's disappointment when he realized how far removed his beloved wife was from his ancestral faith. His outburst gave vent to many feelings that could not be spoken.

In his biblical commentary, *Zeror ha-Mor*, R. Abraham Sabba explains that God's remembrance of Rachel resulted not from anything that she had done; rather, ironically, this act came about only when Rachel had despaired of achieving her wish.

> *And God remembered Rachel.* This statement intimates that all of her efforts and diligence were useless: not her giving her maidservant [to Jacob], nor her purchasing the mandrakes from her sister, as mandrakes would have taken effect immediately. God, however, arranged matters so that a year, two, or three passed, during which time Issachar, Zebulun, and Dinah their sister were born. Only then did God remember Rachel. It therefore states "God remembered her," as if she had been forgotten, in order to emphasize to her that attempting to manipulate nature was futile; [she conceived] only through the name of God who communicated to her. (*Zeror ha-Mor*, Gen. 30:22)

Rachel's voice, therefore, though similarly driven by the desire for motherhood, was unlike that of Hannah. While the latter was reassured by her husband, Elkanah, of his love for her, Rachel cried out in anguish and was not comforted by Jacob. In her case the dominant voice was that of Jacob, callously shouting her down. Her appeal unanswered, it took years before she was remembered by God. Rachel's cognizance of her total reliance upon the Almighty might have served as an important object lesson for us all on the Day of Judgment; unfortunately, later events indicate that she did not internalize this message. Her voice is so jarringly discordant with those of the other two female protagonists of Rosh Hashanah that the Rabbis did not include her story in the scriptural passages of the day.

However, in the haftarah of the second day of every New Year we do hear Rachel's haunting voice; not the voice that skirmished with Jacob over the searing issue of infertility, but rather the voice that echoed from a far-off hilltop in the mountains of Benjamin—the voice of Rachel weeping as described by the prophet Jeremiah.

The haftarah of Jeremiah 31 stands in contradistinction with all other chapters of the book. Jeremiah of Anatoth was the most tragic of the prophets. His burdensome task was to be the harbinger of destruction and exile. Jeremiah's scathing words reflect both his intense anguish and, at the same time, his profound hopes regarding the fate of the nation. Most of the book deals with Jeremiah's prophetic attempt to warn his people of imminent disaster and to restore their spiritual rectitude. However, despite his dedicating 40 years to unswerving and zealous preaching, he was unsuccessful in achieving his aim. The Temple was destroyed and the nation exiled.

Chapter 31 is the brighter side of Jeremiah. This chapter of consolation focuses on the themes of return and reversal of fortune. God promises that one day He will rebuild the nation that has been destroyed and firmly replant the uprooted within their borders. There will be dancing as the multitudes return from the ends of the earth; the blind, the lame, the pregnant, the birthing mothers—all will come home:

> In a vast throng they shall return here.
> They shall come with weeping,
> And with compassion will I guide them.
> I will lead them to streams of water,
> By a level road where they will not stumble.
> For I am ever a Father to Israel,
> Ephraim is My first-born.
> (Jer. 31:8–9)

In addition to the physical restoration and return, Jeremiah describes the forthcoming contrition of the nation and its heartfelt desire to repent and return, as well as God's readiness to reforge His spiritual bond with His children:

I can hear Ephraim lamenting:
You have chastised me, and I am chastised
Like a calf that has not been broken
Receive me back, let me return,
For You, O LORD, are my God.
Now that I have turned back, I am filled with remorse;
Now that I am made aware, I strike my thigh.
I am ashamed and humiliated,
For I bear the disgrace of my youth.
Truly, Ephraim is a dear son to Me
A child of affection!
Whenever I have turned against him,
Still, I fondly remember him.
That is why My heart yearns for him;
I will have compassion on him
declares the LORD.
(Jer. 31:18-20) [author's translation]

The Talmud explains that these were the verses that inspired the selection of Jeremiah 31 as the haftarah of the second day of Rosh Hashanah. They strike an almost wistful tone in describing the everlasting love and compassion that God had and will always have for His beloved son Israel, which endures despite sin and betrayal. Fond memories of the loyal bonds of yesteryear soften God's current wrath, and will bring Him to forgive the nation and enable their spiritual rebirth. As Rashi notes: "It is *because* 'I fondly remember him' that 'I will have compassion on him' " (B. Meg. 31a).

At the fulcrum of this prophecy, though, is one of the most striking images in all of biblical literature—the portrait of Rachel crying. Let us listen carefully to her voice, and to that of the prophet whose depiction of her has left its indelible imprint upon Rosh Hashanah for all times.

> Thus said the LORD:
> A cry is heard in Ramah. Wailing, bitter weeping. Rachel weeping for her children.
> She refuses to be comforted
> For her children, who are gone.
> (Jer. 31:15)

A voice is heard in Ramah—seemingly, the ancient site adjacent to today's town of A-Ram, a short distance north of Jerusalem. Why does Jeremiah hear Rachel's voice specifically in that place? Jeremiah was not a Jerusalemite; he was a resident of the city of Anatoth. On the road from Anatoth to Jerusalem, Jeremiah would pass by Ramah, where he no doubt noticed a large ancient stone memorial. Since the Middle Ages, tradition has placed Rachel's burial place just north of Bethlehem; however, the biblical account states otherwise. Mentioned in 1 Samuel 10:2 is "the tomb of Rachel in the territory of Benjamin at Zelzah." This description corresponds to the location of Ramah in the hill country of Benjamin to which Jeremiah refers, and to that ancient memorial. It is placed just off the main north-south axis road that winds its way through the hills of Judah and Samaria, the heartland of biblical Israel. Rachel had died in childbirth during Jacob's return journey along that road from the house of Laban to his home in Beersheba, shortly after the family had stopped at Bethel. Instead of bringing her body to rest in the family tomb in the Cave of Machpelah in Hebron, only a few days' journey distant, Jacob chose to bury her on the road to Ephrath, and to set a memorial on her tomb there (Gen. 35:19–20). This was such an unexpected decision that years later, when reunited with Joseph in Egypt, Jacob chooses to make mention of it (Gen. 48:7) and to offer a much-needed explanation as to why he decided on this particular locale. The Rabbis explained that Jacob intentionally chose to bury Rachel on that road because of a prophetic insight:

Since he foresaw that eventually the Temple would be destroyed and his sons would be taken off into exile, they would appeal to the Ancestors, asking them to pray for them, to no avail. When they would pass on the road and embrace the tomb of Rachel, she would appeal for mercy on their behalf. She would call out to God: "Listen to my weeping and have mercy on my children; pay the debt due to me." Immediately God would listen to her voice and to her prayer, as it says: "Wailing, bitter weeping: Rachel weeping for her children." (*Pesikta Rabbati* 3:2)

If Rachel were buried in Bethlehem, south of Jerusalem, this midrash would make no sense; the exiles would not have passed her tomb on their way north to captivity in Babylon. The tomb site known by Jeremiah is a more appropriate identification, and a reason that Jeremiah spoke of Rachel as crying at Ramah.

But it is likely that Jeremiah prophesied about Rachel's voice being heard in Ramah not only because of his earlier familiarity with that place, but because of a chilling incident that happened to him there after the destruction of Jerusalem. Ramah loomed large in Jeremiah's consciousness since it was the *Umshlagsplatz* of the Babylonian exile. In Jeremiah, chapter 40, we are told that there the exiles were officially given their walking papers and sent off to Babylon. It was in Ramah that the prophet himself had an encounter with personal and national destiny, and it was there that he made a fateful choice:

The word that came to Jeremiah from the LORD, after Nebuzaradan, the chief of the guards, set him free at Ramah, to which he had taken him, chained in fetters among those from Jerusalem and Judah who were being exiled to Babylon. The chief of the guards took charge of Jeremiah, and he said to him, "The LORD your God threatened this place with this disaster; and now the LORD has brought it about. He has acted as He threatened, because you sinned against the LORD and did not obey Him. That is why this has happened to you. Now, I release you this day from the fetters which were on your hands. If you would like to go with me to Babylon, come, and I will look after you. And if you don't want to come with me to Babylon, you need not. See, the whole land is before you: go wherever seems good and right to you." But [Jeremiah] still did not turn back." Or go to Gedaliah son of Ahikam son of Shaphan, whom the king of Babylon has put in charge of the towns of Judah, and stay with him among the people, or go wherever you want to go." The chief of the guards gave him an allowance of food, and dismissed him. So Jeremiah came to Gedaliah son of Ahikam at Mizpah, and stayed with him among the people who were left in the land. (Jer. 40:1–6)

Jeremiah, who had dedicated a lifetime to saving his people, was at that point totally crushed. Although he had predicted the punishments the nation had just endured, even he could not have imagined the atrocities he had recently witnessed. He had been unsuccessful in his mission; he sat among the chained and weeping prisoners, the evidence of his failure. " Oh, that my head were water, My eyes a fount of tears! Then would I weep day and night for the slain of my poor people!" (Jer. 8:23). Together, they had arrived at death's door. The kindest sentence they could hope for was to be banished forever from their homeland. At Ramah, Jeremiah's prophetic foresight failed him. The seer could only wonder what the future held in store for him and for his nation. His angst was unbearable.

It was at that point that he was approached by Nevuzaradan, the chief executioner of Babylon. Jeremiah's eyes saw black; surely, his end had come. But to his great astonishment, Nevuzaradan drew near, unlocked his chains, and spoke respectfully to the prophet of the Lord. Jeremiah found it difficult to believe what was taking place as he listened to the Babylonian royal executioner validate everything he had preached through the years, vindicating him and his religious integrity. Furthermore, the Babylonian gave Jeremiah the freedom to go wherever he wished. Given this unexpected choice, Jeremiah decided to cast his lot with the remnant of the people who would stay in the land. Although he would be forced to confront the painful diminution of the nation and the country's utter desolation, he chose to minister to those few who would try to regroup and rebuild a modest Jewish presence, preserving the memories of kingdoms past.

Sitting among the exiles at Ramah, prophetic cadences swept through Jeremiah's mind. Suddenly Rachel appeared to him in a vision. He heard her voice, weeping not for her vanished youth, but for the children lost to her forever. When Rachel the mother died in childbirth, she was deprived of her two children, Joseph and Benjamin. Now Rachel, in her role as national matriarch, was being deprived of the Children of Israel. The mainstay of the Northern Kingdom of Israel, prophetically called Ephraim, were the descendants of Rachel's son Joseph; the Southern Kingdom, though founded by rulers from the tribe of Judah and so named, contained the tribe of Benjamin, whose territory notably included Jerusalem. Symbolically, Rachel is the queen-mother who longs for the reunification of the two kingdoms. But the image of Rachel as sketched by Jeremiah was integrally connected to her personal life and the prophet's strong identification with it. At that contemplative moment, his prophetic spirit was moved to recall the woman who had tried to transform her fate into destiny by building her family and had sorrowfully failed. Struck down by pain, loss, and defeat, Jeremiah's mind was filled with the image of Rachel, the ancestress of the nation whose life and death were marked by tragedy. Not only Jeremiah, but all those present at Ramah— including the exiles-to-be—could at that moment identify with the pathetic figure of Rachel. The prophet couched his words of consolation to them in a message of comfort to her.

Restrain your voice from weeping,
Your eyes from shedding tears;
For there is reward for your labor
declares the LORD:
They shall return from the enemy's land.
And there is hope for your future
declares the LORD:
Your children shall return to their country. (Jer. 31:16–17)

Let us pause for a moment to consider the associations that Jeremiah would have awoken in his listeners at Ramah by invoking the name of Rachel and directing consolation to her. Examining verse 14 carefully, we note Jeremiah's turn of phrase: "Rachel crying for her *sons* (plural), for *he* is gone (singular)." The grammatical dissonance was intentional, because the word *einenu*, "he is gone" is a *leitwort* in the biblical account of Rachel's life.

Rachel's personal life was one defined by presence and absence. When she finally became a mother after years of barrenness, she named her first son Joseph—literally, "He will add." She said: "May the Lord add another son for me" (Gen. 30:24). What a strange declaration upon the birth of a first child! One would expect her to say a *Shehehiyanu* —to praise the Lord for having given her life, sustained her, and brought her to this day! Instead, she spoke of her past chagrin and longing for another child. How are we to understand this bewildering statement, this obliviousness to the present moment? Is it that having finally been given a life, she feels that she is the mistress of her fate and can therefore steer her future course? Or does she now believe that the intense desire between her and Jacob revolved around the children who had been missing from her life? With this lack now partially filled, perhaps she was left insecure about Jacob's love. Had Rachel now become Leah, suddenly gripped by the sense that only the number of children she was to bear would assure her of Jacob's unwavering devotion? Or might it be that only once she had a child did she understand, as do all new parents, just how much she had to lose?

In the end, she who so desperately longed for motherhood died in childbirth; at the very moment that she was granted a life she was taken from this world. As she breathed her dying breath, the midwife reassured her: "Have no fear, for it is another boy for you" (Gen. 35:17). This declaration resounds with painful irony: Rachel's wish had come true, she has been given an additional son—but he was one she would not live to raise. Death placed her squarely in the present, ridding her forever of her earlier illusions.

The word *einenu*, the marker of absence, continues as a refrain in the lives of Rachel's children. When Joseph is torn away from his doting father and thrown into a pit by his jealous brothers, we are told that Reuben attempted to rescue him: "When Reuben returned to the pit and saw that Joseph was not in the pit, he rent his clothes. Returning to his brothers, he said, 'The boy is gone (*einenu*)! Now what am I to do?' " (Gen. 37:29–30). Interestingly, Jacob's refusal to be comforted about Joseph's disappearance is described with the words *va-yema'en le-hitnahem*, "he refused to be comforted" (v. 35), using the same words later employed by Jeremiah to describe Rachel's refusal to be comforted for the loss of her sons: *me-ana le-hinahem*.

Many years later, when the brothers go down to Egypt to procure food for the family during the years of famine, they introduce themselves to the viceroy of Egypt—who is in fact their long-lost brother—as follows: "We your servants were twelve brothers, sons of a certain man in the land of Canaan; the youngest, however, is now with our father and one 'is no more' (*einenu*)" (Gen. 42:13,32). This haunting refrain of *einenu* is used by Jacob as well when the brothers return without their brother Simeon. "Their father Jacob said to them, 'It is always me that you bereave: Joseph is no more (*einenu*) and Simeon is no more (*einenu*), and now you would take away Benjamin. These things always happen to me!' " (vv. 36–38). When Judah steps forward and confesses the sins of the past, again he focuses upon *einenu*, on the missing piece:

"Later our father said, 'Go back and procure some food for us.'

We answered, 'We cannot go down; only if our youngest brother is with us can we go down, for we may not show our faces to the man if our youngest brother 'is not with us' (*einenu*). Your servant my father said to us, 'As you know, my wife bore me two sons. But one is gone from me, and I said: Alas, he was torn by a beast!' . . . Now if I come to your servant my father and the boy is not with us (*einenu*)—since his own life is so bound up with his—when he sees that the boy is not with us, he will die. . . . For how can I go back to my father if the boy is not with me (*einenu*)? Let me not be witness to the woe that would overtake my father!" (Gen. 44:25–34) [author's translation]

And so we see that the echo of *einenu* reverberates throughout the stories of both of Rachel's sons, Joseph and Benjamin. What is so powerful and ironic about this refrain is that in both cases, their absence is illusory. Joseph is missing to his father and brothers, but we the readers are well aware that he is alive and well and living in Egypt. Benjamin is only imagined to be gone as his family members agonize over his peril. His mother died on the road, his older brother died on the road; Benjamin, they fear, will do the same. Indeed, both sons and their descendants, along with all of Jacob's family, are fated to be lost in slavery in Egypt. Yet from that iron furnace of oppression they will be redeemed, and will return to their land—much as Jeremiah says, "The children shall return to their country."

Rachel's tragic life story stirred the soul of the prophet from Anatoth, a city of banished priests (1 Kings 2:26). Rachel was fated not to play out her role as a mother; passing by Ramah on his way to Jerusalem, Jeremiah was reminded of the role he would not play in the Temple. He was "a priest from Anatoth," defined by what he was not, by the sacred tasks he could not perform. The self-realization for which his soul yearned—religious leadership and pristine spiritual ministry abounding in blessing and hope—remained pathetically beyond his reach. Like that of Rachel, his life had been full of frustrations and tragedy. He, too, had tried to alter the course of destiny, but had been forced to accept his fate, placing himself in God's hands. His family life, like hers, had been replete with concessions. Jeremiah was the only prophet of Israel forbidden to marry and to father children.

> The word of the LORD came to me: You are not to marry and not to have sons and daughters in this place. For thus said the LORD concerning any sons and daughters that may be born in this place, and concerning the mothers who bear them, and concerning the fathers who beget them in this land: They shall die gruesome deaths. They shall not be lamented or buried; they shall be like dung on the surface of the ground. They shall be consumed by the sword and by famine, and their corpses shall be food for the birds of the sky and the beasts of the earth. (Jer. 16:1–4)

This prohibition and its dreadful basis were conveyed by Jeremiah to the people in a public prophecy and served as a sign that there was no hope. The evil decree of destruction and exile would not be averted. On a human level, though, Jeremiah must have undergone great personal anguish at the thought that he would be cut off from the future, without descendants to carry his name or maintain his inheritance. Well could he relate to Rachel's suffering during her years of barrenness, and to her bitter pain at dying before seeing her sons grown! Her tale resonated with his life; her tears were his own. So Jeremiah strove to find for Rachel some consolation in the future, some glimmer of hope that all was not in vain. He looked ahead beyond loss and destruction and proclaimed: "there is reward for your labor . . . there is hope for your future" (Jer. 31: 16-17).

The Rabbis, however, went a step further. They assigned Rachel an active role in this story by transforming her into the facilitator of the redemption. It was she, they averred, who petitioned for the return of the people to their homeland. They pointed out that her burial place was strategically positioned as a way station of hope. Furthermore, they dramatized the idea, describing Rachel rising from her tomb to plead the case of the nation in light of her own waivers, compromises, pain, and self-abnegation. The midrash (*Eikhah Rabbah*, Proem 24) begins with a description of Jeremiah helplessly witnessing the destruction of Jerusalem and the exile of the nation. The prophet seeks partners to commiserate with him and to come to the defense of the Jewish people. This midrash depicts Jeremiah pleading with Abraham, Isaac, Jacob, and Moses to awaken from their graves to pray and weep for the people of Israel. They assent, and their cries reach the heavenly angels who rend their garments and weep over the tragedy. All this, however, is of no avail; none are able to annul the evil decree. No one, that is, except Rachel.

At that moment, the Matriarch Rachel broke forth into speech before the Holy One Blessed be He and said: "Sovereign of the Universe! It is revealed before Thee that Thy servant Jacob loved me exceedingly and toiled for my father on my behalf for seven years. When those seven years were completed and the time arrived for me to wed my husband, my father planned to switch me with my sister. It was very hard for me, because the plot was known to me and I disclosed it to my husband; and I gave him a sign whereby he could distinguish between me and my sister, so that my father should not be able to make the substitution. After that, I relented, suppressed my desire, and had pity upon my sister, that she should not be exposed to shame. In the evening, they substituted my sister for me with my husband, and I delivered over to my sister all the signs which I had arranged with my husband so that he should think that she was Rachel. More than that, I went beneath the bed upon which he lay with my sister, and when he spoke to her she remained silent and I made all the replies in order that he should not recognize my sister's voice. I did her a kindness, was not jealous of her, and did not expose her to shame. And if I, a creature of flesh and blood, formed of dust and ashes, was not envious of my rival and did not expose her to shame and contempt, why should Thou, a king who lives eternally and art merciful, be jealous of idolatry in which there is no reality and exile my children and let them be slain by the sword and their enemies have done with them as they wished." Forthwith, the mercy of the Holy One, Blessed Be He, was stirred and He said, "For thy sake, Rachel, I will restore Israel to their place." And so it is written: "A cry is heard in Ramah." (Jer. 31:15)

This midrashic overlay portrays Rachel as the defender of the people of Israel. Her personal experience serves to justify her demands. She speaks of her exemplary ability to overcome the jealousy that raged in her heart toward her sister, Leah, who married Jacob in her stead. The precedent she set, she asserts, is worthy of divine emulation. She challenges the Almighty to overcome His jealousy and forgive Israel their infidelity. Joshua Levinson has suggested that the midrash pays tribute to Rachel's moral grandeur: "Rachel's ruse is neither for personal gain nor intended to promote national goals but is, rather, motivated by an intensely personal and moral concern" (Levinson, 518). There can be little question that she demonstrates total empathy with Leah and willingly accommodates Leah at great self-sacrifice.

However, the midrash has placed Rachel's contention in the context of a dialogue with God. "And if I, a creature of flesh and blood, formed of dust and ashes, was not envious of my rival and did not expose her to shame and contempt, why should Thou, a king who lives eternally and art merciful, be jealous of idolatry in which there is no reality and exile my children and let them be slain by the sword and their enemies have done with them as they wished?" Rachel's claim is the height of audacity; nothing could be more ridiculous. Demanding of the Master of the Universe to overcome His jealousy of other gods is tantamount to asking Him to renege on the basis of monotheism. The implausibility of such an argument leads the reader to seek Rachel's substantive claim elsewhere. Rachel speaks of love.

In order to understand the power of her appeal, let us consider three dimensions of Rachel's love. The first was her profound love of Jacob. Rachel's young life revolved around that love. She dreamed of consummating it through marriage and instead was forced to see her dream detained for years. Yet the certainty of the love and the intensity of the ardor between Rachel and Jacob mitigated the harshness of seven long years of waiting. Rachel, by all rights, could speak with self-assurance of love; her survival had been a testimonial to that love. Love had provided the anchor for her relationship with Jacob and had allowed them to weather all storms. Only love was capable of conquering jealousy, pain, and years of paralyzing loneliness. As Rachel described her love the analogous picture came into full focus. God's love of His people and their love in return would overcome His rage. His response was immediate; His love prevailed, and He said, "Rachel, for you, I shall bring the Children of Israel home."

However, there is another way to view the love that Rachel enacts in this midrashic theater. Rachel's love of Jacob was superseded by her love and concern for her sister. Rachel mercifully gave the signs to Leah so that she could surreptitiously replace Rachel on her wedding night. In a certain sense, the choice Rachel made between her husband and her sister represents the dichotomy between selfish love and selfless love. Through this act, Rachel nobly transcended self. It is little wonder that the masters of Midrash have Jeremiah appeal to Rachel to state her case. The conflict that she experienced between her love of Jacob and her love of Leah reflects Jeremiah's conflicting empathies between his love of God and his love of Israel.

In a most unusual comment, Rabbi Levi Yitzhak of Berditchev suggests a third dimension of love. Rachel not only gave of her own love; she cultivated love in others.

And he came to Rachel as well and loved Rachel because of Leah (va-yavo va-ye'ehav gam et Rahel mi-Leah). It should be understood that the primary reason Jacob was in Laban's house was because of Rachel. As is well known, it was because of Rachel that Jacob also married Leah. In that sense, Rachel caused Jacob to marry Leah. Moreover, he loved Rachel herself, but loved her even more since she brought him to love Leah as his wife. That is the meaning of the phrase, "and he also loved Rachel because of Leah [mi-Leah]"—that is to say, Leah was his wife and Rachel brought it about so he loved Rachel for that as well. (*Sefer Kedushat Levi ha-Shalem*, Gen. 29:31)

Although this explanation is far from the literal sense of the text, it allows for a deeper understanding of why it was Rachel who was successful in pleading the case for Israel. Rachel opened up God's heart once again to love His children, the unlikely recipients of His grace.

Jeremiah 31, the prophecy of consolation, is replete with love. "The LORD revealed Himself to me from afar. Eternal love I conceived for you then; therefore I continue My grace to you" (Jer. 31:3) [author's translation]. How appropriate, therefore, to find Rachel on center stage in this prophecy. Just as she loved and struggled, so did Jeremiah. And just as Jeremiah loved and struggled, we are told that the Almighty Himself was conflicted because of love as well. *Pesikta de-Rav Kahana* 13:9 describes His deliberation at Ramah as follows:

God said to Jeremiah: "Either you go with them to Babylonia and I will stay here, or I will go with them and you stay here." To which Jeremiah responded, "Master of the Universe, if I go with them I am of no use. Rather, You, their Creator, should accompany them. That will be beneficial."

Kol be-Ramah nishma—the voice of Rachel is heard at Ramah. Targum Jonathan translates the phrase *kol be-Ramah* as *be-rum almah*, "a voice is heard in the world on high." Every Rosh Hashanah, God listens to the voice of Rachel contained in the immortal words of

Jeremiah. Though it is a faraway voice coming from a distant hilltop, it does not go unheard. It harmonizes love and faith and assures us that there is reward for our labor, and ultimately, hope for our future.

Chapter Four

⌗

The Symphony
of Return

⌗

The historical significance of Rosh Hashanah is shrouded in mystery. As opposed to the other Jewish festivals, it is not singled out in the Torah as a milestone date in the history of the Jewish people. The Rabbis offered a variety of suggestions as to what took place on that day: Rosh Hashanah was the day of Adam's reprieve; the day that Joseph was released from prison; the day the edict of slavery in Egypt was rescinded; and the day that Sarah, Rachel, and Hannah conceived. All of these incidents are examples of judgments that were dramatically reversed. These cases illustrate that hope can shine forth even when all seems lost. Yet nowhere in the Bible are we told that any of these occurrences in fact took place on Rosh Hashanah. There are, however, two significant historical events that are recorded in the Bible as having transpired on the first day of the month of Tishrei: one is the building of the altar upon the return to Zion, described in Ezra, chapter 3, and the second is the *hak'hel*—a public gathering for the reading of the Torah, carried out by Ezra and recorded in Nehemiah, chapter 8.

For the Rabbis, the public study of Torah was central and *hak'hel* was the paradigm of this notion. As we shall see, what Ezra and

Nehemiah succeeded in achieving in the *hak'hel* ceremony was reso-
nant with their own agenda of saving the Torah by engaging the
entire community, through love, understanding, and observance.

The Rabbis teach that on one occasion, R. Yohanan b. Beroka and
R. Eleazar b. Hisma set out to visit their teacher R. Joshua in Pekiin.
When they arrived, R. Joshua asked them to share with him some
innovative idea they had learned. Taken aback by this request, they
turned to their rebbe and said, "But we are your disciples and your
waters do we drink!" Refusing to take no for an answer, he insisted,
"Even so, it is impossible for a *beit midrash* to be without some novel
teaching!" He then asked them whose *Shabbat* it had been, hoping to
hear words of Torah from the most recent discourse that had been
delivered that week. They answered that it had been the week of R.
Eleazar b. Azariah, who had spoken about *hak'hel*, the commandment
of publicly reading the Torah before the entire nation, as outlined in
Deuteronomy 31:

> And Moses instructed them as follows: Every seventh year, the
> year set for remission, at the Feast of Booths, when all Israel
> comes to appear before the LORD your God in the place that
> He will choose, you shall read this Torah aloud in the presence
> of all Israel. Gather the people—*men, women, children,* [italics
> added] and the strangers in your communities—that they may
> hear and so learn to revere the LORD your God and to observe
> faithfully every word of this Torah. Their children, too, who
> have not had the experience, shall hear and learn to revere the
> LORD your God as long as they live in the land that you are
> about to cross the Jordan to possess. (Deut. 31:10–13)

The biblical commandment stipulates gathering all of Israel—
men, women, and children—to hear the Torah publicly read by the
king on the holiday of Sukkot. R. Eleazar b. Azariah had questioned
the curious fact that men, women, and *even* children were expected to
attend. He offered the following rationale:

The men came to learn, the women came to listen; but why did the little children have to come? He answered: in order to grant reward to those that bring them. (B. Hag. 3a)

When the students completed the *derashah* (teaching), R. Joshua was so overwhelmed, he exclaimed: "There was a precious pearl in your hand and you sought to deprive me of it!?" One wonders if R. Joshua's enthusiastic reaction was precipitated by R. Eleazar's encouragement to bring children to hear the Torah in order to grant reward to their parents, since we are told (in J. Yev. 1:6) that his Torah education began just that way: "I remember that his [R. Joshua's] mother used to bring him in his cradle to synagogue so his ears would absorb words of Torah."

The heartwarming incident in which this *derashah* is framed illustrates the dynamic teacher-student relationship that existed between R. Joshua and his disciples. Although R. Joshua was an eminent scholar, he elicited ideas from them. How propitious that the exposition that they recounted to him referred to *hak'hel*—the commandment to gather the people in order to publicly share in the Torah. The ceremony magnificently acknowledges that Torah belongs to the entire nation. By asking his students to share their Torah with their master, he impressed this noble idea upon them.

But there is more here than meets the eye. R. Joshua asked his pupils whose *Shabbat* it had been, meaning, who had delivered the discourse. He was referring to the fallout that resulted from the deposition of the *Nasi* (the head of the Sanhedrin), Rabban Gamliel II. Initially, Rabban Gamliel had been replaced by R. Eleazar b. Azariah. After reconciliation between the sages, Rabban Gamliel was formally reinstated as *Nasi*. It was decided, however, that the two would take turns delivering the discourse on alternate weeks. Notably, this was not the only change that took place when R. Eleazar assumed the position of *Nasi*. The Talmud reports that on the day R. Eleazar was appointed *Nasi*, the academy was opened to all who wished to study without restriction, contrary to the previous ruling of Rabban

Gamliel that "no disciple whose true character does not correspond to his outer bearing may enter the *beit ha-midrash*" (B. Ber. 28a). On that day, hundreds of benches were added to the *beit ha-midrash* and there was no law about which any doubt was not elucidated. Hence, R. Eleazar's exposition of the commandment of *hak'hel* was in complete consonance with his new policy and his overarching educational philosophy.

The last two mitzvot in the Pentateuch relate to the dissemination and glorification of Torah. The mitzvah of *hak'hel* is the penultimate biblical commandment. The final mitzvah commands every adult male in Israel to write his own copy of the Torah. B. *Sanhedrin* 21b stipulates that even in the event that a man's father left him a Torah scroll, he is required to write his own. Thus, the Torah becomes the personal legacy of everyone. The mitzvah of *hak'hel* bears testimony to the fact that Torah belongs to the collective as well as to the individual.

> The *hak'hel* ceremony was an impressive one. Once every seven years, at the end of the sabbatical year, on the festival of Sukkot, the Torah was read with great pomp and circumstance. Trumpets were blown throughout the city of Jerusalem to gather the masses. A large pulpit was constructed and placed in the women's court of the Temple. The king mounted the stand to read to all those assembled. The Torah was then handed from the sexton of the assembly to the head of the assembly, who in turn handed it to the captain, who handed it to the High Priest, who gave it to the king. The king arose and began to read aloud from the book of Deuteronomy, alighting upon select passages such as the *Shema*, the imprecations and the blessings, and the covenant at Sinai. Indeed, the ceremony was patterned after that very first *hak'hel*—the giving of the Torah. In fact, twice in the book of Deuteronomy revelation at Sinai is expressed in terms of *hak'hel*. "The day you stood before the LORD your God at Horeb, when the LORD said to me: 'Gather (*hak'hel*) the people to Me that I may let them

hear My words, in order that they may learn to revere Me as long as they live on earth, and may so teach their children' " (Deut. 4:10). And subsequently, "And the LORD gave me the two tablets of stone inscribed by the finger of God, with the exact words that the LORD had addressed to you on the mountain out of the fire on the day of the Assembly *(yom ha-kahal)*" (9:10).

Maimonides explains the rationale behind the public reading of the Torah in Sinaitic terms as well:

Even converts who are unfamiliar with the Torah must prepare their hearts and their ears to listen with reverence, trepidation, and trembling joy *like the day the Torah was given at Sinai.* Even great men of wisdom, who know all of Torah, must listen with an intense degree of concentration. And one who is unable to hear (attend) should direct his heart towards this reading, since Scripture's intention was to reinforce true wisdom. And one should consider himself as if he was commanded then and there: hearing the Torah from the mouth of God Himself. (*Mishneh Torah*, Hag. 3:6)

The detailed halakhic explanations of *hak'hel* thereafter offered by Maimonides presuppose a regular course of events; that is to say, once every seven years, *hak'hel* took place. One would like to believe that from the time Moses performed the very first *hak'hel*, a cycle began and the practice was implemented regularly in the month of Tishrei. In fact, there were long stretches in Jewish history when it is clear that this practice was not upheld, years during which Torah was abandoned. At those junctures, the reading of the Torah by the king was a rare and unexpected event. In large measure, examining instances when *hak'hel* was periodically reinstated provides a deeper understanding of its value and meaning.

In 622 B.C.E., for example, a critical assembly (*hak'hel*) was held by

King Josiah of Judah. This gathering was a serious turning point in the religious life of the nation. In the 18th year of his reign, King Josiah sent Shaphan the scribe to Hilkiah the priest to supervise the refurbishing of the Temple. In the course of that project, Hilkiah found a Torah scroll, which he brought to Shaphan. Shaphan, in turn, brought the scroll and read it to the king. When the king heard the words of the Torah, he rent his garments and sent a delegation to the prophetess Huldah for an emergency religious consultation. The prophetess confirmed the ominous threat that loomed over the errant nation, but assured Josiah that his tears, remorse, and penitent actions would spare him the wrath of God. Josiah, a man of action, inaugurated a new epoch in the religious history of Israel. Although he was the son of the idolatrous king Amon, and grandson of notorious King Manasseh who had led Israel astray for 52 years of worshiping foreign gods, Josiah made a clean break. He purged Israel of foreign practices that included everything from solar and astral cults to Asherah and Molekh worship, necromancers, and mediums, all imported in the wake of Assyrian dominion. Josiah saw fit to remove and destroy all traces of this widespread idolatrous contamination. In addition, we are told that Josiah called all of the people together and read them the Torah.

> At the king's summons, all the elders of Judah and Jerusalem assembled before him. The king went up to the House of the LORD, together with all the men of Judah and all the inhabitants of Jerusalem, and the priests and prophets—*all the people, young and old* [italics added]. And he read to them the entire text of the covenant scroll which had been found in the House of the LORD. (2 Kings 23:1)
>
> Scripture describes how after renewing the covenant, Josiah moved the people to positive action, commanding them to offer the Passover sacrifice that had been neglected for generations. They took up his challenge with utmost devotion, reminiscent of the above-mentioned words of Maimonides:

"they prepared their hearts and their ears to listen with reverence, trepidation, and trembling joy, like the day the Torah was
given at Sinai." It is therefore not surprising that the praises of
Josiah were sung to the tune of Moses: "There was no king like
him before who turned back to the LORD with all his heart and
soul and might, in full accord with the Torah of Moses; nor did
any like him arise after him" (2 Kings 23:25).

Josiah's reformation in the 7th century B.C.E. rescued Torah from
oblivion. His *hak'hel* was a revival meeting that restored Torah as the
inheritance of the entire nation. Reflecting upon this heartening incident, the Rabbis asserted that even when the religious life of the
people is at its lowest spiritual ebb, one never knows who will turn
the tide:

> *If you shall keep this mitzvah which I have commanded you.* Lest
> you say: But there are the sons of wise men, the sons of the
> elders, the sons of prophets . . . we have been taught: "If *you*
> shall keep this mitzvah"—all are equal in Torah . . . As it says,
> "*You* stand this day, all of you, before the Lord your God, your
> tribal heads, your elders and your officials, *all the men of Israel,
> your children, your wives,* even the stranger within your camp,
> from woodchopper to water drawer to enter into the covenant
> of the Lord your God." . . . If they hadn't been present at this
> assembly, wouldn't Torah have been forgotten in Israel? If it
> had not been for Shaphan in his time, Ezra in his time and
> Rabbi Akiva in his time, wouldn't Torah have been forgotten
> in Israel? (*Sifrei Devarim, Eikev* 12)

Three historical characters are singled out as responsible for saving Torah from perdition: Shaphan, Ezra, and Rabbi Akiva. This
midrash selected representatives from three historic time frames: the
Roman, Persian, and Babylonian eras. At each critical juncture, a personality is credited with saving the day. One needs little convincing

that Rabbi Akiva was central to the vitality and perpetuity of Torah in his time. He was, after all, the founding father of Rabbinic Judaism. His trailblazing hermeneutics, as well as his legal traditions, continue to inform and inspire to this day. His contribution was so innovative that B. *Menahot* 29b stages a visit of Moses to Rabbi Akiva's *beit midrash*, in which the great lawgiver himself asks God why He presented the Torah through his agency if a giant such as Rabbi Akiva was destined to arise. Moreover, Rabbi Akiva himself took personal responsibility for preserving Torah by defying the Hadrianic edict that outlawed its study and teaching. In the face of adversity, Rabbi Akiva continued to spread Torah publicly in Israel and paid for that steadfastness dearly—through martyrdom. Indeed, had it not been for Rabbi Akiva, Torah would have been lost from Israel.

Returning to the first character credited in the *Sifrei Devarim* with assuring the continuity of Torah, we are taken by surprise. It was not the great king and religious revolutionary Josiah who is celebrated, but rather his scribe Shaphan. Perhaps the midrash desired to draw a parallel between Ezra *ha-sofer* (the scribe) and Shaphan *ha-sofer* (the scribe). However, the idea communicated by this choice is far deeper.

As we mentioned above, the biblical narrative describes the Torah scroll as found by Hilkiah the priest. He promptly handed it over to Shaphan the scribe, who brought it to the king. The transfer of the Torah from hand to hand is reminiscent of the *hak'hel* ceremony. However, the mood in Israel was not one of delighting in the word of the Lord. After over 50 years of neglect of Torah and active idol worship, we anticipate that Shaphan would take the ancient scroll and place it in a *genizah* (a storeroom or depository for worn-out or damaged Hebrew documents or books that contain the name of God and so cannot be discarded), burying it along with the obsolete practices it described. The Torah, he discovered, speaks in a language that long before had become foreign to the people. To read it to them was to risk having the holy words of God fall on deaf ears, making a further mockery of the sacred ancient traditions. Even if he himself was loyal to his ancestral faith, he risked his life confronting the king of Judah with the Torah of Moses—a litany of allegations against him, his forefathers, and the entire nation. Shaphan could have taken the path of least resistance, the more prudent route. Rather, he decided to bring the Torah to the king by himself—both its harsh words of rebuke and its gentle words of comfort. He hoped that the power of Torah would impact on the hearts of the leader and his people. The courage of Shaphan's convictions was rewarded by the favorable response of King Josiah. Furthermore, Shaphan's descendants were singled out during this period of idol worship as loyal adherents to the Torah. His son Ahikam saved the prophet Jeremiah from the angry mob (Jer. 26:24), and his grandson Gedaliah ben Ahikam ben Shaphan was appointed the governor of Judea after the Babylonian destruction (39:14). King Josiah may have organized hak'hel and read the Torah to the entire nation; however, Shaphan was the paragon of belief that Torah belongs to one and all, and a sterling attestation to the fact that one never knows who may be elected to save Torah.

The second historical figure singled out in the Sifrei Devarim is Ezra the Scribe. He, too, is credited with saving the Torah. In order to appreciate his contribution, some background is required. In the year 538 B.C.E., the Persian king Cyrus proclaimed his beneficent decree inviting the Jews under his jurisdiction to return to Zion and rebuild the Temple. Babylonian Jewry did not rise as one man to meet this challenge. It seems that only the minority of Jews living in Babylonia opted to pack their bags and return home. In the first wave, it is estimated that approximately 50,000 men of conviction and purpose "whose spirit had been roused by God . . . to build the house of the LORD that is in Jerusalem" (Ezra 1:5) made the move. Those who stayed behind strengthened their hands by providing financial support. The first stage in the restoration of Zion was connected with the political leadership of

Zerubavel and inspired by the prophets Haggai and Zechariah who encouraged the nation to rebuild the Temple. Although the Persians had originally welcomed the initiative, trouble was not long in coming. The Samaritans in the north accused the newcomers of sedition and hence appealed to the Persians to retract their royal permission to rebuild the Temple. Consequently, the building was suspended between 536 and 528 B.C.E.

Moreover, the country no longer flowed with milk and honey; over time it had become "a land that consumed its inhabitants." There was trouble in the south from the Edomites who had taken advantage of the years of exile to encroach on the territory of Judea, infiltrating through the Negev as far as the city of Hebron. The Israel to which the community had returned spanned but 25 miles from north to south. Unrelenting troubles plagued the returning exiles during the early years of the Restoration. The newcomers were dogged by famine, crop failure, and pestilence. It would take another 18 years until the poor, harassed, and dispirited people would once again take up the challenge of rebuilding the Temple.

Help arrived in the form of leaders from Babylonia. Nehemiah, who had attained high office in the court of Artaxerxes I, was given permission to visit Jerusalem and help the community. Upon arrival, he found the people dejected and the country in stark distress.

Nehemiah was bombarded by challenges. As his first project, he undertook the rebuilding of the city walls of Jerusalem. It was Nehemiah who provided the returning remnant with a political administration, bolstering them to better weather the storms of internal stress and external hostility. He remained for 12 years, attempting to enact social reform, before returning to Babylonia. When he came back to Jerusalem a second time, he found that conditions had seriously deteriorated and the need for religious reform was acute. He immediately understood that it was vital to reorganize the community, reestablish the nation's ethnic purity, and revitalize its spiritual life.

But Nehemiah also understood that he could not do all this on his own. He brought Ezra the Scribe to save the day.

Who was Ezra the Scribe? We are first introduced to him in chapter 7 of the book of Ezra, where his roots are traced all the way back to Aaron the High Priest. Scripture also connects him with Moses: "Ezra came up from Babylon, a scribe expert in the Torah of Moses" (Ezra 7:6). The two vital roles of priest and lawgiver were fused in the person of Ezra. Remarkably, the Rabbis elevated him even further, describing Ezra as being as great as Moses:

> R. Yossi says: Ezra was worthy of having the Torah presented to Israel through him, had Moses not preceded him. In regard to Moses, Scripture states: "And Moses went up to God" (Exod. 19:3), and with regard to Ezra, Scripture states: "This Ezra ascended from Babylon." Just as the ascension spoken of here in the case of Moses refers to receiving the Torah from God, so too the ascension spoken of there in connection with Ezra refers to receiving the Torah. In regard to Moses, it states: "And God commanded me at that time to teach you statutes and laws," and with regard to Ezra it states: "For Ezra readied his heart to seek the Torah of his God and to fulfill it and to teach in Israel the statutes and the law" (Ezra 7:10) [author's translation]. But even though the Torah was not given through Ezra, the script was changed by him, as it is stated, "The changed writing was written in Aramaic and expressed in Aramaic" (Ezra 4:7). (B. San. 21b)

The conclusion of this talmudic passage refers to an earlier statement about changes made by Ezra in the biblical script and language:

> Mar Zutra, and some say Mar Ukva, said: originally, the Torah was presented to Israel in *Ivri* (ancient Hebrew) script and the holy language (Hebrew); it was given to them again in the days of Ezra in the *Ashuri* (square Hebrew) script and the Aramaic

language. The Israelites chose for themselves the *Ashuri* script and the holy language and left for the commoners (Cuthim) the *Ivri* script and the Aramaic language.

The Talmud implies that Ezra took stock of his constituency's inability to read and understand Hebrew and as a result adapted the Torah to their needs, through innovative—and somewhat radical—steps. In so doing, he was successful in preventing Torah from being lost. R. Meir Simcha of Dvinsk, in his biblical commentary *Meshekh Hokhmah*, explains Ezra's decision to change the script as a vehicle by which Torah was made accessible to the masses, and even connects him to our old friend, Rabbi Eleazar ben Azariah:

In the Jerusalem Talmud at the end of the first chapter of *Yevamot*, we are told [regarding Rabbi Eleazar b. Azariah] . . . that he was a tenth-generation descendant of Ezra, and "his eyes were like his eyes." This refers to the fact that Ezra changed the script. In truth, it would be proper for Torah to be given into the hands of the priests, the Levites, and the elders who possess treasured perfection, and to the ascetics who dwell in Jerusalem. Anyone wishing to approach the Torah should come to Jerusalem. . . . Therefore the Torah was (originally) written in *Ivri* script so that it should not be learned by the unworthy . . . so that the young should not lord it over the old and claim, "I too understand and know the secrets of knowledge as do you." However, Ezra in his time saw that the dispersion of Israel among the nations [had caused them] to have forgotten the basics of Torah. . . . It was therefore more appropriate to write the Torah in a language understood by all who were desirous of knowing, [as it says], "Wisdom cries aloud in the streets" (Prov. 1:20) and thereby achieves the worthy goal of spreading wisdom in the Land. . . . He [Ezra] made the decision [to change the script] through the holy spirit inspired from on high. This was [also] the case with Rabbi Eleazar ben

Azariah, who immediately upon becoming the *Nasi*, said that all who wish to enter may enter [the *beit midrash*] and four hundred benches were added [to the *beit midrash*]. So too in other sources, one finds that he [Rabbi Eleazar ben Azariah] explained, for example, "And the children to give reward to those who brought them" (B. Hag. 3a). At every juncture he seriously stressed the dissemination of Torah and the proliferation of students. That is what is meant by the expression "his eyes [Rabbi Eleazar ben Azariah's] were like his eyes" [Ezra's], that is to say his vision, his overall perception, as in the expression "the eyes of the community" or "your eyes are like doves." His outlook regarding leading the people was like that of Ezra the Scribe. (*Meshekh Hokhmah*, Deut. 31:9)

According to Rabbi Meir Simcha of Dvinsk, when it came to teaching Torah to the Jewish people, Rabbi Eleazar ben Azariah and Ezra saw eye to eye.

But returning to the book of Ezra, itself, we find Ezra's noble acts of religious leadership summed up as follows: "For Ezra had dedicated himself to study the Torah of the LORD so as to observe it, and to teach laws and rules to Israel" (Ezra 7:10). Ezra's efforts were intended to reconstitute the spiritual life of the nation according to the standards of Torah. Scripture records the many challenges he successfully met. He reinstituted the proper celebration of festivals, such as Passover (6:22) and Tabernacles (Neh. 8:17–18). We are told that these were not perfunctory rituals, but groundbreaking events: "The Israelites had not done so from the days of Joshua son of Nun to that day—and there was very great rejoicing" (v. 17). In addition, Ezra brought about many fundamental religious changes. In his day, alienation, ignorance, and assimilation were rampant. In response, he combatted Sabbath desecration and tried to educate his constituency. However, Ezra's major challenge was that of intermarriage. He required of the people to set aside their foreign wives and children and engage in endogamy, in order to restore Israel's identity and continuity. In this respect, he spiritually renewed the community and assured their survival: "Had it not been for Ezra, Torah would have been forgotten from Israel."

The Rabbis embellished the scriptural picture, portraying legal decisions made by Ezra and implemented in his time. B. *Bava Kamma* 82a credits him with instituting the reading of the Torah on Monday and Thursday mornings, thus exposing the common folk to Torah on the days they came to market. He also introduced the reading of the coming Torah portion at the Sabbath *Minchah* service, thereby whetting the congregation's appetite for the Torah reading of the following week. His practicality and awareness of the people's need for education and understanding are reflected in these innovations that made Torah an integral part of daily life. But Ezra also made the Torah accessible to men, women, and children through a moving *hak'hel* ceremony described in Nehemiah, chapter 8:

When the seventh month arrived—the Israelites being [settled] in their towns—the entire people assembled as one man in the square before the Water Gate, and they asked Ezra the scribe to bring the scroll of the Torah of Moses with which the LORD had charged Israel. On the first day of the seventh month, Ezra the priest brought the Torah before the congregation, men and women and all who could listen with understanding. He read from it, facing the square before the Water Gate, from the first light until midday, to the men and the women and those who could understand; the ears of all the people were given to the scroll of the Torah. Ezra the scribe stood upon a wooden tower made for the purpose. . . . Ezra opened the scroll in the sight of all the people, for he was above all the people; as he opened it, all the people stood up. Ezra blessed the LORD, the great God, and all the people answered, "Amen, Amen," with hands upraised. Then they bowed their heads and prostrated themselves before the Lord with their faces to the ground . . . and the Levites explained the Torah to the people, while the people stood in their places. They read from the scroll of the Torah of God, translating it and giving the sense; so they understood the reading. (Neh. 8:1–8)

Ezra gathered the entire nation as one, built a tall platform, and, as their religious leader, read them the Torah. This was a transformational experience in their religious lives and a turning point in the history of the nation. In his book *Revelation Restored*, David Weiss Halivni explains:

After ages of straying from the path of God—after their bitter repentance in exile—the people gathered close; willing and attentive, they were prepared, finally, for revelation. This was the age in which idolatry ceased in Israel; it was also the end of prophecy. Once the nation had embraced a book, no need remained for the admonitions and the visions of the prophets. Interpretation took the place of revelation. (Halivni, 83)

Precisely what did Ezra read to them on that fateful day? Did he read the *Shema*? The blessings and imprecations? The prohibition against intermarriage? The account of the covenant at Sinai? The text does not specify chapter and verse, but rather states: "They read from the scroll of the Torah of God translating it and giving the sense; so they understood the meaning" (Neh. 8:10). The Rabbis noted that the experience was not a rhetorical tour de force but rather a complete educational experience.

"They read from the scroll of the Torah of God"—this refers to Scripture; "translating it"—this refers to Targum; "giving the sense"—this refers to punctuation; "so they understood the reading"—this refers to cantillation. (B. Meg. 3a)

In this parsing of the verse, each word was used by the Rabbis to describe the innovative tools and techniques that were introduced by Ezra in his role as scribe, concerned with the proper reading and interpretation of Scripture. This explication of Ezra's public reading is in line with another fascinating Rabbinic comment: "Why is it [the king's Torah scroll] called *Mishneh Torah*? Since Torah is destined to change [*atidah le-hishtanot*]" (*Sifrei Devarim*, Deut. 17:18). A most remarkable play on words! *Mishneh* Torah, because the Torah is destined *le-hishtanot*—to change. One might argue (as does Rashi) that the predicted change in Torah was that Ezra altered the language and the script. Yet the changes offered by Ezra far transcended the technical. Ezra changed the destiny of Torah, in that he was able to radically alter the approach of the people by touching the hearts and souls of everyone present at that *hak'hel* gathering. This becomes evident by carefully examining what he said to the people on that fateful day.

The entire nation had gathered together in the square before the Water Gate. Scripture notes that the people actually asked Ezra to bring the scroll of the Torah of Moses. It is hard to know just what they had in mind. They may have anticipated a social gathering in Jerusalem with a modicum of religious content. It is therefore not surprising that when Ezra blessed the Lord, the people perfunctorily answered "Amen." However, one wonders whether they were prepared for what happened next. First, Ezra held up the Torah for the people to see (reminiscent of the Sephardic custom of performing *hagbahah*, raising the Torah scroll prior to the Torah reading, as opposed to the Ashkenazic custom of doing so after the Torah reading). Ezra began to read the scroll, and as he did, the Levites interspersed among the crowd simultaneously translated everything he said. Suddenly, the sacred words were no longer locked in an ancient dialect beyond their comprehension. The more they heard, the more they became cognizant of how far they had drifted from the word of God. The men, the women, and the children of Israel cried and cried. Ezra, Nehemiah, and the Levites turned to the assembly and declared:

"This day is holy to the LORD your God: you must not mourn or weep," for all the people were weeping as they listened to the words of the Torah. He [Ezra] further said to them, "Go, eat choice foods and drink sweet drinks and send portions to whomever has nothing prepared, for the day is holy to our LORD. Do not be sad, for your rejoicing in the LORD is the source of your strength." (Neh. 8:9–10)

The inhabitants of Zion had once been dreamers. Long ago, though, they had relinquished hope that their tears of sadness would reap joy. Ezra was determined to help them regain faith in their destiny. Standing with his people in Jerusalem, he orchestrated the last movement in the symphony of return.

The first movement had been composed many years earlier by Jeremiah in his prophecy of consolation. It, too, contained tears and joy:

They will come with weeping and with supplication I will guide them. . . . They shall come and rejoice on the heights of Zion. . . . I will turn their mourning to joy. I will comfort them and cheer them in their grief. (Jer. 31:9–13) [author's translation]

Jeremiah had predicted the lament of the returning exiles: that they would make their way, crying as they came. Perhaps their wailing was to be an expression of the residual pain that they would sustain in exile. Alternatively, their tears would result from the excitement of return, or from a deep understanding of what had been lost. Now, Jeremiah's prophecy had been realized. The people had come home, but the process was far from complete.

The second movement of tears and exhilaration is described in Ezra, chapter 3. When the nation gathered to celebrate the laying of the foundation of the Temple, we are told:

Many of the priests and Levites and the chiefs of the clans, the old men who had seen the first house, wept loudly at the sight of the founding of this house. Many others shouted joyously at the top of their voices. The people could not distinguish the shouts of joy from the people's weeping, for the people raised a great shout, the sound of which could be heard from afar. (Ezra 3:12–13)

The elders remembered well the magnificent edifice that Solomon had constructed. The Second Temple would be a ramshackle hut compared to its palatial splendor. The disappointment of that older generation was proportional to their expectations. Yet the crowd also included those who had not seen the First Temple. For them, at long last, the foundation of the Temple had been laid. It was the day that they had waited for. Despite the modest beginning, the importance of this occasion could not be underestimated. One is reminded of Theodor Herzl's diary entry on August 29, 1897: "If I were to sum up the [Zionist] congress in a word which I shall take care not to publish it would be this. At Basel I founded the Jewish state. If I said this out loud today, I would be greeted by universal laughter. In five years perhaps and certainly in fifty years everyone will perceive it." Fifty-one years later, the State of Israel was established.

Similarly, the significance of the laying of the Temple foundation in 538 B.C.E., would only be understood in the fullness of time. It was not simply the first stage in the construction of the House of the Lord, which would be completed 18 years thereafter; it was the germination of the spirit of the nation and the assurance that "the eternity of Israel would not be lost." Perhaps those who cried with joy implicitly understood this point. The text notes that the mélange of gladness and sadness made the laughter indistinguishable from the tears. And yet, the passage ends with the shout heard from afar. Presumably, the joy of the present moment, tinged with the hope for the future, drowned out the nostalgic weeping over the past.

The third and final movement of tears and gladness is recorded in

Nehemiah, chapter 8. It was then that the pain was the most intense. The grave disappointment the people experienced was with themselves. They were helpless in the face of their own spiritual vacuity. Ignorance and assimilation had consumed them. Their sense of worthlessness resounded in every powerful word Ezra uttered. How then was he able to reassure his people? What was it that he taught them at this stage? How did he move them from maudlin penitence to rejoicing? How could they segue from tears to joy?

Again we turn to the ceremony of *hak'hel* for the answer; not the *hak'hel* of the past but the *hak'hel* of the present. *Hak'hel* is performed every year by the Ethiopian Jewish community in Israel, in their central holiday known as *Sigd*. According to the Ethiopian tradition, Yom Kippur represents only the beginning of a personal redemptive process. For 50 days following that auspicious day, until the 29th day of Heshvan, the community works toward collective repentance, culminating in the *Sigd* (meaning "to bow"). The entire community dresses in white, leaves the village, and makes its way up a mountain as if ascending toward God. Throngs of men, women, and children begin a march of return, praying that just as they have returned to Him, He too will return to them.

The Ethiopians explain that the very first *Sigd* took place in the time of Ezra and Nehemiah, as described in Nehemiah, chapters 8 and 9. Their holiday is patterned after the biblical template. The day begins solemnly, with the community fasting until midday. The procession up the mountain is led by their religious leaders (*kessim*), walking with the Torah (*Orit*). All of the people walk with rocks on their heads as a sign of submission. The tone is somber, laden with a true sense of contrition and inadequacy. When they arrive atop the mountain, they place the stones in a circle, circumscribing the location of their *hak'hel* ceremony. At that point, portions from Scripture are read, including the giving of the Torah at Sinai and selections from the book of Nehemiah. The *Orit* is written in Ge'ez, the holy tongue, but just as in the time of Ezra, the texts that are read are translated into the spoken languages Amharic and Tigrignan, and, in recent years, also into Hebrew. After the readings and the prayers, the *kes* says words of rebuke and blesses the people, just as Ezra did. He then reminds them of the need for devotion, performance of the commandments, and the return to Jerusalem. The people cry, bow, and pray. When the ceremony is over, the shofar is blown and the *Orit* is returned to the synagogue. Singing, dancing, and rejoicing follow. The similarity between the *Sigd* and the *hak'hel* of Ezra is remarkable in many respects. Notably, it is consonant in its combination of the tones of sadness and happiness.

It is essential, however, to emphasize that the *hak'hel* of Ezra was not performed on the 29th of Heshvan, or even on the festival of Sukkot as described in Deuteronomy. Ezra's *hak'hel* took place on Rosh Hashanah. What was the nature of Rosh Hashanah in Ezra's time and how did it evolve?

The Geonim of the 9th and 10th centuries presented two positions on the tenor of the day. Those of *Eretz Yisra'el* and the yeshivah of Sura in Babylonia (according to Sar Shalom Gaon and Zemach Gaon) stressed the gravity of the Day of Judgment, and instituted the custom to fast on both days of Rosh Hashanah (and for that matter, on the 10 Days of Repentance including Shabbat Shuvah!). Conversely, the tradition in the Babylonian academy in the city of Pumbeditha, recorded by Hai Gaon, forbade fasting on Rosh Hashanah, based on the verses from Nehemiah: "Go, eat choice foods and drink sweet drinks and send portions to whomever has nothing prepared, for the day is holy to our Lord. Do not be sad, for your rejoicing in the Lord is the source of your strength" (Neh. 8:10). Saadiah Gaon arrives at the same conclusion. He posits that Rosh Hashanah is a *mikra kodesh*, a holiday in every respect, and hence a day of celebration as described in the book of Nehemiah. Natronai Gaon suggested a compromise solution. The first day of Rosh Hashanah he declared to be a day of feasting, and the second, a day of fasting.

The custom that won out was that of celebration. That geonic position echoes the opinion of the Rabbis of the Jerusalem Talmud:

"Or what great nation has laws and rules as perfect as all this Torah. . ." (Deut. 4:8). R. Hama said: What nation is like this one? It is the way of the world that when a man knows that he has to appear in court, he wears black, enshrouds himself in black, and grows his beard, since he has no idea if he will be acquitted. But Israel is not like that: they wear white, wrap themselves in white, shave, eat, drink, and rejoice, since they know that God will perform miracles for them. (J. RH 7:2)

For Ezra, though, the dissonance did not require any halakhic harmonization. The people's tears were a welcome first step toward return. This notion is eloquently encapsulated in the words of Abraham Joshua Heschel in his book *Man Is Not Alone:*

An inspiration passes, having been inspired never passes. It remains like an island across the restlessness of time, to which we move over the wake of undying wonder. An eagerness is left behind, a craving and a feeling of shame at our ever being tainted with oblivion . . . But there is no man who is not shaken for an instant by the eternal. And if we claim we have no heart to feel, no soul to hear, let us pray for tears or a feeling of shame. (Heschel, *Man,* 79)

Having been "shaken for an instant by the eternal," the people were now ready to take steps toward repentance. Ezra walked them through the process slowly. He began by telling them: "Go eat choice foods and drink sweet drinks." The suggestion to eat, drink, and be merry was a directive to live in the present moment. His point was that all of their inadequacies were a thing of the past. Only by focusing on the present could they appreciate how far they had come. This modular appreciation would enable them to smile through their tears. It was, after all, Rosh Hashanah, a new beginning in the life of the community of returnees, and there was true cause for celebration. But, how might eating, drinking and rejoicing make up for their spiritual deficit? Heschel adds a profound spiritual dimension that may be applied to Ezra's command:

> Life passes on in proximity to the sacred, and it is this proximity that endows existence with ultimate significance. In our relation to the immediate we touch upon the most distant. Even the satisfaction of physical needs can be a sacred act. Perhaps the essential message of Judaism is that in doing the finite we may perceive the infinite. It is incumbent on us to obtain the perception of the impossible in the possible, the perception of life eternal in everyday deeds. (Heschel, Man, 265)

Next, Ezra instructed the assembled to reach out to others, "and send portions to whoever has nothing prepared, for the day is holy to our LORD" (Neh. 8:10). In doing this, Ezra related directly to their feeling of emptiness. As he shared his Torah with the spiritually depleted, he impressed upon them that there was something that they, too, could share. Those who had provender could give to others. Heschel continues:

> Happiness, in fact, may be defined as the certainty of being needed. But who is in need of man? The first answer that comes to mind is a social one—man's purpose is to serve society or mankind. (Heschel, Man, 194)

Through the sacred act of giving, the nation could achieve holiness. But the emphasis was on more than just sharing food; it was on interacting. Ezra taught Israel to bond together in corporate holiness. Through kinship, they would find solace, purpose, and fulfillment.

Ezra understood that the law required a community to receive it, and Ezra had established that community through acceptance. He had reached out to them, not as some idealized image of what he hoped they would be, but as who they really were. The act was not only decisive, it was electrifying. The people responded by demonstrating their feeling of kinship with their fellow Jews—another gesture of acceptance. These stepping-stones would lead to approval in the eyes of God. Carefully investigating Ezra's words may explain what ultimately unlocked the floodgates of happiness:

> Go, eat choice foods and drink sweet drinks and send portions to whomever has nothing prepared, for the day is holy to our Lord. Do not be sad, for your rejoicing in the LORD is the source of your strength (*ki hedvat Adonai hi ma'uzkhem*). (Neh. 8:10)

Ezra's words echo the wisdom of Ecclesiastes. "Go, eat your bread in gladness, and drink your wine in joy; for your action was long ago approved by God" (Eccles. 9:7). *Kohelet Rabbah* elaborates:

> Rabbi Levi explained the verse as referring to Rosh Hashanah and Yom Kippur. It can be likened to a county who is in debt to the king. The king sends his tax collector. As he is within ten miles of the place, the elders emerge and praise the king. He reduces the tax by a third. He then continues, and when he is within five miles the average citizens come out and praise him; he reduces another third. But when he arrives, *the men, the women, and the children* come out and praise him, and it is then that he cancels the debt. And he says: "Whatever was, was; hereon, we begin a new accounting." So on the eve of Rosh Hashanah the elders fast and God forgives a third . . . between Rosh Hashanah and Yom Kippur, some fast and God forgives another third of their iniquities. On Yom Kippur, when *men, women, and children* all come together and fast, God forgives them all. (*Kohelet Rabbah* 9:7)

The assembly of men, women, and children bonded through common purpose, devotion, and love created what has been called an "ever-widening holiness franchise." On that first momentous Rosh Hashanah when Ezra gathered the community of Israel, they were solidly bound together through Torah—to one another, and to the merciful God of Israel, who had granted them a new beginning. Although they stood crying, deep in their hearts they knew: having sown with tears, they would reap with gladness. Ezra was telling the people of Zion at that auspicious *hak'hel* that starting a new accounting was cause for celebration! However, implicit in his call for rejoicing was that God was happy for them and with them.

One way to translate the somewhat obscure phrase *ki hedvat Adonai hi ma'uzkhem* is: "for God's happiness is the source of your strength." God's reprieve not only afforded the nation reassurance, hope, and joy; it brought gladness to the Almighty. But classically the phrase "*ki hedvat Adonai hi ma'uzkhem*" is translated, "Rejoicing in the Lord is the source of your strength." How does one rejoice in the Lord? *Shir ha-Shirim Rabbah* offers the following explanation:

> "We shall rejoice and revel in You" (Songs 1:4). Rabbi Aben explained, "This is the day that the LORD has made to rejoice and revel in" (Ps. 118:24) [author's translation]. We do not know in what we are supposed to rejoice—the day, or the Lord. Solomon came and resolved the issue: We are to rejoice in You, O Lord, rejoice in Your salvation, in Your Torah, in Your reverence. (*Shir HaShirim Rabbah* 1:31)

The same point is made even clearer in *Seder Eliyahu Rabbah*, which lyrically describes how rejoicing in the Lord derives from the transformational experience that we undergo, through the power of Torah.

> "We shall rejoice and revel in you": In the fact that You have elevated *us*, sanctified *us*, praised *us*, and exalted *us*, and that

You have bound *us* with the great binding power of Torah, to the ends of the earth. (*Seder Eliyahu Rabbah* 7:3)

On Rosh Hashanah and whenever the community of Israel unites, we all celebrate God's embrace, and rapture in His delight and with His delight. Little wonder that despair turns to felicity. In His presence we are elevated, sanctified, praised, exalted, and bound through the great power of love and Torah that extends to the ends of the earth.

Chapter Five

❧

From the Fathomless Depths to the Windows of Heaven

❧

The well-known custom of *Tashlikh* is among the many rituals associated with Rosh Hashanah. Communities assemble near a body of water, symbolically casting away their sins and reciting biblical passages related to repentance. Although there are various biblical selections and meditations that are included in the ceremony of *Tashlikh*, the central text, indeed the one from which *Tashlikh* derives its name, is taken from the book of Micah: *Ve-tashlikh bi-metzulot yam kol hatotam*: "And cast all their sins into the depths of the sea." The heartfelt prophetic plea of the prophet Micah reads as follows:

Who is a God like You,
Forgiving iniquity
And remitting transgression;
Who has not maintained His wrath forever
Against the remnant of His own people,
Because He loves graciousness!

He will take us back in love;
He will cover up our iniquities,
And You will hurl (*ve-tashlikh*) all their sins
Into the depths of the sea.
You will give truth to Jacob
Kindness to Abraham
As You promised on oath to our fathers
In days gone by. (Micah 7:18–20) [author's translation]

The earliest mention of *Tashlikh* is recorded by Rabbi Jacob Moellin (Maharil) (1360–1427), the most formidable German halakhic authority of his time:

The custom of going down to the seashore or the river after the meal on Rosh Hashanah to cast our sins into the depths is based on an incident recorded in *Midrash Tanhuma*. *Tashlikh* recalls the *Akedah* (the binding of Isaac) in which Abraham passed through the river until it reached his neck and cried out, "Deliver me, O God, for the waters have reached my neck" (Ps. 69:2). Satan became a river to prevent Abraham from going through with the *Akedah*. (*Minhagei Maharil*, RH 9)

The rationale provided by the Maharil for *Tashlikh* pertains to the midrashic tale of Abraham's peregrination to the *Akedah*. The old man, burdened by anguish and doubt, set off to sacrifice his only son. En route, he was accosted by Satan, the personification of all of Abraham's compunctions, who questioned both his motives and the moral implications of his actions. Thoroughly unsuccessful in weakening Abraham's resolve, Satan attempted to thwart Isaac's determination. However, Isaac's unwavering moral fortitude only compounded Satan's frustration.

At this point in the midrashic narrative, Satan transforms himself into a roaring river, attempting to extinguish the fire in Abraham's soul by placing himself as an insurmountable obstacle in his path. Undaunted, Abraham proceeds and enters the river. As the water level begins to rise from his knees to his neck, he turns his eyes heavenward and cries out,

> "Master of the Universe! You have chosen me and glorified me, and revealed Yourself to me. You have told me that I am one just as You are One, and that it is my mission to spread the message of Your unity in the world. You have commanded me to sacrifice Isaac; I have not hesitated in upholding Your command, but now 'the waters have reached my neck' (Ps. 69:2). If Isaac or I drown, who will be Your messenger of monotheism in the world?" God replied, "Abraham, you shall unify My name in the world," and He upbraided the spring (the river's source). The river dried up, and they stood on terra firma. (*Midrash Tanhuma*, *Va-yera'*, 22)

At the river's edge, performing *Tashlikh*, we remember Abraham. We call to mind the many elements that impeded his path in the service of the Lord and his exemplary ability to uphold the divine command in spite of all deterrents. Abraham's unflinching devotion serves as a powerful source of inspiration. By the roaring river, we invoke the merit of our father Abraham as we stand in judgment. Through awakening the memory of the *Akedah*, the Maharil has transformed the river into a symbol of all the forces in life that we must resist and overcome.

Rabbi Mordechai Jaffe (1535–1612) suggested that the fish swimming in the water provide the key to understanding *Tashlikh*:

> It is customary to go down to a place where one can see fish (in the water) to remind us that we are like fish caught by the fisherman's net; the net of death and judgment. This should give us pause to seriously contemplate repentance. (*Levush ha-Tekhelet*, 596)

Jaffe uses Ecclesiastes 9:12 as the basis of his explanation:

And a man cannot even know his time. As fishes are enmeshed in a fatal net and as birds are trapped in a snare, so men are caught at the time of calamity when it comes upon them without warning.

Man is humbled by the image of unsuspecting creatures caught by fatal nets and snares. In like measure, our fate hangs in the balance. The tenuous and unpredictable nature of life is brought home to us through this ritual.

And so Rabbi Jacob Moellin and Rabbi Mordechai Jaffe, standing on the banks of the rivers in Mainz and Prague, respectively, understood *Tashlikh* as serving to remind man of life's trials and tribulations. Although the test of the *Akedah* suggests that, against all odds, man can triumph in his spiritual battles, the sobering image of helpless creatures unknowingly destined for defeat drives home the idea of our total dependence upon God's mercy.

Whereas the setting for the ritual in the above-cited texts is the banks of the river, Rabbi Hayyim Hezekiah Medini (1832–1904), hailing from Israel, a land of few rivers, describes the recitation of *Tashlikh* near a spring.

The Rabbis of blessed memory (B. Hor. 12a) stated that kings are to be anointed by a spring in order to assure the continuation of their monarchy. As it says, "The king said to them, 'Take your lord's men . . . and bring him (Adonijah) down to the Gihon [a spring]" (1 Kings 1:33) [author's translation]. And our Rabbis of blessed memory would say the prayer (*Tashlikh*) before the *Malkhuyot* prayer as if to anoint the Lord king over us. Of course, this is only symbolic and intended for us so that the yoke of the kingship of heaven and the purity of spirit which we have taken upon ourselves on Rosh Hashanah shall continue far beyond. (*Sedei Hemed*, RH, #3, 111)

The talmudic reference mentioned above bases the precedent of the anointment of kings by a wellspring on the story of David's son Adonijah. By extension, *Tashlikh* becomes a ceremony of the proclamation of the kingdom of heaven. Having recognized God as our king, our souls are cleansed, and we may begin the New Year in a state of purity.

Rabbi Moses Isserles (Rema) suggested yet another powerful lesson learned from the ritual of *Tashlikh*:

The custom of Israel becomes Torah; such is the case pertaining to going down to the water to recite, "And You will hurl all their sins into the depths of the sea." This is because from the depths of the ocean we become aware of the creation of the universe . . . we go down to the ocean to witness how God placed a boundary for the mighty waters at the seashore. We go down on Rosh Hashanah, the Day of Judgment, so that each one of us will recall the Creation and understand that God is the King of the Universe. That is why we recite, "And You will hurl all their sins into the depths of the sea." He who truly contemplates the depths of the ocean realizes that the world is renewed, and he will thereby come to an awareness of the existence of God and recant all of his sins, and be forgiven. It is in this manner that one's transgressions are cast into the sea. (*Torat ha-Olah* III:56)

Rema has moved us beyond rivers and springs to the grandeur of the ocean. The fathomless deep, the roaring waves, and the incessant rhythms of the tide impress upon every soul the omnipotence and infinity of the Master of the Universe and call us to place Him at the center of our world.

These represent a few of the symbolic explanations offered for the ceremony of *Tashlikh*. They present *Tashlikh* performed by three bodies of water, each with its own symbolic value. Maharil and Levush performed *Tashlikh* at the banks of the river, *Sedei Hemed* by a spring, and Rema standing on the seashore. Rema's explanation seems most compelling—Ve-**tashlikh** bi-metzulot yam kol hatotam: "And You will hurl all their sins into the depths of the sea"—the very sea to which Rema referred.

Let us carefully consider Micah's words:

Who is a God like You,
Forgiving iniquity
And remitting transgression;
Who has not maintained His wrath forever
Against the remnant of His own people,
Because He loves graciousness!
He will take us back in love;
He will cover up our iniquities,
And You will hurl [Ve-tashlikh] all their sins
Into the depths of the sea. (Micah 7:18–19)
[author's translation]

Who was Micah and to whom did he direct his prophecy? Micah lived in Judea during the 8th century, along with Hosea, Isaiah, and Amos, and prophesied during the Assyrian period. It would seem that Micah, the younger contemporary of Isaiah, lived after the exile of the 10 tribes and witnessed the siege of Jerusalem and its miraculous deliverance. Micah addressed a number of prevailing societal ills. He railed against corruption in Jerusalem. He condemned false prophets, dishonest priests, and rapacious leaders. Micah censured them not only for their actions but for their arrogance and misrepresentation of God's eternal presence in their midst:

Hear this, you rulers of the House of Jacob,
You chiefs of the House of Israel,
Who detest justice
And make crooked all that is straight.

Who build Zion with crime,
Jerusalem with iniquity!
Her rulers judge for gifts,
Her priests give ruling for a fee,
And her prophets divine for pay;
Yet they rely upon the LORD, saying,
"The LORD is in our midst;
No calamity shall overtake us."
Assuredly, because of you
Zion shall be plowed as a field,
And Jerusalem shall become heaps of ruins,
And the Temple Mount
A shrine in the woods. (Micah 3:9–12)

These offenses described by Micah were not limited to the ruling class; they filtered down to the Jewish people at large. However, beyond denouncing their acts of social injustice, Micah encouraged and inspired his constituency by instructing them in the fundamentals of humanity:

He has told you, O man, what is good,
And what the LORD requires of you:
Only to do justice
And to love goodness,
And to walk humbly with your God. (Micah 6:8)

But Micah's prophecies do not end on this high note. His was an uphill struggle. His attempts to change the actions of his people met with little success, but this did not deter him from his efforts to alter their attitudes. His final prophecy, which has become the central text of *Tashlikh*, gives expression to Micah's singular theology.

Micah arrived at an awe-inspired realization of the magnitude of God's infinite mercy. Man is rudely awakened by an understanding of the hopelessness of his plight. His spiritual limitations and human frailties leave him powerless without God's grace. It is this salient message that the prophet sought to impart.

> Though I have fallen, I rise again;
> Though I sit in darkness, the LORD is my light.
> I must bear the anger of the LORD,
> Since I have sinned against Him,
> Until He champions my cause
> And upholds my claim.
> He will let me out into the light;
> I will enjoy vindication by Him. (Micah 7:8–9)

This point may not be immediately obvious but it becomes clear when we compare the final message of Micah, the core of *Tashlikh*, with the closing prophecy of his older contemporary Hosea, which we read as the haftarah of Shabbat Shuvah, the Sabbath between Rosh Hashanah and Yom Kippur.

> Hosea implores the people to repent:
> Return, O Israel, to the LORD your God,
> For you have fallen because of your sin.
> Take words with you
> And return to the LORD.
> Say to Him:
> Forgive all guilt
> And accept what is good. (Hosea 14:2–3)

His words represent the classic doctrine of repentance. Irrespective of the nature of their sin, Hosea assures the people that they can mend the breach, restore the covenant, and find their way back to the Almighty. The ways of the Lord are open to those who choose to stride in a new direction. The prophet clarifies the issue as a simple matter for those cognizant of the religious advantage they have been offered:

> He who is wise will consider these words,
> He who is prudent will take note of them.
> For the paths of the LORD are smooth;
> The righteous can walk on them,
> While sinners stumble on them. (Hosea 14:10)

It is little wonder that Hosea 14 was chosen as the haftarah for Shabbat Shuvah. As Michael Fishbane has noted:

> The haftarah readings emphasize the activity of repentance, the external acts (verbal and behavioral) that announce and activate a transformation of religious life. The inward journey "toward" God is left for the individual worshipper along with the "words" that must be taken to heart and spoken with integrity. According to one later master [the teachings of Rabbi Aryeh Leib of Gur, *Sefat Emet*, in his teaching for Shabbat Shuvah (1880)] this journey is a return to one's spiritual Source—to a transcendental point of integration symbolized on earth by the Sabbath. This day is thus the ideal time for repentance or returning to God and most especially is this so for the great Sabbath of Repentance—Shabbat Shuvah. (Fishbane, 329)

But let us take another look at Micah's declaration:

> He will take us back in love;
> He will cover up our iniquities,
> And You will hurl (*ve-tashlikh*) all their sins
> Into the depths of the sea. (Micah 7:19) [author's translation]

Micah makes no mention of *teshuvah*. If Hosea tells the people, "Take words with you and return to the LORD," Micah would concur with Ecclesiastes: "All words are wearisome, man has nothing left to say" (Eccles. 1:8). At the end of his arduous prophetic career, Micah is battle-weary. He no longer speaks to the people in terms of repentance. He has exhausted all of the possibilities for change. He's been down that road too many times. And yet Micah does not give up. His hope is firmly rooted in God's limitless compassion.

How well we understand Micah's spiritual fatigue. Struggling with our evil inclinations we have, more often than not, lost. We have waged wars against injustice and been vanquished by forces beyond our control. Trying to effect change in ourselves and in others has met with little success. And so we implore God, as did Micah in his prophetic valedictory, to remit transgression, to absolve us of iniquity, and to cast our sins into the fathomless depths. We beg Him for truth and kindness for the sake of Abraham and of Jacob: Abraham who withstood the river's rage, and Jacob who blessed his children that they should be like the fish swimming freely in uncertain waters.

How appropriate that it is this passage from Micah that we read for *Tashlikh*. The *teshuvah* to which we aspire is like the ocean tide. It approaches and pulls back. It seems within reach but often proves beyond our grasp.

Tashlikh in this respect is echoed in the special liturgy of Hoshana Rabbah known as *Hoshanot*. Consider for a moment the fundamental difference between *Hoshanot* and the *Selihot*, the backbone of the liturgy of the 10 Days of Repentance. In the *Hoshanot*, there is no confessional, no mention of sin and repentance; only a desperate appeal to God to rain down His salvation upon us as a magnanimous expression of His mercy: "Redeem us, O Lord, for Your sake our God; Hoshanah!"

These verses from the book of Micah are not only read during the *Tashlikh* ceremony, they make an additional appearance in the High Holy Day liturgy. They are added to the haftarah of the *Minhah* service of Yom Kippur and read immediately after the book of Jonah. They culminate with the verse:

> You will give truth to Jacob,
> Kindness to Abraham
> As You promised on oath to our fathers
> In days gone by. (Micah 7:20) [author's translation]

This final note leaves the reader wondering what the prophet meant. One can well understand the request for "kindness to Abraham." Micah himself refers to God in terms of His love of graciousness, and assures us that He will take us back in love. From the setting of the sun at *Tashlikh* until the setting of the sun on Yom Kippur, we are encouraged by the words of the prophet that the Almighty will not maintain His wrath forever.

But how are we to understand his second request—"give truth to Jacob"? What is it that we are asking for? Moreover, why request truth, which throughout the *mahzor* is equated with the standard of justice. We have had our share of painful truths in life. We now yearn for graciousness.

Perhaps what Micah intended is that we implore God to help us not lose that which we cherished. Life has washed away many of the truths we thought immutable and unwavering. Our experiences have undermined so much of what we held to be honest, faithful, just, and lasting. The prophet's words become our prayer for the ability to restore the unalterable and rebuild the trustworthy. We hope to find the resilience to withstand the turbulence that shakes our very existence. We beg God to restore our faith, and to replace our despair with certainty—to verify the rightness of our path. This powerful prophecy proclaims: Do not doubt or falter, but rather stand strong in the face of adversity and the devastation that threatens our worlds. Let integrity enlighten life and extinguish falsehood. We ask that the sum total of our fears, losses, and frustrations not impinge upon our relationships in our families, with our friends, and with all those who are dear to us. Our prayers are for the stability and perspective that will allow us to draw comfort from that which is good in our lives and enable us to continue to see the essence of beauty in the essentials of truth.

Only by persevering in this course can we raise ourselves from the fathomless depths and peer through the windows of heaven.

Ten Days of
Repentance/Aseret
Yemei Teshuvah

Chapter Six

⸙

The Last Psalm

⸙

"Seek the Lord while He can be found, call to Him while He is near" (Isa. 55:6): R. Abbah bar Abuyah said these are the ten days between Rosh Hashanah and Yom Kippur. (B. RH 18a)

These days of close religious encounters are days of *teshuvah*—repentance. It is during this period that we seek God's light, yearn for His shelter, and strive to realign our relationship with Him.

The ten days of *teshuvah* culminating in Yom Kippur are filled with moments of retrospection. *Teshuvah*, the Hebrew word for repentance, also means return. The Days of Awe flash us back to the year past. However, it is on Yom Kippur that our entire life passes before our eyes. In addition to looking back, we are catapulted toward our death—from dust to dust.

In his article "Teshuva and Authenticity," Yehudah Gellman makes the following observations:

We are unable to anticipate our *own* death. We are deprived of its center of authenticity until it is upon us. . . . That is why the Holy One, Blessed be He, gave us Yom Kippur. Yom

Kippur is an attempt at simulation, a confrontation for each of us with his own moment of death. . . . The very act of fasting . . . simulates in the individual a turning towards death. He begins a process which, if it were to continue would bring about his own death. . . .

The conceptual analogue between turning toward death and Yom Kippur is preserved in the nature of the judgment of Yom Kippur. . . . Contrary to popular conceptions, the *teshuvah* of Yom Kippur does not relate to the wrongdoings of the previous year, as such. The unit of time over which we must confess our sins is the whole of our past lives. (See Maimonides, *Teshuvah* 2:8.) . . . On Yom Kippur I must look at the whole of my life and confront it as I must when turning towards death. . . . As Yom Kippur approaches I cease eating and drinking . . . [and] don the raiments of the dead, and in that posture confront the whole of my life and its bearing on eternity. In this enactment exists the possibility of turning into myself, withdrawing from the entanglements and attachments of life, into an authenticity which makes *teshuvah* possible. In this state of mind I say the confession said by the person who is dying. (Gellman, 251-252)

The 10 Days of Repentance are described in the *mahzor* as days of *teshuvah*, *tefillah*, and *tzedakah*. We raise our voices and passionately declare: "repentance, prayer, and charity cancel the stern decree." We do our best to mend our ways, engage in acts of *tzedakah*, and actively immerse ourselves in the world of prayer, imploring God for *teshuvah*, which also means response. Our hopes are fervent but our goals often not attained. We often do not receive the response for which we hope.

Yearning, retrospection, and prayer blend during the 10 days between Rosh Hashanah and Yom Kippur. This coalescence is exemplified in the persona of one great man whose name was David.

Many are the characters in Scripture who challenged death with supplication; however, David, King of Israel, nobly confronted death through his many voices of prayer.

In the book of Kings, David's death is described in singularly mundane terms. "King David was now old, advanced in years; and though they covered him with bedclothes, he never felt warm" (1 Kings 1:1). The text goes on to tell us that David took a concubine, Abishag of Shunam, in an effort to alleviate his discomfort, with limited success. In the larger framework, this vignette forms part of a royal succession narrative. David's son Adonijah, a pretender to the throne, was displaced by Solomon after David's death, and subsequently lost his life when he asked Solomon for the hand of Abishag. A curious midrash preserved in the Talmud (B. Ber. 62b), however, sees great significance in the Bible specifically telling us of David's inability to stay warm. Earlier in his life, as a fugitive from King Saul's insane and murderous jealousy, David snuck into a cave where Saul was sleeping and cut off a corner of his cloak. As a punishment, garments provided David with no relief in his old age. Perhaps this midrash is trying to tell us that all things that we do when young and impetuous come back to haunt us at the end of our days.

Lying under the covers that brought him no warmth, David had ample opportunity to reminisce about the many events of his younger years. Few biblical characters led lives as illustrious as King David. From the outset he was a man among men. His defeat of Goliath instantly cast David in the hero's role. His sweet music brought relief to King Saul during his bouts of depression, and his military prowess brought security and well-being to the nation. Long before he ascended the throne, David had displaced Saul as leader in the eyes of the people. But his success also made him a victim, relentlessly persecuted by Saul. David's resulting exile and tribulations forged his character and sensitized him to the suffering of others. His monarchy was characterized by mercy and justice—until the day he faltered.

While strolling on the palace rooftop, David caught sight of a beautiful woman—Bathsheba, the wife of Uriah the Hittite, one of his commanders. David coveted his neighbor's wife, succumbed to the temptation of adultery, and had his lover's husband killed. From that point onward David's life began a downward spiral. Having destroyed the household of Uriah and Bathsheba, his own household was taken apart, piece by piece. For the sins of adultery and murder he paid heavily with the lives of his children, and ultimately with the dastardly rebellion of his beloved son Absalom. It is little wonder, therefore, that the final scenes in the life of David, described in 1 Kings 2, are nowhere near as glorious as the earlier ones. Forty years of achievement are summed up as follows: "So David slept with his fathers, and he was buried in the City of David. The length of David's reign over Israel was forty years; he reigned seven years in Hebron and thirty-three years in Jerusalem" (1 Kings 2:10–11). As biblical scholar Yair Zakovitch has pointed out, this is an exceedingly dry and forlorn obituary for such a distinguished life.

While the book of Kings chooses to present David's political biography through a moral lens, Scripture offers other renditions of his life. His spiritual biography is recounted in the book of Psalms, in which many of the pivotal events of his life find expression through prayer. Another biblical book, Chronicles, assesses David's leadership from a very different perspective. In Chronicles, the last chapter in the life of David is portrayed as his finest.

Chronicles describes David's activities before his death. Unlike the account in Kings, he is not depicted as lying feebly on his deathbed instructing Solomon to settle his unfinished accounts and avenge his adversaries. The portrait of the king in Chronicles is far nobler. David is portrayed as delivering two farewell speeches. The first (1 Chron. 22) is principally addressed to his son Solomon. He called upon him to build a house for God and focused on the provisions for proper worship. David recalled the circumstances that prevented him from building the Temple. Through his valiant efforts on the battlefield, Israel had arrived at a *pax Davidica*, which warranted the building of the Temple. Ironically, as a warrior held accountable for spilling much blood, David was disqualified from that holy task. His son Solomon, a man of peace, merited the assignment. David instructed Solomon to exercise discretion and understanding and to observe God's laws as the key to success. David then outlined the preparations he had made for the Temple by stockpiling materials and preparing skilled laborers. He left little for his son to do other than to execute the monumental project.

Next, David summoned the leaders of the people, putting the sacral and political administration of Israel in place before his departure. He began with the priests and Levites, assigning them responsibilities in the Temple service, such as keeping charge of the sanctuary and conducting the liturgy. He continued by establishing the secular administration of the nation, appointing military officials, tribal leaders, stewards, and personal advisers to the king.

Having done all that, David delivered another farewell address, which appears in 1 Chronicles 29. This time, he directed his remarks to the entire congregation of Israel. He publicly shared his unfulfilled dream of building a resting place for the Ark of the Covenant. He called upon the people to affirm Solomon as his successor. Most important, he actively involved the people in the grand undertaking of building the House of the Lord. The Chronicler again describes the careful steps that David took to prepare Solomon for his noble assignment. David is presented as the exemplar par excellence of generosity. He dedicated his own personal fortune to the Temple and inspired the people to respond in kind. Along with the blueprints, which he handed over to him, David bestowed upon Solomon a dazzling collection of vessels and raw materials: gold, silver, fine woods, precious stones, and marble. David's contributions of 3,000 talents of Ophir gold and 7,000 talents of refined silver are matched and exceeded by 5,000 talents of gold, 10,000 talents of silver, 18,000 talents of copper, and 100,000 talents of iron contributed by the people. This spectacular demonstration of generosity created an atmosphere of wholehearted rejoicing. Through his example, David taught the nation that rendering unto God all that is due Him need not be merely a material display of surface piety but, given the right intentions, could provide them with an access route to the Divine.

Consider the narrative setting of this event—the very last day of David's life. David did not lament that which life had withheld from him, nor rage against the dying of the light. Instead, he was fully focused on maximizing his religious legacy to the nation he had ruled, in fulfillment of the great hopes with which he ascended the throne years before. David divested himself of all worldly possessions, in essence preparing to enter the heavenly court. David faced his death as the ultimate retrospective. For many, death comes without warning, terminating the journey long before its desired end. For others, senescence offers a capstone experience, allowing those privileged few to reach their point of departure with grace and dignity. David was among the blessed who had the opportunity to make one stop prior to death—to assess and accept all that happened and all that should not have taken place. It enabled him to be reconciled to his passions, his decisions, with family and foes. It provided him with perspective.

Having done so, he then performed an inspiring act of spirituality—he lifted his voice in a final prayer (1 Chron. 29). In this last psalm, David explores the theology of immanence and transcendence.

David blessed the LORD in front of all the assemblage;

David said, Blessed are You, LORD, God of Israel our father, from eternity to eternity. Yours, LORD, are greatness, might, splendor, triumph, and majesty—yes, all that is in heaven and on earth; to You, LORD, belong kingship and preeminence above all. Riches and honor are Yours to dispense; You have dominion over all; with You are strength and might, and it is in Your power to make anyone great and strong. Now, God, we praise You and extol Your glorious name. Who am I and who are my people, that we should have the means to make such a freewill offering; but all is from You, and it is Your gift that we have given to You. For we are sojourners with You, mere transients like our fathers; our days on earth are like a shadow, with nothing in prospect. O LORD our God, all this great mass that we have laid aside to build You a House for Your holy name is from You, and it is all Yours. I know, God, that You search the heart and desire uprightness; I, with upright heart, freely offered all these things; now Your people, who are present here—I saw them joyously making freewill offerings. O LORD God of Abraham, Isaac, and Israel, our fathers, remember this to the eternal credit of the thoughts of Your people's hearts, and make their hearts toward You. As to my son Solomon, give him a whole heart to observe Your commandments, Your admonitions, and Your laws, and to fulfill them all, and to build this temple for which I have made provision." (1 Chron. 29:10–19)

The chapter is familiar to most by way of the siddur. Some of these verses are an integral part of the daily morning prayers, forming the conclusion of the initial phase of the service, the *Pesukei de-Zimra* (the verses of song). The chapter also contains elements that have been incorporated into the *Modim* prayer, the *U'va l'Tziyyon* prayer, *Hoshanot*, and the verses recited when taking the Torah out of the ark. Clearly, David's last words play a significant role in the foundation of our liturgy. In order to appreciate why, let us examine their biblical context.

David began by acknowledging the transcendent majesty of the Lord in a blessing that he offers to God before the entire congregation:

David blessed the LORD in front of all the assemblage; David said, "Blessed are You, LORD, God of Israel our father, from eternity to eternity. Yours, LORD, are greatness, might splendor, triumph, and majesty—yes, all that is in heaven and on earth; to You, LORD, belong kingship and preeminence above all. Riches and honor are Yours to dispense; You have dominion over all; with You are strength and might, and it is in Your power to make anyone great and strong." (1 Chron. 29:10–12)

What is the significance of David beginning his oration in this fashion? Biblical scholar William Johnstone has noted that David opens by addressing God not familiarly through the immediacy of his own experience, but as the historical God of Israel, and calls on Him as the King of Kings. Why does David do so? Because David, the founder of monarchy, tried to teach his people that the human experience of kingship can convey by analogy something of the power and awesome splendor of God. Mortal rulers, at that time and in our own, are feared and adulated by their subjects. David says to the people: Take those feelings that you have developed toward me as your monarch, multiply them a thousandfold, and begin to get a sense of how you should relate to the Master of the Universe.

The Rabbinic interpretation of David's last prayer fine-tunes these notions. David describes greatness, might, splendor, triumph, and majesty as belonging to the Lord alone. If greatness is exclusively God's, where does that leave us? The Rabbis offer a two-tiered explanation. The first is the opinion of R. Shila:

R. Shila exclaimed, "Thine, O Lord is the greatness and the power"—Blessed is the All Merciful who has made earthly royalty on the model of the heavenly, and has given you dominion and made you lovers of justice. (B. Ber. 58a)

We are charged to emulate God's ways and seek justice. David's demonstration of power through kingship, which he transferred to his son at this juncture, carried with it this important message. But Rabbi Akiva goes a step further:

"Thine, O Lord is the greatness"—this refers to the cleaving of the Red Sea. "And the power"—this refers to the smiting of the first-born. "And the glory"—this refers to the giving of the Torah. "And the victory"—this refers to Jerusalem. "And the majesty"—this refers to the Temple (B. Ber. 58a).

By transposing all of the divine attributes into historic time, Rabbi Akiva has suggested that God's qualities, though unattainable by man, find expression in His covenantal relationship with Israel. We have been beneficiaries of His unfathomable greatness, might, glory, and triumph. By dubbing David's words in this fashion, Rabbi Akiva posits that this most accomplished of kings, when relinquishing his control and confronting his total dependence, understands that he has been involved in something far greater than his own personal accomplishments.

In the next part of the psalm, David skillfully interweaves reflections on mortality, transience, and material wealth. Taking stock of the possessions he has amassed in his lifetime, David's prayer turns from blessing to thankfulness. Yet this too is tinged with authentic humility, verging on sadness, that nothing was ever really his. God enabled everything.

> Now, God, we praise You and extol Your glorious name. Who am I and who are my people, that we should have the means to make such a freewill offering; but all is from You, and it is Your gift that we have given to You. For we are sojourners with You, mere transients like our fathers; our days on earth are like a shadow, with nothing in prospect. O LORD our God, all this great mass that we have laid aside to build You a House for Your holy name is from You, and it is all Yours. (1 Chron. 29:13–16)

The Rabbis unpack the implications of this perspective for our own quotidian religious practice:

> A heavenly Voice will in the future cry aloud on the top of the mountains and say: whoso has wrought with God let him come

and receive his reward. . . . Or it is the Holy Spirit that says: who hath given Me anything beforehand? Yet I shall repay him. Meaning, who offered praise to Me before I gave him breath? Who performed circumcision in My name before I gave him a male child: Who made a parapet for My sake before I gave him room? Who prepared a *lulav* for My sake before I gave him money? Who made fringes for My sake before I gave him a *tallit*? Who set apart *pe'ah* for My sake before I gave him a field? Who set apart *terumah* for My sake before I gave him a threshing floor? Who set aside *hallah* for My sake before I gave him dough? Who set aside an offering for Me before I gave him cattle? (*Va-yikra Rabbah* 27:2)

Feeling the burden of performing the commandments and the material resources they require, the observant Jew may feel that too much is demanded of him. The Rabbis' response echoes David's statement: all that we possess is a gift from God, and the modest resources we are asked to dedicate to His service pale beside His generosity to us. In the succinct formulation of the Mishnah (Avot 3:8): "Give Him that which is His, since you and all you own is His, as David says: 'But all is from You, and it is Your gift that we have given to You' " (1 Chron 29:13).

Observations about the value of wealth, however important for maintaining perspective in life, are not the most profound statement in this part of David's psalm. Rather, we are taken and shaken by his observation about the totality of life: "For we are sojourners with You, mere transients like our fathers; our days on earth are like a shadow, with nothing in prospect" (1 Chron. 29:15). If that is the conclusion of a man who wrote the Psalms and ruled over Israel, what shall we say?

The Rabbis were not content to describe the state of human existence in such a discouraging fashion. Not surprisingly, they assert that our lives are futile, if, and only if, we do not engage in Torah. The specter of death that haunts our brief and fleeting days is blinded by the luminescence of Torah. But the Rabbis also point to another passageway out of the shadows: that we lift our voices in prayer, intoning the immortal song of the immortal soul. Ironically, they ascribed this revolutionary concept to David.

> What is *maskil l'David be-heyoto ba-meara tefillah?* A *maskil* of David, while he was in the cave—a prayer. When Saul and David were in the cave, he realized that man is not sustained by wealth, wisdom, or strength but by prayer; David became wise (*maskil*) and realized that he possessed nothing but prayer. (*Midrash Tehillim* 142:1)

This midrashic passage relates to the early period in David's life. Pursued by King Saul, David twice found himself trapped in the oppressive darkness of a cave, the footsteps of the royal guard advancing toward him. The walls closed in; there was no place to turn. At that darkest moment David achieved an unprecedented degree of clarity, realizing that wisdom, wealth, and might were meaningless. In the blackest night, the individual possesses nothing at all, nothing but prayer.

One might argue that this operative conclusion was a simple one for David. After all, his foxhole prayers were answered; both times, he exited the cave unscathed. However, in the final scene of the book of Chronicles, David's relationship to prayer takes on a different character. Facing death with serenity and courage, David extolled the virtues of prayer and at the same time shared with his people the experience of a prayer that went unanswered. Building the Temple, a house of prayer for all nations (1 Kings 8:41–43), was unquestionably a noble cause. How could such a sincere and enthusiastic initiative have been refused? David might have found a modicum of comfort in the fact that his son would merit the task, but God's resounding "no" never left him. What does it mean to a loyal servant of God to have a prayer rejected? With the wisdom afforded by age, he came to realize that a negative response is also an answer. It was not the one he had hoped for, but the very fact that God had related to his request was also an expression of their special rapport.

David the king, who founded the eternal monarchy of Israel, was not the first leader to have his prayer refused. According to R. Tzadok ha-Cohen of Lubin, Abraham, the founder of the nation of Israel, offered the first petitionary prayer in the Bible—a prayer that ostensibly went unanswered.

> In this Torah portion (Genesis 18), we find the first prayer, the prayer, which Abraham offered for Sodom. Earlier generations didn't have any sense that one might utter prayer to change a decree. Noah, who heard that the Holy One, Blessed Be He, intended to bring a flood upon the world, did not even consider praying to revoke the decree. However, when God informed Abraham that He was planning to punish Sodom, he prayed for them. Now even though God knew that the prayer would be ineffectual since He would not find ten righteous people, even so his prayer was successful in saving Lot, from whom David my servant was descended. [Relating to the verse "I have found David, My servant" (Ps. 89:21)], *Midrash Rabbah* says: "Where did I find him? In Sodom." King David, of blessed memory, was the root of all prayer, as it says: "And I am prayer" (*va'ani tefilati'*); he was the (*shaliah tzibbur*), the emissary of prayer for the community of Israel. (ha-Cohen, 225)

Rabbi Zadok's comment is based on *Bereshit Rabbah* 41:4: "R. Yossi b. Yitzhak said: 'There were two "finds" (*metzi'ot*)—Ruth the Moabite and Na'ama the Ammonite'; R. Yitzhak said, 'I found my servant David.' Where did I find him? In Sodom.' " The basic connection between these characters is clear. Lot survived the destruction of Sodom and Gomorrah and subsequently sired Moab. Generations later, Ruth the Moabite entered the annals of Jewish history, and David was her great-grandson. That would explain the arresting statement that God found David in Sodom. R. Tzadok ha-Cohen, however, goes beyond that. Abraham invented petitionary prayer in pleading for Sodom. That form of dialogue between man and God was perfected by David, who thereby became the *shaliah tzibbur* (emissary of prayer) of Israel for all generations.

In order to appreciate the link between Abraham and David suggested by R. Zadok, let us consider the nature of their respective prayers. Abraham prayed not for himself, but for others, in the unique framework of a dialogue initiated by God. The Lord had resolved not to destroy Sodom until He revealed to Abraham that which He was about to do (Gen. 18:17). But this was not to be a one-sided announcement. The Rabbis point out that God *consulted* with Abraham. The prophet Amos makes the astonishing statement, "The LORD God does nothing if He has not shared His counsel with His servants the prophets" (Amos 3:7) [author's translation]. Abraham, who was described as being a prophet (*navi*) (20:7), was not only privy to God's intentions, but allowed—and perhaps even expected—to challenge them.

> Abraham came forward and said, "Will You sweep away the innocent along with the guilty? What if there should be fifty innocent within the city; will You then wipe out the place and not forgive it for the sake of the innocent fifty who are in it? Far be it from You! Shall not the Judge of all the earth deal justly?" (Gen. 18:23–25)

Lest we say that this boldness in criticizing God's justice reflects a flaw in Abraham's appreciation of God's standards or in his own humility, we are immediately apprised of both God's agreement with Abraham's argument and Abraham's keen understanding of his human limits:

> And the LORD answered, "If I find within the city of Sodom fifty innocent ones, I will forgive the whole place for their

sake." Abraham spoke up, saying, "Here I venture to speak to my Lord, I who am but dust and ashes." (Gen. 18:26–27)

Recognizing the inherent finitude of man and yet daring to shake the heavenly throne in heartfelt appeal—in this incongruent duality of the human condition lies the secret of prayer, discovered by our father Abraham and bequeathed to his descendants.

Another lesson may be learned from this account, though, and it is a sobering one. Abraham's prayer failed to achieve its intended goal. Was the entire enterprise, then, not merely an exercise in futility? What was the efficacy of prayer if in the end Sodom and Gomorrah were overturned?

In truth, the most important change achieved by prayer is not in the course of events in the external world but in the soul of the person who prays. Through the act of prayer, Abraham became acutely aware of his responsibility and limitations as well as the responsibilities and limitations of others. Abraham's prayer came from a place of genuine compassion and altruism and helped Abraham himself achieve a newfound degree of understanding, humility, and acceptance.

> Prayer deals not with the discovery of new knowledge and the enrichment of the human intellect with their truth, but with the utilization of already attained knowledge, and to deepen through the power of feeling the imprint of moral knowledge on the powers of the soul. (Kook I: 20)

Furthermore, prayer utterly transforms the existing relationship between the supplicant and the Almighty, revealing new dimensions of that bond. God, the Judge of all the earth, rendered the final decision on Sodom, but Abraham's closeness to Him grew through submission and acceptance of that decree. Moreover, it was God who had solicited Abraham's input. Contrast God's initiation of the dialogue with Abraham here with His abrupt confrontation of Adam after the fall: "Where art thou?" The negotiation over Sodom was not an invitation for confession or reality testing by God as prosecutor, but rather a discussion initiated by God with His beloved servant Abraham—in essence, an invitation to him to share in the moral governance of the world. The effectiveness of prayer is defined by the outgrowth rather than the outcome. Parameters and positioning are sharpened and fate is accepted—it is then that prayer begins.

What was Abraham thinking after this exchange? We do not know. Perhaps he resigned himself to a more profound awareness of how he was nothing but dust and ashes. Yet we are told in Genesis 20:17 that Abraham prayed again for the recovery of Abimelech and his household; this time, his prayer was answered. *Bereshit Rabbah* notes that this is the first time the word *vayitpalel* is used in the Torah.

> *Vayitpalel Avraham.* And Abraham prayed to God. R. Hama the son of R. Hanina said that from the beginning of the book (Genesis) until now, no one used the term *vayitpalel*; when our father Abraham prayed, the knot was untied. (*Bereshit Rabbah* 52:13)

This midrash credits Abraham with "untying the knot." Exactly what this phrase means is unclear. Perhaps R. Hama is thinking of prayer as a spiritual instrument of great power, which had remained bound up in its exalted wrappings since the beginning of time. Along came Abraham, empowered by the intimacy of prayer he had experienced at Sodom, and unpacked this wondrous process for use in all situations of human need, in yearning for the fulfillment of simple desires as much as in matters of destiny. It took the boldness of Abraham to unravel the mystery of prayer—to untie the knot.

And what was God thinking after His dialogue with Abraham in Sodom? One can only wonder what effect was rendered on the Almighty. The Torah concludes the episode with a most unusual verse, which serves as the springboard for such speculation.

> When the LORD had finished speaking to Abraham, He
> departed; and Abraham returned to his place. (Gen. 18:33)

The verse is perplexing. Why inform us that the Lord took leave of Abraham and why tell us that Abraham returned to his place? *Midrash Tanhuma* elaborates:

> When the Lord had finished speaking to Abraham, He depart-
> ed; note the humility of God. Rabbi Berachya said, ordinarily
> when two people converse and they want to take leave of one
> another, the less important asks permission of the more impor-
> tant. . . . However, when the Holy One Blessed Be He spoke
> to Abraham and wanted to take leave, He, as it were, requested
> Abraham's permission. (*Midrash Tanhuma*, Va-yera' 8)

In this midrashic passage, God is portrayed as being humbled and awe-struck by the valor of Abraham. He responds as the unimportant person in deference to Abraham. In a different midrash, His reverence for Abraham is expressed in His lingering, hoping that through Abraham's prayer, He would find some merit to save Sodom. We must not underestimate the courage of these midrashic texts, which dare to portray God as halted in His tracks and left deeply moved, even con-templative, by Abraham's prayer.

As for Abraham, he returned to his place. Presumably, he just went home. However, R. Naftali Zvi Yehudah Berlin explains the phrase in terms of the experience of prayer. Prayer had been a lofty prophetic interlude. Abraham, in communication with God, had been elevated to a different level. He had become, as Abraham Joshua Heschel says, the "object of divine thought." The reverberation of that meeting of minds and hearts would fill the lull that followed as Abraham and God went their respective ways, and the experience would leave an indelible mark on Abraham's religious psyche.

Let us now return to Reb Tzadok ha-Cohen's fascinating idea that

Abraham's failure to save Sodom was transformed into a triumph of the spirit. Through Abraham's prayer, someone (Lot) was physically saved; metaphysically, however, someone was created—David the *shaliah tzibbur* of *klal Yisra'el* (emissary of prayer of the community of Israel). Abraham set into motion the next movement in the symphony of prayer. He created the climate of prayer that enabled the emergence of King David, who would compose the poetic substance of that personal dialogue with God.

The points of convergence and divergence between Abraham and David are instructive. Like Abraham, David proposed a most reasonable request, which was denied. In 2 Samuel 7 / 1 Chronicles 17, we are told that David conceived the idea of building a permanent Temple and shared his plans with the prophet Nathan, who initially concurred enthusiastically. God, though, immediately revealed His disapproval to the prophet, who conveyed this disheartening oracle to the king. For David, the rejection of his sincere offer to serve God through building His Temple was a crowning blow. How did he respond to the news? He was not silenced, nor did he "return to his place." He immediately went to God's place:

Then King David came and sat (*va-yeshev*) before the LORD. (2 Sam. 7:18)

This detail is significant both spatially and symbolically. It echoes the opening passage in 2 Samuel, chapter 7, where David expressed his dismay that "here I am dwelling in a house of cedar, while the Ark of the Lord sits (*yoshev*) in a tent." Moreover, God Himself had undermined David's initiative using this very term: "From the day that I brought the people of Israel out of Egypt to this day, I did not dwell (*lo yashavti*) in a house!"(2 Chron. 7:6). David's sitting before the Lord in prayer was a clear and humble act of capitulation to God's will. *Midrash Tehillim* emphasizes this point by injecting an additional nuance into the word *yashav*:

As it says, "King David came and sat before God." Is it permitted to sit before God? Man prays standing, as it says, "Phineas stood and prayed." What then is the meaning of "David sat before God?" His heart found peace in prayer (*sheyashav lebo be-tefillah*), as it says, "You will settle their hearts, You will incline Your ear." (Ps. 10:17) [author's translation]

David tried to make peace with the dashing of his hopes through prayer. Like Abraham, his pronouncements highlight the incongruent duality of the human condition and of the predicament of prayer. David resorted to deference, doxology, and demand. He cried:

What more can David say to You? You know Your servant, O Lord God. For Your word's sake and of Your own accord You have wrought this great thing, and made it known to Your servant. You are great indeed, O LORD God! There is none like You and there is no other God but You, as we have always heard. . . . And now, O LORD God, fulfill Your promise to Your servant and his house forever; and do as You have promised. (2 Sam. 7:20–22, 25)

In his groundbreaking work, *Narrative Art and Poetry in the Book of Samuel*, J. P. Fokkelman points out that when God denied David the right to build the Temple, He compensated him with the assurance that his dynasty would be eternal. The mortal, who thought the initiative was his and adopted the stance of a benefactor, became the beneficiary. David acquiesced to the Lord's rejection of his initiative, but the outpourings of his soul were not contained by his disappointment. He was still able to articulate his plea that God keep His promise to his house. This blend of yielding with insistence is a mark of David's faith and demonstrates prayer at its best. David and God had reached an understanding. Like Jacob his forefather, David would not let God go until He had blessed him for all time to come.

As we have noted, David was not allowed to build the Temple

because of his martial pursuits. The prophet Nathan had informed him, "you shall not build a House or My name, for you have shed much blood on the earth in My sight" (1 Chron. 22:8). The Rabbis found this explanation inadequate. After all, David's military actions were all in the service of the Lord and in defense of the people of Israel. Why should David be denied the opportunity to serve God with all his might and all his means just because of his earlier dedication to God's will? The masters of Midrash, therefore, posit that a far more significant concern underlay God's restraining order: the transfer of the Temple's construction to Solomon was intended to prevent the future destruction of the nation. In a remarkable passage in *Pesikta Rabbati* 2:6, the Rabbis portray God as telling David: "If you build [the Temple], it will endure and stand and never be destroyed." David replied, "But that is a good thing!" The Holy One, Blessed Be He, said to him, "It is revealed and known unto Me that Israel will sin, and then I shall cool My fury upon [the Temple] and destroy it, and Israel will be saved."

Esther Menn observes that:

David is granted prophetic insight into the fate of the Temple, and he is also privileged to discuss the significance of its destruction in other dialogues with God. David thereby becomes not only the first human to envision the Temple . . . but also the first to learn of its tragic destiny and its ultimate restoration. As a prophetic figure . . . David has a perspective that uniquely encompasses the entire course of the Temple's history. (Menn, 314)

This penetrating analysis of the midrashic text serves to reinforce the concept of prayer being the ultimate intimate discourse with the Lord. By denying David his wish, the people will be saved. David's rejection is thus transformed by the Rabbis into his election and the answer to his prayer into prophetic revelation. Ironically, an unrequited prayer became the vehicle for Israel's salvation. Instead of a house of prayer, David's legacy would be prayer that would act as the saving grace of Israel for all times.

This midrash is instructive in highlighting the parallel between Abraham and David. For both pioneers of prayer, supplication is closely linked with revelation. Only because they allow themselves to stand before God in all their human vulnerability, without any pretensions of strength or mastery, are they granted the insight of revelation. God's truth flows to them instantly because they have prepared their hearts through prayer. Indeed, as it were, God Himself cannot but respond in kind. In the simple but powerful biblical formulation: *Sod Ha-Shem l'yeriav*, the counsel of God is open to those who revere Him.

There is another facet of *tefillah*, though, that synthesizes the two unidirectional acts of supplication and revelation, and it is one that is perhaps the most relevant to modern man. Shalom Carmy describes how prayer reveals not only God's mind but our own.

> The gesture of prayerful petition affects us by redeeming from nescience our hidden hopes and visions. Praying, we do not manipulate God, nor do we withdraw all desire for the fulfillment of our legitimate needs. We strive to discover, in dialogue with God, through the unique verbal enterprise defined as prayer, what our needs truly are, no more and no less than God's will for us. (Carmy, 21)

Returning now to 1 Chronicles 29—David's final address, with which we began—we witness how this earlier encounter in David's life had transformed him. David's preparations for the Temple to be built by Solomon, described in 1 Chronicles 28–29, might be seen as representing a form of bargaining, like that of Abraham: a compromise, allowing him some share in the Temple he was not permitted to build. However, his parting words transport him elsewhere. David was a changed man. His own desire to build the Temple metamorphosed into a profound understanding of his role in service of the nation and their performance of that task.

In a sense, David was granted the honor of laying the foundations of the Temple—not its physical substrate, but its spiritual basis: the groundwork for the inner sanctum of prayer. David began his farewell address by blessing God before the assembly. He ends it by turning to the people and instructing *them* to pray.

> David said to the whole assemblage, "Now bless the LORD your God." All the assemblage blessed the LORD God of their fathers, and bowed their heads low to the LORD and the king. (1 Chron. 29:20)

What did David teach the people about prayer that they did not know before? Perhaps simply to dare to pray. This spiritual audacity is captured in the following midrash.

> The Holy One, blessed be He, will make a great banquet for the righteous . . . after they have eaten and drunk, the cup of Grace will be offered to our father Abraham, that he should recite Grace, but he will answer them, "I cannot say Grace, because Ishmael issued from me." Then Isaac will be asked, "Take it and say Grace." "I cannot say Grace," he will reply, "because Esau issued from me." Then Jacob will be asked: "Take it and say Grace." "I cannot say Grace," he will reply, "because I married two sisters during [both] their lifetimes, whereas the Torah was destined to forbid them to me." Then Moses will be asked, "Take it and say Grace." "I cannot say Grace, because I was not privileged to enter *Eretz Yisra'el* either in life or in death." Then Joshua will be asked: "Take it and say Grace." "I cannot say Grace," he will reply, "because I was not privileged to have a son." . . . Then David will be asked: "Take it and say Grace." "I will say Grace and it is fit-

ting for me to say Grace," he will reply, as it is said, "I raise the cup of deliverance and invoke the name of the Lord" (Ps. 116:13). (B. Pes. 9b)

This passage leaves the reader puzzled about what appears to be David's sheer arrogance. Was David more worthy than all the rest? Had he not suffered his own personal and national misfortune? What could be more ignominious than the Bathsheba affair? His son Amnon had raped his half-sister, David's beautiful daughter Tamar, and then been murdered by his own brother. And could there be any greater personal tragedy than Absalom's rebellion and death? David had known his fair share of troubles. Yet it is he who lifted his cup and praised God, for he understood prayer in its fullest sense. Prayer had allowed David to find his way through marshes of paradox and to engage in battles of hopes and doubts, giving expression to passionate feelings, reaching the depths of his soul and sometimes the heights of transcendence. From the lowest ebbs he strove upward, knowing full well that heaven's infinite reach exceeded his mortal grasp. In the throes of helplessness, David came to replace the plans he had for God with the plans God had for him. It was in prayer that he found inner agreement with the God of heaven and earth, and the strength that emboldened him to proceed and face his death with equanimity.

Unlike the book of Kings, 1 Chronicles 29 concludes David's valedictory address by telling us that he died be-seva tovah—at a ripe old age. The same expression was used for Abraham (Gen. 25:8). Perhaps we can conclude that David had come to the same resolution as did Abraham: at peace with God, with his life, and with his accomplishments.

David successfully transformed all of Israel into his spiritual heirs and his personal dialectic of prayer into the template for all worship. The Rabbis lyrically describe David's long-range legacy, which has transcended time.

Let me dwell in your tent forever. Did David really think he would live forever? No, but he asked the Holy One, Blessed Be He, May it be Thy will that my songs and praises be said in synagogues and houses of study forever. (*Midrash Tehillim* 61:3)

The passion of King David for the House of Prayer turned every house of worship and study into a temple frequented in each generation by the compositions of the "sweet singer of Israel." The spatial notion of stability and permanence that inspired David to make his initial request found expression in new and continuous venues for David's literary immortality—his prayer.

The focus of prayer is not the self. A man may spend hours meditating about himself, or be stirred by the deepest sympathy for his fellow man, and no prayer will come to pass. Prayer comes to pass in a complete turning of the heart toward God, toward His goodness and power. It is the momentary disregard of our personal concerns, the absence of self-centered thoughts, which constitute the act of prayer. Feeling becomes prayer in the moment in which we forget ourselves and become aware of God. When we analyze the consciousness of a supplicant, we discover that it is not concentrated upon his own interests, but on something beyond the self. The thought of personal need is absent, and the thought of divine grace alone is present in his mind. Thus, in beseeching Him for bread, there is one instant, at least, in which our mind is directed neither to our hunger nor to food, but to His mercy. This instant is prayer. (Heschel, "Prayer," 167–168)

Abraham Joshua Heschel gives expression to the soul's quest for God. The human spirit soars beyond its impermanent confines, seeking the Lord while He can be found and calling to Him when He is near.

Yom Kippur

Chapter Seven

⚛

Shattered Tablets, Broken Hearts

⚛

The cornerstone of our penitential liturgy, from the predawn *Selihot* of the month of Elul through *Ne'ilah* at the closing of the gates on Yom Kippur, is what is classically known as the *Sh'losh Esreh Midot*—the 13 Divine Attributes of Mercy.

The repeated recitation of these attributes was not seen merely as an incantation that would automatically induce divine mercy, but as a guide to repentance. Rabbi Moshe Cordovero, the 16th-century author of the mystical work *Tomer Devorah*, stresses that the Talmud (B. RH 17a) portrays God as saying: "Let them *carry out* this service (the invocation of the attributes) before Me;" that is, not only to recite them, but to be inspired by God's example to similar acts of mercy, *imitatio Dei*. In the wake of such a moral transformation, man may indeed merit forgiveness.

An expression of this idea is found in the concluding stanza of the *selihah* for the eve of Rosh Hashanah, titled "The Thirteen Attributes," composed in the 13th century by the liturgist Rabbi Shlomo ben Menachem: "If all have indeed repented wholeheartedly and come to beseech Thee through each proper attribute, please concur in Your pardon; act, Lord, for Your sake and forgive Your assembly, return on behalf of Your servants, the tribes of Your lot."

However, this formula of divine attributes reaches its liturgical crescendo in the denouement of Yom Kippur, the *Ne'ilah* prayer. As is well known, Yom Kippur is not only the climax of the 10 Days of Repentance; it is also the most important liturgical day of the year. In the final hour of Yom Kippur, the declamation of the attributes becomes the refrain that is desperately and incessantly chanted, expressing our last hope for mercy.

In the Bible, the attributes are first introduced in Exodus, chapter 34, when the second tablets of the law are given to Moses. Rabbinic literature makes the claim that the auspicious day on which God magnanimously gave Israel a second set of tablets to replace those that had been smashed was Yom Kippur. Exploring the story of the two sets of tablets that Moses brought down the mountain enhances our understanding of Yom Kippur. The story begins as follows:

His heart fearful and full of foreboding, Moses headed down the rough and craggy path from the summit of Sinai to the plain below, where the Israelites were encamped. The Almighty had already told him what awaited:

> Hurry down, for your people, whom you brought out of the land of Egypt, have acted basely. They have been quick to turn aside from the way that I enjoined upon them. They have made themselves a molten calf and bowed low to it and sacrificed to it, saying: "This is your god, O Israel, who brought you out of the land of Egypt!" (Exod. 32:7–8)

Despite this warning, not until Moses actually witnessed this travesty with his own eyes did the shock set in. Only a few days earlier, Moses had left the nation at a spiritual zenith as he ascended the mountain. He returned to find them having plummeted into an idolatrous frenzy. The raucous sounds and images of the wanton worship of the Golden Calf extinguished the exalted visions and voices of

Sinai. Standing above the people, Moses reacted with intemperate anger:

> As soon as Moses came near the camp and saw the calf and the dancing, he became enraged; and he hurled the tablets from his hands and shattered them at the foot of the mountain. (Exod. 32:19)

The shattering of the Tablets of the Covenant is one of the classic moments of drama in the Bible. We recount the story twice yearly, in our synagogue reading of Exodus in the winter, and in the passage from Deuteronomy, in which Moses retells the event that we read every summer. The familiarity of the tale inures us, perhaps, to the question that leaps out from the page of Scripture: how could Moses have allowed himself to destroy the tablets? Dismayed though he may have been by the people's sin, "the tablets were God's work, and the writing was God's writing, incised upon the tablets" (Exod. 32:16)— no small matter. The Rabbis amplify the unique nature of the Tablets, listing them among the 10 items that God created at twilight, just before the onset of the first Sabbath (M. Avot 5:6), and asserting that they had been fashioned out of sapphire hewn from under the Throne of Glory (*Midrash Tanhuma, Eikev*, 9). How then could Moses have taken the liberty of destroying divine objects? Other options were available to him. Why not ascend the mountain and return the tablets to their rightful Owner? In fact, why bring them down in the first place? Having been informed of the trouble that awaited him, Moses could have simply gone down, sorted out the fiasco of the calf and dealt with the tablets at some later stage. How are we to understand his destructive audacity?

Through the ages, numerous explanations have been offered to account for the shattering of the tablets. The simplest is that Moses lost control and broke the tablets in a fit of rage. Yet Moses' purposive and measured actions in the following stages of the story indicate that he broke the tablets not in a moment of fury but with planned intent.

In his Torah commentary *Ha-Emek Davar*, Rabbi Naftali Zvi Yehudah Berlin argues that Moses acted as a disciplinarian, depriving the nation before their very eyes of an invaluable treasure of which they no longer were worthy. No other action would have been equal to the deserved measure of punishment.

Other commentators suggest that Moses' intention was not to punish the people but to educate them. Their worship of the Golden Calf—a physical object—indicated that they were capable of doing the very same thing to the Tablets of the Covenant. Moses was compelled to impress upon the people how misguided they were. He therefore had no choice but to smash the tablets, thereby proving that sanctity is not in stone, but in the word of God. Better, thought Moses, to leave the people with no emblematic symbol of immanent divinity in their camp than to introduce a stumbling block that might encourage future fetishism.

A third approach views Moses not as disciplinarian or educator, but as defense attorney. To prevent God from punishing the people, Moses shattered the tablets in order to annul the covenant that they had violated. The midrash in *Avot de-Rabbi Natan* (I:2) compares the tablets to a marriage contract about to be delivered to a woman who has been unfaithful to her betrothed. Understanding that delivery of the contract would finalize the marriage and cause the woman to be punished for adultery, the merciful messenger therefore destroys it. This notion is in consonance with the ancient Near Eastern reality in which pacts were annulled through this method. As Nahum Sarna points out, in Akkadian legal terminology to "break the tablet" means to invalidate an agreement. Realizing that the tablets contained the divine laws and commandments that were beyond the people's ability to uphold, Moses destroyed them, thereby freeing the people from their obligations and protecting them from greater sin and punishment.

Although the breaking of the tablets is in many ways the dramatic climax of this story, its most soul-stirring elements are elsewhere. Let us leave the shards of the tablets scattered about Moses' feet and return to the summit of Mount Sinai, to the moment when God reveals to Moses that the people have stumbled. Listening carefully to the tenor of God's words, the reader is struck by the stark contrast between God's fit of pique and Moses' calm.

The LORD spoke to Moses, "Hurry down, for *your* people, *whom you brought out of the land of Egypt* [italics added], have acted basely. They have been quick to turn aside from the way that I enjoined upon them. They have made themselves a molten calf and bowed low to it and sacrificed to it, saying: 'This is your god, O Israel, who brought you out of the land of Egypt!' " The LORD further said to Moses, "I see that this is a stiffnecked people. Now, let Me be, that My anger may blaze forth against them and that I may destroy them, and make of you a great nation." (Exod. 32:7–10)

God's attitude is strange and unexpected. How absurd for the Almighty to turn to Moses and call Israel *his* people whom *he* brought out of the land of Egypt! Who's in charge here? When did Israel stop being God's nation and become Moses'? The exchange is reminiscent of parents arguing over a child's misbehavior, with the father accusatorily rebuking the mother about the actions of "your son." Moreover, God's final statement, "Now let Me be, that My anger may blaze forth against them and that I may destroy them" colors God as impetuous and lacking in self-control. It also seems utterly incongruous: does God need Moses' permission to get angry?

On the other hand, Moses reacts in a surprisingly reasoned manner. Having just spent 40 days and 40 nights on Mount Sinai without food or drink, Moses is hungry and tired. As if it were not enough to be faced with the crisis of Israel's idolatry, Moses is now confronted with an unparalleled expression of God's wrath. No one could have faulted Moses for resigning his commission and leaving the responsibility for the nation in someone else's hands. Instead, Moses displays spiritual maturity of the highest order.

First, he restores objectivity with a simple adjective shift, replying to God: "Let not Your anger, O LORD, blaze forth against *Your* people, whom *You* delivered from the land of Egypt with great power and with a mighty hand" [italics added] (Exod. 32:11). Moses wastes no time in reorienting the conversation and realigning the connections between the dramatis personae. He gently reminds God of His mercies that led to the Exodus and of His commitment to the people throughout the ages. After initially defusing God's wrath, Moses presents two cogent arguments as to why destroying the nation at this stage would be counterindicated: the first relates to the rumors that would ruin God's credibility in the eyes of the world. The annihilation of the Israelites would confirm the suspicions of the Egyptians that God's intentions had, from the start, not been honorable:

> Let not the Egyptians say, "It was with evil intent that He delivered them only to kill them off in the mountains and annihilate them from the face of the earth." Turn from Your blazing anger, and renounce the plan to punish Your people. (Exod. 32:12)

Moses' second appeal relates to God's responsibility to the forefathers. Although His covenant with the people may have been annulled, His obligation to the Patriarchs remained.

> Remember Your servants, Abraham, Isaac, and Israel, how You swore to them by Your Self and said to them: I will make your offspring as numerous as the stars of heaven, and I will give to your offspring this whole land of which I spoke, to possess forever. (Exod. 32:13)

Moses' second argument is predicated upon the value of devotion and fidelity. True, the Israelites have been flagrantly disloyal to God by worshipping an idol. But if in recompense God destroys them, He will be guilty of disloyalty as well—of going back on His promise to the Patriarchs. Furthermore, the steadfast and unequivocal loyalty of Abraham, Isaac, and Israel outshines the current infidelity of the Children of Israel. God's covenant with them spans the ages and must not be put aside because of the improper acts of one generation of their descendants. Moses' reasoned and well-tempered words strike a responsive chord in God's heart, and we are told: "And the LORD renounced the punishment He had planned to bring upon His people" (Exod. 32:14).

As courageous as Moses' immediate defense of the people was, what is even more impressive is that the "next day," after having shattered the tablets, destroyed the calf, confronted Aaron, punished the sinners, and assessed the damage, Moses once again took the initiative and pleaded Israel's case before God.

The next day Moses said to the people, "You have been guilty of a great sin. Yet I will now go up to the LORD; perhaps I may win forgiveness for your sin." Moses went back to the LORD and said, "Alas, this people is guilty of a great sin in making for themselves a god of gold. Now if You will forgive their sin [well and good]; but if not, erase me from the book which You have written!" (Exod. 32:30–32)

Previously, when God had suggested to Moses: "Now, let Me be, that My anger may blaze forth against them and that I may destroy them, and make of you a great nation" (Exod. 32:10), Moses simply ignored the offer. At this stage, he relates directly to God's suggestion, adamantly refusing to countenance the proposal and insisting that God forgive the people: "Now, if You will forgive their sin [well and good]; but if not, erase me from the book which You have written!" (32:32).

Which book exactly does Moses have in mind? The medieval Spanish biblical interpreter Rabbi Joseph ibn Kaspi (1279–1340) explains that the book is a metaphor, based on the custom of kings to record the chronicles of their reign and the deeds of their subjects to be rewarded or punished (as does Ahasuerus (Esther 2:23)). Moses is saying that if God destroys the people, all of his own accumulated merits are worthless in his eyes. The Talmud (B. RH 16b) develops this metaphor into one of the main themes of the Days of Awe. There are three books, we are told, opened on Rosh Hashanah: one for the righteous, one for the evil, and one for those whose judgment is uncertain. The righteous are immediately inscribed in the Book of Life, the evil are immediately inscribed in the Book of Death, and those in between are given a reprieve from Rosh Hashanah till Yom Kippur. The Rabbis explain that when Moses exclaimed "Erase me from Your book," he was referring to the Book of Life: if the people will die, so must I. He conjoined his fate with theirs, hoping that God's affection for him would avert His punishment of the nation. Nachmanides (1194–1270) takes the idea one step further, explaining that Moses was offering not to die with the people, but to die in their stead.

Another Rabbinic view explains that the book in question is the Torah itself:

> He said to the Holy One, Blessed Be He, the entire Torah that You have given me is comprised of "And God said to Moses," "Speak to the Children of Israel," "Command the Children of Israel," "Tell the Children of Israel." If you wipe them out, what shall I do with Your Torah? Therefore he [Moses] said, "Erase me from Your book," for without Israel there is no story. (*Shemot Rabbah* 47:9)

The Talmud adds a third dimension:

> "I will make of thee a great nation." R. Eleazar said: Moses said before the Holy One, Blessed Be He: "Sovereign of the Universe! Seeing that a stool with three legs cannot stand before Thee in the hour of Thy wrath, how much less a stool with one leg! And moreover, I am ashamed before my ancestors, who will now say: See what a leader He has set over

them—he sought greatness for himself but he did not seek mercy for them." (B. Ber. 32a)

The stool of three legs is, of course, the nation descended from the three Patriarchs—if with all of their merits, their descendants may come to be destroyed, what hope is there for a nation I might found? But the Rabbis have here supplied an additional, psychological dimension to Moses' dramatic outburst. Although Scripture credits Moses with pure altruism, compassion, and courage, the Talmud focuses on Moses' eye toward his reputation as a leader for posterity. Will his actions at this juncture not be interpreted as selfish on his part? The Rabbis of the talmudic age, who as spiritual leaders in times of suffering and persecution could well have sympathized with Moses' dilemma, may have interpreted his choice in accordance with their own leadership experiences.

But returning to the biblical text, in a moment's reflection, we realize how amazing Moses' words really are. This is the same Moses who less than two years earlier had stood trembling and totally lacking in confidence at the very same location—the burning bush at Mount Sinai. Then, God repeatedly commanded him to take the Israelites out of Egypt. In response, over and over again, Moses vigorously objected to the assignment based on his lack of qualifications: "I have never been a man of words . . . I am slow of speech and slow of tongue" (Exod. 4:10). God convinces him to take the assignment only by assuring him that his words would come from God Himself and would be spoken with the aid of his brother, Aaron. And now, in the greatest crisis that Moses and his people have ever confronted, face-to-face with the towering fury of God and forces of destruction that the world had never experienced, Moses finds his voice. With pathos and eloquence, he rises to the occasion, countering God's destructive intent, cunningly crafting arguments to defuse His wrath, declaiming words that shook the heavens as he puts his life on the line: "If that is Your intention, erase me from the book which You have written!" The man Moses was indeed grown great.

Moses' courageous spiritual maturity again stands in stark contrast with the next expression of God's response to the Golden Calf incident.

> Then the LORD said to Moses, "Set out from here, you and the people that you have brought up from the land of Egypt, to the land of which I swore to Abraham, Isaac, and Jacob, saying, 'To your offspring will I give it'—I will send an angel before you. . . . But I will not go in your midst, since you are a stiff-necked people, lest I destroy you on the way." (Exod. 33:1–3)

What a strange resolution God offers Moses! He has acceded to Moses' appeal that the nation not be annihilated (albeit reserving the right to visit further punishment on them; in a sense, a suspended sentence (Exod. 32:34). Yet though the Israelites will continue on to the Promised Land, God will not travel among them. This compromise assumes that (a) God is willing to forgive the people their past and future trespasses, to fulfill His covenant with the Patriarchs, but (b) were His presence in proximity to them, He would be unable to control His fury, with retribution sure to follow—as He reiterates: "If I were to go in your midst for one moment, I would destroy you" (33:5).

Again, the image of God presented here is that of a petulant child unable to curb his anger, who resorts to distancing himself from a source of annoyance. It is an act of disengagement that could not be more different from Moses' embrace of the nation despite their faults. Could God really not control His anger in the presence of the people? And if He were further removed, would it suddenly become appropriate for Him to ignore Israel's iniquities?

Rather, God's response is a sign of His love for Israel. Just as a lover injured by infidelity withdraws brokenhearted into isolation, here too God projects a future in which being among the people in their rejection of Him is simply too painful to bear; hence, His presence became veiled. If after the revelation at Sinai we are told, "and they saw the God of Israel: under His feet there was the likeness of a pavement of sapphire, like the very sky for purity" (Exod. 24:10), now "Man may not see Me and live" (33:20).

Previously, Moses' petition was based on the covenant with the forefathers and concern for God's reputation. These points were sufficient to allay God's anger to the extent of sparing the people their deserved punishment. These contentions were insufficient, however, to repair the breach between the sinful nation and their Redeemer, whom they had grievously injured through their idolatry, to the point that God needed to withdraw His numinous presence. Realizing the radical difference to the destiny of Israel that would be affected by the withdrawal of God's presence, Moses refuses to accept the act as a fait accompli. He twice petitions God to reverse His decision (Exod. 33:16, 34:9)—and surprisingly, God agrees to Moses' request. What led God to change His mind?

Moses addresses God's withdrawal in two ways. First, Moses asks God to appear to him personally. If taken as a request for mystical revelation, this makes little sense in the context of the story. However, if we understand Moses' appeal as continuing his advocacy on behalf of the people, we might say that Moses tried to reengage God and the nation gradually. God in His pain had withdrawn; now, Moses was attempting to entice Him out of His isolation, first by revealing Himself once again to His loyal servant Moses, and later perhaps to the people once again. In light of this interpretation, Moses' second appeal—"And see that this nation is Your people"—which otherwise is totally disjointed, begins to make sense.

With His faith in man renewed by the spiritual majesty that Moses had achieved, at that moment, God was willing to reveal Himself in the world once again. Taking the replacement tablets in his hands, Moses ascended the mountain and stood before God in the cleft of the rock on Sinai (Exod. 33:22). There, the Attributes of Divine Mercy were revealed to the world. But by whom?

One school of thought, beginning with the talmudic sage R. Yochanan of Tiberias, reads the text as indicating that these qualities of God's mercy were taught to Moses by God.

"And the Lord passed before him and proclaimed." R. Yochanan said: Were it not written in the text, it would be impossible for us to say such a thing. This verse teaches us that the Holy One, Blessed Be He, drew His *tallit* around Him like the cantor of a congregation and showed Moses the order of prayer. He said to him: Whenever Israel sins, let them carry out this service before Me and I will forgive them. (B. RH 17a)

R. Yochanan's portrayal of God revealing the attributes while wrapped in a *tallit* like a cantor hints that only because of these attributes are the gates of prayers open to sinners. God shares this knowledge with Israel, thus allowing them to approach Him in supplication, then and in all generations to follow. The revelation of the Attributes of Mercy is itself an act of mercy.

An alternative reading of the biblical text is offered by the midrash in the 47th chapter of *Pirkei de-Rabbi Eliezer*, and it is breathtaking in its boldness. It was not God who revealed these attributes to Moses, but rather Moses who revealed them to God: "When He passed before him . . . Moses . . . began to shout, 'The Lord, the Lord, a God compassionate and gracious. . . . ' " At first, this notion seems incredible: how is it possible that a mortal might reveal to God an aspect of His own being? And yet, throughout the tale, it is Moses who is the voice of temperance and kindness, standing in stark contrast to God's volatile anger and retributive intent. Note, too, that in the earlier biblical narratives of Genesis and Exodus, God is not portrayed as acting mercifully. Only by Moses' proclamation that these qualities are aspects of His divine nature does God renounce "the punishment He planned to bring upon His people" (Exod. 32:14). In this reading, Moses' declaration brought to actuality God's qualities of mercy, which had not previously found expression in the confines of this world.

The reason that Moses was capable of this great revelation is that he himself embodied the same qualities of mercy that he attributed to God. Recall that in the initial dialogue, Moses asks God to be merciful and compassionate, not only for the sake of Israel but for the sake of His public image and for the sake of His promises to the Patriarchs. Moses is concerned that God not suffer: what will become of Your great name? What will be with Your covenant? Moses' mercy and concern are so great that they reached out to God Himself in His moment of pain and distress.

Consider also that Moses was, no doubt, personally devastated by the people's idolatry, which shattered the validation he had achieved at Sinai as prophet and lawgiver. Nevertheless, Moses immediately reacted as a selfless leader. Rising above self-pity and resentment toward the people, Moses compassionately pleaded the case of Israel. Add to this Moses' incredible act of self-abnegation in refusing God's offer that he become the founder of a new chosen people, and we are not surprised that such a man might teach even God about the meaning of mercy.

Radical as this notion might appear, it seems to have struck a chord with rabbinic theology. In one of the most sublime and moving passages in the Talmud, we are made privy to a reminiscence of R. Ishmael the High Priest, describing one of his visitations to the Holy of Holies in the last years of the Second Temple:

> How do we know that the Holy One, Blessed Be He, prays? Because it says, "I will bring them to My sacred mount. And let them rejoice in My house of prayer" (Isa. 56:7). It is not said, "their [house of] prayer" but "My [house of] prayer," hence you learn that the Holy One, Blessed Be He, prays. What does He pray? R. Zutra b. Tobi said in the name of Rav: May it be My will that My mercy may suppress My anger and that My mercy may prevail over My other attributes so that I may deal with My children in the attribute of mercy, and on their behalf, stop short of the limit of strict justice.

It was taught: R. Ishmael b. Elisha said: "I once entered into the innermost part of the sanctuary to offer incense and saw Akathriel Jah the Lord of Hosts seated upon a high and exalted throne. He said to me: 'Ishmael My son, bless Me.' I replied: 'May it be Thy will that Thy mercy may suppress Thy anger, and Thy mercy may prevail over Thy other attributes so that Thou may deal with Thy children according to the attribute of mercy and may on their behalf stop short of the limit of strict justice!' And He nodded to me with His head.' " (B. Ber. 7a)

The idea that God would desire the blessing of a mortal is almost too extreme to comprehend. And yet, it will not escape the reader's notice that R. Ishmael's blessing is precisely what Moses had proclaimed to God generations earlier—that mercy is the essence of His being. All else that we proclaim about God, that He is mighty, omnipotent, awe-inspiring, vast, grand, and so on, is self-evident. Seemingly, though, even God is grateful for our intercession on behalf of His mercies. Contrary to the Bard's saying, the quality of mercy is indeed strained. It is so hard to come by that God Himself prays for it.

The innermost part of the sanctuary that R. Ishmael entered was the Holy of Holies, and the day he did so was Yom Kippur, the only day of the year that even he, as High Priest, was allowed to set foot there. Foremost on his mind at the moment was concern for Israel, for the forgiveness of their sins, for their atonement, and for their welfare. Suddenly, he was vouchsafed a vision of God, who on that day sat in terrible judgment with the Books of Life and Death open before Him. Seemingly, despite God's limitless power, the task of deciding the world's fate weighed heavily upon Him. R. Ishmael was moved to compassion and blessed God that His mercies might be revealed at that moment. In doing so, R. Ishmael echoed the actions of Moses our Teacher, who, on the selfsame Yom Kippur (so the Rabbis tell us) so many years before, blessed God by revealing His attributes of mercy for the first time.

If God prays, it is only a short midrashic step to assert that He also wears tefillin. In the cleft of the rock on Sinai, Moses was to be shown a minor aspect of God's presence, described in Exodus 33:23 as God's back. The Rabbis assert that this aspect of God that Moses saw was the knot of His tefillin (which in more conventional tefillin is on the back of the head). If our tefillin contain scrolls in which *Shema Yisra'el* is written, what is found in God's tefillin? The Rabbis reply that it is a passage from 1 Chronicles 17:21: "And who is like Your people Israel, a unique nation on earth?" God shows Moses the knot of His tefillin, the bond that ties Him to Israel. It is another confirmation of His internalization of Moses' message of mercy and reconciliation.

Unique though the nation of Israel might be, its sudden descent into idolatry was a self-inflicted spiritual wound of major proportions. It revealed that they were capricious, irresponsible, and ungrateful; indeed, as Moses calls them elsewhere, "the least of all peoples." And yet, despite their shortcomings, the next stage of the incident reveals that they had the potential to rise above their faults. Between God's original statement that He would no longer accompany the nation and His later retraction of that threat came not only Moses' mediation, but a simple act by the people that did not go unnoticed by God.

When the people heard this harsh word, they went into mourning, and none put on his finery. The LORD said to Moses, "Say to the Israelite people, 'You are a stiffnecked people. If I were to go in your midst for one moment, I would destroy you. Now then leave off your finery, and I will consider what to do to you.' " So the Israelites remained stripped of the finery from Mount Horeb on. (Exod. 33:4–6)

In this enigmatic passage, the people mourn the loss of God's presence in their midst. Commentators are divided as to the meaning of "removing finery." Some claim that they took off their festive clothing, which they had worn to receive the Torah, recognizing their demotion in status. Others suggest that they took off their jewelry, since it had been used to make the Golden Calf. But the Rabbis explain that the people had been doubly crowned at Sinai for their agreement to obey—*na'aseh*—and to heed—*nishma*—the words of God. These crowns were now taken away; the people were literally crestfallen.

At that juncture, Scripture tells us, "They went into mourning." The chasm that they had opened between Israel and God was painfully real to them. The Rabbis embellish the profundity of their bereavement:

> "Draw me after you, let us run!" (Songs 1:4)—This verse [metaphorically describes] the withdrawal of the divine presence from their midst and they longed to run after it. . . . When all of the troubles befell them in the case of the Golden Calf, they did not mourn, but when Moses informed them that God would not be amongst them, "the nation heard this dreadful matter and they mourned." (*Shir ha-Shirim Rabbah* 1:24)

The shards of the tablets lay strewn on the ground beneath the mountain. One can only imagine the sobriety of that moment: the feelings of failure, of loss, and of despair. Perhaps they felt, as we do when we say in the liturgy for the Days of Awe, that "Man is like a pot shard that breaks, the grass that withers, the flower that fades, the shadow that passes, the cloud that vanishes, the breeze that blows, the dust that floats, and the dream that flies away."

Wayward as they were in raising an idol to serve as an object of the kinds of rituals they had seen practiced by pagan peoples, they did so not out of evil intent, but more likely out of folly. Too late, they became acutely aware of the fallout of that willful act. Their pursuit of vanity had led them to waste an incredible opportunity, never before offered in the history of mankind—the chance to become "a kingdom of priests and a holy nation." To their credit, the Israelites immediately grasped that they had just undergone a supreme loss—the departure of God's presence. And so they mourned. They wept for the special relationship with God that they were sure could never be restored. The tablets had indeed been shattered, but far more broken were the people's hearts.

Not only Moses' compassionate intercession, but this expression of sincere remorse might have been what led God to change His mind and to continue His relationship with Israel. Suddenly and unexpectedly, the word of God came to Moses once again:

> Carve two tablets of stone like the first, and I will inscribe upon the tablets the words that were on the first tablets, which you shattered. (Exod. 34:1)

How might there ever be other tablets "like the first," which had been shaped and inscribed by God? *Midrash ha-Gadol* (Exod. 34:1) supplies the answer: Indeed, they were not like the first—they were greater. Miraculous as the first tablets were, they were a unilateral symbol of the covenant, reflecting only God's commands and not Israel's acceptance of them. The second tablets, that Moses fashioned and God inscribed, were a far better basis for the relationship that needed to be built between God and Israel.

The sight of the shattered tablets upon the ground brought the people of Israel back to their senses. In the end, their role as a catalyst of repentance superseded their original intended status as a static symbol of the covenant. What became of those broken pieces? The Talmud (B. Men. 91a) explains that they, too, were placed in the Ark of the Covenant. Two sets of tablets would always accompany the nation, one whole and the other broken. This would serve as eternal testimony to the fact that restoration is possible. Even after devastating downfalls, we have it within our power to rise again, to find the road back.

In the end, though, the tablets remained but an external symbol of a truth that the People of Israel need to find within themselves. No physical object, not even one fashioned and given by God, can guarantee that we are, and will forever be, the People of the Covenant.

Only when that pact becomes a truly integral part of what we are will our relationship with God be secure. This truth was beautifully expressed by the prophet Jeremiah, in whose time the nation focused too much on the ritual of the Temple and not enough on their own morality and spirituality. He spoke of a future for Israel in which we will live and breathe the covenant.

> See, a time is coming—declares the LORD—when I will make a new covenant with the House of Israel and the House of Judah. It will not be like the covenant I made with their fathers, when I took them by the hand to lead them out of the land of Egypt, a covenant which they broke, so that I rejected them—declares the LORD. But such is the covenant I will make with the House of Israel after these days—declares the LORD: I will put My Teaching into their inmost being and inscribe it upon their hearts. Then I will be their God, and they shall be My people. No longer will they need to teach one another and say to one another, "Heed the LORD"; for all of them, from the least of them to the greatest, shall heed Me— declares the LORD. (Jer. 31:31–34)

Once, when God initiated His covenant with us, He inscribed His holy words in letters of fire on tablets of stone. But in the fullness of time, He offers to inscribe His words directly on the chambers of our hearts. All we need to do is let them in.

Chapter Eight

❧

Eleh Ezkerah

❧

The fulcrum of the Yom Kippur liturgy, found in the *Musaf* prayer, is the *avodah* (literally, "the service"). It describes in great detail the Temple rituals of sacrifice and atonement performed by the High Priest in days of yore. In one of the rites, he was brought two he-goats. By casting lots, he marked one for God and the other for *Azazel*. The first goat was offered as a sacrifice for the sins of the people. Subsequently, at the climax of the ritual, the High Priest laid his hands on the head of the second goat and confessed the transgressions of the House of Israel. The scapegoat was then sent off to be cast over a precipice in the wilderness, carrying with it the sins of the nation. This symbolic act of collective atonement and expiation gave graphic expression to the nature of Yom Kippur: "For on this day, atonement shall be made for you to cleanse you of all your sins; you shall be clean before the LORD" (Lev. 16:30). These acts were followed by additional sacrifices and ablutions of the High Priest, who entered the awesome realm of the Holy of Holies to burn incense before the presence of the Almighty. Purified and renewed, he and the people rejoiced in the Creator of the universe: "Happy the people that is so situated! Happy the people whose God is their LORD!" The High Priest concluded the day with a heartfelt prayer, asking the Lord to grant the house of Israel a year of abundant blessing.

155

These and other rituals of atonement, which we reenact liturgically in great detail, are discordant with our modern experience and perhaps foreign to our worldview. Nevertheless, they contain within them profound messages, totally consonant with this most sanctified of days. We learn about purity, holiness, sin, and expiation. These rites stress the importance of renewal, brotherhood, and communal responsibility. It is therefore understandable that these passages form a central part of the day's liturgy.

Notably, the Yom Kippur afternoon service does not end there. Immediately following the *avodah*, we are introduced to what is perhaps the most enigmatic passage in the *mahzor*; a *piyyut* (liturgical poem) about 10 martyrs, titled *Eleh Ezkerah* ("These I Shall Remember").

> These martyrs I well remember, and my soul is melting with secret sorrow. Evil men have devoured us and eagerly consumed us. In the days of the tyrant, there was not reprieve for the ten who were put to death by the Roman government. (Birnbaum, 838)

This *piyyut* is based on midrashim composed in the 5th or 6th century of the Common Era, and describes 10 great Torah leaders who suffered martyrdom during the Roman period.

Eleh Ezkerah employs literary license in portraying the executions of all 10 rabbis as occurring, en suite, at the same time—although in fact they were not even contemporaries. By collapsing historical boundaries, the author leads the reader to be even more appalled by this chilling sequence of murders. The *piyyut* goes into graphic detail about the torturous deaths of all 10 and concludes with the following passage, beseeching God to yield to our entreaties in the merit of these martyrs:

> This has befallen us; we narrate it repeatedly, pouring out our downtrodden and grievous hearts. From on high, heed our supplication; Thou O Lord art a merciful and gracious God.

Gracious One, look down from heaven; see the spilled blood of the saintly, look upon Your curtain and remove all stains of guilt. O God, Thou art the King who dost sit on the throne of mercy. We have sinned, our Rock, forgive us our Creator. (Birnbaum, 844)

At this point in the synagogue service, hunger and fatigue have begun to set in, and our power of concentration has waned. Yet suddenly we are called to attention by this disturbing lament, as it impinges upon the tenor of the day and of the prayer service. The 10 martyrs of whom we speak are familiar to us from Tisha b'Av. We read about them in a *kinnah* (lament) titled *Arzei ha-Levanon* ("The Cedars of Lebanon"):

The cedars of Lebanon, the noble of the Law, great champions in Mishnah and in Talmud, mighty in strength who toiled (at their books) in purity. Behold the ten martyrs that were massacred by the dominion (of Rome); their blood has been shed and their strength failed, O for these do I weep, and my eye gushes forth (in tears). When I remember this, I cry out bitterly (for) the choice (flower of) Israel, the holy vessels, the crown, and diadem; pure in heart and holy, they died a dreadful death. (Rosenfeld, 125)

The relevance of reading such a lament on Tisha b'Av is clear. On the anniversary of the destruction of the Second Temple by the Romans, it is befitting to honor the memory of mighty Torah luminaries who were also executed by the Romans. However, by recalling their martyrdom on Yom Kippur, the emphasis is shifted from politics to theology. Indeed, it made sense for Jews under Roman rule—the audience of the author of *Eleh Ezkerah*—to grapple with theodicy, given the senseless death that characterized their reality. However, what significance could this hold for a modern reader on Yom Kippur? Perhaps, by engendering our outrage at the death of innocents, *Eleh*

Ezkerah gives expression to the lack of theological clarity we face in our lives. On a day of deep introspection, when we may be preoccupied with our own pain, crises, and losses of the past year, we are asked to recall the history of our people, full of unending suffering and tragedy. This outlook may help us see the problems of our lives from a different viewpoint.

However, *Eleh Ezkerah* is far more complex and cryptic than one might expect from a simple homily on perspective. Consider the peculiar set of circumstances that led to the execution of the 10 martyrs. The Roman emperor, casually leafing through the Bible, is struck by the following passage: "He who kidnaps a man—whether he has sold him or is still holding him—shall be put to death" (Exod. 21:16). He notes that Joseph's brothers, who kidnapped and sold him, were never punished. He then curiously commands that his palace be filled with shoes, and summons the Rabbis to clarify the legal matter. They confirm that indeed he who kidnaps must be put to death. The emperor then demands that 10 sages be killed as punishment for the transgression of Joseph's brothers. The Rabbis ask for a three-day reprieve, during which time they send Rabbi Ishmael up to the heavenly tribunal to ascertain the legitimacy of this demand for vicarious atonement. Shockingly, Rabbi Ishmael is informed that these great rabbis are fated to be executed for the crime of others.

The oddities herein abound. Why would the Roman emperor be leafing through the Bible? Of what concern was it to him that a crime committed long ago went unpunished? Why did he fill his palace with shoes? What was the nature of Rabbi Ishmael's mysterious mystical ascent? But the most significant question of all is: since when is vicarious atonement a concept approved of by the heavenly tribunal? In Jewish tradition, "a person shall be put to death only for his own crime" (Deut. 24:16), not for the sins of others!

The *piyyut* is predicated on the assumption, inherent in a simple reading of Genesis, that the brothers were not punished during their lifetime for selling Joseph. Therefore, subsequent generations suffered in their stead. Rabbinic literature, however, both supplies an account of their own atonement and punishment, and explains the long-range effects of their felony.

R. Yannai posited that the sin of the tribes who sold Joseph was not atoned for until they died, as it says: "Then the LORD of Hosts revealed Himself to my ears: 'This iniquity shall never be forgiven you until you die' " (Isa. 22:14). Moreover, through the sin of selling Joseph, the Land of Israel was struck by famine for seven years (*Pirke de-Rabbi Eliezer* 37).

Shemot Rabbah 30:7 claims that the punishment extended beyond the lifetime of Joseph and his brothers. Four hundred years of enslavement in Egypt are midrashically linked to this unconscionable crime. The basis of this claim lies in the notion of measure for measure. Having sold their brother into slavery, the Children of Israel were punished in like fashion. *Midrash Tehillim* 10:3 posits that throughout the generations, Jews are to relate to this dastardly deed and its severe consequence in their annual recitation of the haggadah of Pesach: "R. Hanin said: The Holy One, Blessed Be He, said to the tribes: since you sold him into slavery, as it says, 'Joseph was sold as a slave' (Ps. 105:17), by your lives! Every year you shall read [in the haggadah] 'And we were slaves to Pharaoh in Egypt.' "

The Rabbis highlighted the repercussions of the sale of Joseph in order to educate their constituency regarding the dangers of brotherly discord. Echoes of this idea made their way into the world of biblical interpretation. For example, the prophet Amos described the crimes of Israel as follows: "because they sold the righteous for silver and the needy for a pair of shoes" (Amos 2:6) [author's translation]. Amos's exhortation was directed toward man's inhumanity to man in his day. And yet, both in Targum Jonathan to Genesis 37:28 and in *Pirke de-Rabbi Eliezer* 38, this verse was interpreted as a reference to Joseph's brothers, who sold him for silver to buy shoes! These commentaries established the brothers' criminal offense as a precedent whose impact was felt throughout the ages.

In the late 15th century, the Spanish exegete Rabbi Abraham Sabba took careful note of the cry of Reuben upon discovering that

Joseph (having been drawn out by the Ishmaelites) was not in the pit into which his brothers had cast him. In his estimation, that piercing scream continues to claim retribution forever:

> . . . his bitter cry: "And what will become of me" (Gen. 37:30) [author's translation] is lament and mourning. I think that he cried for his brother and lamented . . . [demanding] "God of retribution, LORD, God of retribution, appear!" (Ps. 94:1) . . . And God heard his cry, as our sages have taught that this cruelty caused the death of the Ten Martyrs, and [the death of] ten [righteous men] in every generation, and the sin still stands. (*Zeror ha-Mor*, Gen. 37:30)

Despite these isolated texts, the concept of vicarious atonement, whereby innocent victims suffer to atone for the sins of others, is far from mainstream in Judaism. In fact, this notion was so disturbing that it raised eyebrows early on.

The 16th-century Italian historiographer and talmudist Gedaliah ben Joseph ibn Yahya, in his monumental work *Shalshelet ha-Kabbalah*, expressed his consternation as follows:

> My entire life I was perplexed by the *piyyut* which we say on the Day of Atonement and Tisha b'Av apparently in all the *mahzorim* and in all languages. These texts present the death of the Ten Martyrs as resulting from the sale of Joseph . . . This raises many questions . . . how could the brothers' descendants receive their punishment? After all, the prophets cry "Sons shall not die for the sin of their fathers!" (Deut. 24:16) . . . Since the ten tribes were together when they sinned, how is it that the ten victims of punishment were not together at their execution? They did not live at the same time. Moreover, only nine perpetrators [brothers] were present at the sale of Joseph, as Reuben and Benjamin were not present, so why were 10 rabbis martyred? . . . All of these doubts, in my humble esti-

mation, bring me to the conclusion that "our forefathers inherited lies" (Jer. 16:19) in believing that "fathers eat sour grapes and the teeth of the sons are put on edge" (Ezek. 18:2). In fact, not all of the sages listed were executed, only some of them, as listed in the Gemara: R. Shimon b. Gamliel, R. Akiva, R. Judah b. Baba, Teradyon, and others. They, too, died for their own sins or the sins of their generation, not for the sins of others, and the authors of piyyut made this entire thing up to bring contrition to the hearts of the masses on the Days of Awe; days of affliction and repentance. (Ibn Yahya, 13)

However, what Shalshelet ha-Kabbalah fails to mention is that beyond running counter to normative Jewish theology, Eleh Ezkerah's unsettling premise is emphatically Christian. The New Testament claims that Jesus' suffering and death were vicarious. He himself was sinless, but in order to remove the guilt and penalty for the sins of others, Jesus took them upon himself. How can Eleh Ezkerah legitimate Christian doctrine by attributing the death of the 10 Martyrs to a similar process?

Moreover, Christian writings throughout the generations dredged up the story of the sale of Joseph to indict the Jews vehemently. The 4th-century Church father Ambrose links the story of the sale of Joseph for 20 pieces of silver with that of Judas Iscariot betraying Jesus for 30 pieces of silver (Matt. 26:14). Eleh Ezkerah, in granting that the sins of Joseph's brothers could lead to punishment for many generations thereafter, plays into the hands of Christian claims that Jews must eternally pay the price for their betrayal of Jesus!

These Christian overtones in Eleh Ezerah beg for explication. Judith Z. Abrams, in "Incorporating Christian Symbols into Judaism: The Case of Midrash Eleh Ezkerah," posits that this piyyut dove headlong into the Jewish-Christian fray. In her estimation, the bizarre nature of Eleh Ezkerah was a deliberate reaction to the growing popularity of Christianity.

The etiology for the ten martyrs' deaths bears a strong resemblance to the story of Jesus' death. In both stories, a people carries a sin from a past generation—Original sin in Christianity and the sin of Joseph's sale in Judaism. Only the death of a righteous person, or persons, can redeem the sin and bring salvation. . . .(Abrams, 14-15).

The *Eleh Ezkerah* midrashim were redacted during the fifth and sixth centuries, and reflect the struggles of the Jews who were then suffering at the hands of the Christians. Abrams explains that "[t]his mistreatment produced a Jewish response designed to shore up the people's faith in their own religion, particularly vis-à-vis Christianity. . . . Midrash and Aggadah were particularly suited to this purpose since they allowed the sages to reinterpret historical events and apply their lessons to contemporary problems" (Abrams, 13–15). Her conclusion is that *Eleh Ezkerah* adopts this Christian idea, presenting it to Jews in distress as an acceptable avenue of atonement.

Today, we may marvel at the ingenuity, creativity and bravery of *Midrash Eleh Ezkerah*'s authorship: an authorship which was not afraid to incorporate into Judaism a concept which had been claimed by the Christian community in order to maintain our faith's vigor, as it was forced to deal with the irrevocable loss of atonement through the cult. (Abrams, 16-17)

Sid Z. Leiman takes the advertent Christological overtones of the *piyyut* elsewhere. He directs our attention to a midrashic text that served as the basis for the *piyyut*—*Midrash Eleh Ezkerah*. The midrash begins as follows:

When the Holy One, Blessed Be He, created the trees they grew haughty because they were so tall, and they raised themselves higher and higher. Thereafter, when the Holy One,

Blessed Be He, created iron, they humbled themselves and said, "Woe unto us, now that the Holy One, Blessed Be He, created that which will destroy us." So it was that after the destruction of the Temple, there were *peritzei hador* (upstarts of the generation) who prided themselves, and said, "What have we lost with the destruction of the Temple? After all, we have wise men who lead the world through His Torah and His commandments." Immediately, God placed in the heart of the Roman emperor [the desire] to study Torah from the mouths of the wise men and the sages. (*Midrash Eleh Ezkerah* 2:64)

A parallel version of this midrash adds: "so too, had Israel not taught the Caesar Torah, they would have never come to this" (*Midrash Asarah Harugei Malkhut* 6:19). Leiman explains that the trees represent the Jewish people, and the iron—the Romans. Implicit in this fable is the contention that the trees need fear being cut down only if they themselves provide the wood for the ax handles. By analogy, the Jews are warned that destruction always comes from within. Though the Romans did great physical damage to the Jewish People through the destruction of the Second Temple and the bloody suppression of Bar Kokhba's revolt, a far greater threat to Judaism began when the Jews put a mighty weapon—Torah—into Roman hands. And when did the Jews give Torah to the Romans? When the Roman Empire adopted Christianity, which claimed Scripture for its own. This is literarily described in *Eleh Ezkerah* as the Roman emperor leafing through the Torah. Leiman notes that the reference to *peritzei hador* (the upstarts of the generation), who cynically downplay the destruction of the Temple, refers to early Judeo-Christians, who found complete atonement in Jesus and hence did not view the destruction as a tragedy. According to Leiman, the text of *Eleh Ezkerah* is deliberately riddled with allusions to Christianity. It implicitly polemicizes against Christianity at a time when it may have been too dangerous to do so openly. It also contains hopeful wishes for the restoration of

Judaism, in light of the utmost devotion and self-sacrifice of Israel's eminent rabbis.

Daniel Stökel Ben Ezra makes the opposite claim. He posits that vicarious atonement is not a Christian idea superimposed on a Jewish story. Quite the contrary, the ostensibly Christian notion of vicarious atonement found in *Eleh Ezkerah* is in fact directly attributable to Judaism. Stökel observes:

> Yom Kippur had a decisive influence on the formulation of the early Christian myths of the atoning death of Christ and his permanent intercession in the heavenly holy of holies. . . . Two factors may account for this strong impact of Yom Kippur on early Christian mythology. First Yom Kippur was of central importance for any Jew. It was highly mythologized and connected to eschatological expectations of a priestly redeemer. Its atoning function could be easily connected to the rationale of Jesus' death as vicarious atonement. Second, from a cross-cultural perspective, sacrificial categories are more easily translatable than refined allusions to local mythologies such as those of the Old Testament. It is therefore possible that one reason for the spread of the high-priestly Christology and the scapegoat typology was that they were useful in the Christian mission to the pagans. While the first factor applies to the shaping of the mythology, the second explains its acceptance and elaboration. (Stökl Ben Ezra, 226–227)

Stökl Ben Ezra adds that the Christian notion of atonement through the death of the righteous also has Jewish antecedents: "Just as the Day of Atonement expiates, so too the deaths of the righteous atone" (*Va-yikra Rabbah* 20:21). Thus, *Eleh Ezkerah* is exonerated from having a "non-Jewish" character.

The idea of the death of the righteous as a vehicle of atonement is developed in the kabbalistic concept of metempsychosis. Ibn Yahya outlines the theory in *Shalshelet ha-Kabbalah*:

We could approach it differently, that is, it might befit us to believe, as the kabbalists tell us, in the transmigration of souls, as it says: "Truly, God does all these things two or three times to a man, [to bring him back from the Pit, that he may bask in the light of life]" (Job 33:29–30), explaining it this way. There are sins which are not atonable through repentance, or flagellations, or even through Yom Kippur, not even death can atone for them. Reincarnation, though, completes the punishment of the soul for this kind of sin, thereby enabling the soul to benefit from the glory of the *Shekhinah*. It is through the wisdom and justice of the Holy One, Blessed Be He, not to complete administration of punishment then (in a single lifetime). As the Rabbis taught us and as mentioned by *Zeror ha-Mor*, through the cruelty of the Ten Tribes, the Ten Martyrs were put to death, and ten more in every generation, and the sin still stands. It would seem that their sin was more that of the cruelty with which they treated him than the sale itself. (Ibn Yahya, *Shalshelet ha-Kabbalah*, 14)

This kabbalistic notion of metempsychosis provides a Jewish way of approaching *Eleh Ezkerah*—theologically, rather than historically. The 10 Martyrs were reincarnations of the 10 Tribes, and their martyrdom completed the cycle of punishment for their sale of Joseph. The brothers' death penalty for kidnapping needed to be postponed, for had it been carried out in their time, there would have been no descent to Egypt, no Exodus—indeed, no Jewish People. The transmigration of their souls into those of the martyrs makes the death of the latter a case of justice deferred, rather than justice denied.

These theological solutions to the anomaly of *Eleh Ezkerah* are scholarly and ingenious. However, for the contemporary worshipper encountering the composition on Yom Kippur, such esoteric ideas are hard to grasp and not necessarily inspirational. How are we to relate to this prayer?

Let us return to the point of departure of *Eleh Ezkerah*, to the story of Joseph and his brothers, for a different approach to interpreting this *piyyut*.

> At seventeen years of age, Joseph tended the flocks with his brothers, as a helper to the sons of his father's wives Bilhah and Zilpah. And Joseph brought bad reports of them to their father. Now Israel loved Joseph best of all his sons, for he was the child of his old age; and he had made him an ornamented tunic. And when his brothers saw that their father loved him more than any of his brothers, they hated him so that they could not speak a friendly word to him. (Gen. 37:2–4)

The Joseph story begins by providing the reader with all of the necessary information for that which ensues. This opening passage contains a clear explanation of the causes of enmity between Joseph and his brothers. The narrative introduces Joseph as a tale bearer who infuriated and alienated his siblings. The situation was aggravated by an objective reality which his brothers found impossible to bear— Joseph was indeed Jacob's favorite son. After many painful years of barrenness, Jacob's cherished wife, Rachel, had given birth to Joseph. It stands to reason that merely as the child of desire, Joseph would have been the beneficiary of preferential treatment. However, Rachel's untimely death made Joseph even more precious in Jacob's eyes. We are told that he loved Joseph most because he was "the son of his old age." It is perplexing that this epithet was bestowed upon Joseph; after all, his brother Benjamin was Jacob's youngest son. However, since Rachel died while giving birth to Benjamin, his father was incapable of offering him his love, so Joseph received it all. Such favoritism sowed seeds of jealousy and contempt in the hearts of his siblings. To add insult to injury, Jacob made Joseph an ornamented tunic. This gift expressed his partiality in more ways than one. Jacob did not buy Joseph this tunic—he made it. In the biblical context, the act of making a coat for a child is generally reserved for mothers. Hannah, for example, annually made her son Samuel a little coat (1

Sam. 2:19), enveloping him with warmth and love through the work of her hands. Joseph's mother passed away and so his father took her place and acted toward Joseph in both fatherly and motherly roles. Popularly, this gift is called "the coat of many colors." While commentators are divided as to whether that is the actual meaning of the term *kutonet pasim*, it is clear that it was a sign of undisguised favoritism and a mark of status, setting Joseph above his brothers in the family hierarchy. This menacing source of discord raised the ire of Joseph's brothers to a point where they found it impossible to communicate with him in any civil fashion. And if that were not enough, Joseph was a dreamer, and insisted on reporting his vainglorious dreams directly to his hostile brothers.

They were convinced that "a man is shown in a dream only what is suggested by his own thought" (B. Ber. 55a). As far as they were concerned, dreams foretelling Joseph's ambition, starring the dreamer himself as the axis around whom the universe revolved, were an outgrowth of Joseph's unmitigated arrogance. His delusions of grandeur caused his brothers to seethe with contempt. As long as Joseph and his brothers remained close to home, the volatile situation might have remained under control, but one day Jacob sent Joseph to visit his brothers in the field.

The brothers had chosen to pasture their father's flock in Shechem, the historical capital of Samaria. Scripture informs us that Jacob had purchased meadows there; hence, the brothers' visit to Shechem was not out of the ordinary. But Jacob's decision to send Joseph, the apple of his eye, to check on the welfare of his brothers in Shechem—a place notorious for family disaster (it was there that Dinah had been raped and Simeon and Levi had massacred the city)—was tantamount to casting him to the wolves. Perhaps his own personal experience with his disgruntled brother, Esau, led Jacob to believe that on different turf, brothers could be reconciled, so he took the chance of sending Joseph to Shechem with this in mind. Discretion in this case, though, would have been the better part of valor.

As his brothers espied him approaching, they made plans to do in the dreamer once and for all. "They said to one another, 'Here comes that dreamer! Come now, let us kill him and throw him into one of the pits;' and we can say, 'A savage beast devoured him. We shall see what comes of his dreams!' " (Gen. 37:19–20). Whereas the initial call among the brothers was for manslaughter, those nefarious designs were tempered by their older brother Reuben, who suggested that they simply cast him into a pit and let death come naturally. Actually, as the Bible later reveals, Reuben had every intention of rescuing Joseph when the opportunity allowed. Scripture gives expression to the brothers' gleeful disdain for Joseph's plight in the pit by describing them sitting down to eat, undisturbed by his distress. While all this was happening, a caravan of Ishmaelites passed by, giving Judah the capital idea to sell Joseph rather than kill him; he was, after all, their brother. "When Midianite traders passed by, they pulled Joseph up out of the pit. They sold Joseph for twenty pieces of silver to the Ishmaelites, who brought Joseph to Egypt" (37:28).

Whereas Reuben rent his garment upon discovering that Joseph was gone, the brothers had no need for mourning. They were delighted to have finally defrocked their obnoxious sibling. All that concerned them was not to be implicated in the crime. There was something grotesque in their actions. They took Joseph's tunic, slaughtered a kid, and dipped the garment in its blood. As they ripped his coat to simulate his being ravaged by a wild beast, they played out their repressed fantasies. Now they would use the symbol of his exalted status to signify his "tragic" death. The heartlessness of their scheme is reflected in the description of the report of Joseph's death that they sent to Jacob along with the tattered robe. This was the tunic Jacob had made for Joseph, and it symbolized his deep connection with his beloved son. What satisfaction it brought his other children to know that the bond had been severed forever! Jacob's pain, though, was so overwhelming that it defied the attempts of the other sons (and daughter) at consolation. Their father was adamant in his refusal—"No, I will go down mourning to my son in Sheol" (Gen. 37:35). It was a mortal wound from which Jacob never recovered. For 22 years, Jacob mourned the loss. According to the Rabbis, he was haunted by the reverberation of Joseph's last word to him, *hineni*— "here I am." This word, Abraham's answer to the call of the *Akedah*, was echoed in Joseph's acquiescence to his father's request, sent on an innocent journey that turned out to be the path to his own slaughter. Jacob ate himself up alive, believing that he was responsible for Joseph's death.

Yet Jacob is not to be faulted for sending Joseph away from home and into harm's way. A careful examination of the salient biblical verse reveals that it was not *Jacob* who sent Joseph to Shechem—it was *Israel*. The differential use of the names "Jacob" and "Israel" to denote the third patriarch is always carefully matched to the context in which the name appears. Although Jacob was concerned about the welfare of his sons and his flocks, at this juncture it was Israel who dispatched Joseph. He thereby set in motion the unfolding of the covenant made with Abraham in Genesis 15. Little did Joseph know what awaited him. The biblical saga of oppression and redemption was about to begin, and he was to play the leading role. His journey to Shechem initiated the next stage in the destiny of Israel.

Note the providential nature of all that transpired. After casting Joseph into the pit, the brothers sat down to eat. It was during this interlude that a group of itinerant merchants fortuitously appeared on the scene, and absconded with him. Scripture itemizes the local produce—gum, balm, and laudanum—that was transported in the caravan that took Joseph down to Egypt. Later, we are told that Jacob sent the Grand Vizier of Egypt (who turned out to be his son Joseph!) these very items. Even these minor details point to the hand of Providence. Joseph's dreams also serve as a measure of divine intervention. Initially, his bombastic dreams tore down the structure of the nuclear family; however, they ultimately served as the blueprint for the destiny of Jacob's household and the people of Israel. Providence and inversion of fortune emerge as the overriding themes of the Joseph story. The view through this lens obviates the need to speak in terms of crime and punishment. Joseph and his brothers were merely players in the grand scheme of Jewish history.

The Rabbis gave expression to this idea, describing Joseph's actions as the catalyst for setting God's covenant with Abraham in motion.

> *So he sent him out of the vale of Hebron.* Out of the vale of Hebron? Surely Hebron lies on a mountain, yet you say, Out of the vale of Hebron? Said R. Aha: "He went to bring about the fulfillment of the deep designs which the Holy One, Blessed Be He, had arranged between Himself and His noble companion [Abraham] who is buried in Hebron—'Know well that your offspring shall be strangers in a land not theirs, and they shall be enslaved and oppressed four hundred years' " (Gen. 15:13). (*Bereshit Rabbah* 84:1)

However, from the perspective of *Eleh Ezkerah*, the brothers were not simply passive bystanders in the story of the sale of Joseph. It was they who perpetrated the heinous crime. The *piyyut* does not suggest that the brothers had any merits, contrition, or penitent actions, to redeem them. There would seem to be no way around it: their unforgivable sin required expiation. Again, a close reading of the biblical text indicates that this is not entirely the case. Although the brothers as a group are described as being guilty of this contemptible crime, Reuben, the eldest among them, did attempt to save his brother Joseph:

> But when Reuben heard it, he tried to save him from them. He said, "Let us not take his life." And Reuben went on, "Shed no blood! Cast him into that pit out in the wilderness, but do not touch him yourselves" intending to save him from them and restore him to his father. (Gen. 37:21)

The masters of Midrash extol this action, suggesting that Reuben was rewarded for it. One tradition points out that because Reuben was "the pioneer of lifesaving," the first cities of refuge and atonement were established in his territory. Another view connects his penitence with his descendant, the prophet Hosea, claiming: Hosea will open the way for repentance of Israel, as it says, "Return, O Israel, to the Lord your God" (*Pesikta Rabbati* 3:4).

Years later, the brothers found themselves in a serious predicament with the viceroy of Egypt. He insisted that they bring their youngest brother down to appear before him. At that stage, they fully acknowledged their guilt and sincerely expressed remorse: "Alas, we are being punished on account of our brother, because we looked on at his anguish, yet paid no heed as he pleaded with us." Then Reuben spoke up and said to them, "Did I not tell you, 'Do no wrong to the boy'? But you paid no heed. Now comes the reckoning for his blood" (Gen. 42:21–22). It is important to note that the plain reading of Scripture offers a resolution in the narrative itself. After Jacob dies, Joseph's brothers fear that at long last Joseph will seek revenge and they appeal to him for clemency. Joseph himself not only grants forgiveness; he provides the perspective that exonerates all those involved.

When Joseph's brothers saw that their father was dead, they said, "What if Joseph still bears a grudge against us and pays us back for all the wrong that we did him!" So they sent this message to Joseph, "Before his death, your father left this instruction: So shall you say to Joseph, 'Forgive, I urge you, the offense and guilt of your brothers who treated you so harshly.' Therefore, please forgive the offense of the servants of the God of your father." And Joseph was in tears as they spoke to him. His brothers went to him themselves, flung themselves before him, and said, "We are prepared to be your slaves." But Joseph said to them, "Have no fear! Am I a substitute for God? Besides, although you intended me harm, God intended it for good, so as to bring about the present result—the survival of many people. And so, fear not. I will sustain you and your children." Thus he reassured them, speaking kindly to them. (Gen. 50:15–21)

Thus, the story of Joseph and his brothers shines forth as a magnificent example of a family transformed. It can hardly be seen as a case of crime awaiting punishment. It contains important ethical teachings and sincere illustrations of repentance, growth, and change. What remains unclear, however, is its connection to *Eleh Ezkerah* and Yom Kippur. A fascinating answer is recorded in the ancient Jewish composition the Book of Jubilees, the earliest source to associate the story of Joseph with the holiest day of the year.

And he mourned for Joseph one year and did not cease for he said, "Let me go down to the grave mourning for my son." For this reason, it is ordained for the Children of Israel, that they should afflict themselves on the tenth of the seventh month— on the day the news that made him weep for Joseph came to Jacob his father—that they should make atonement for themselves thereon, with a young goat on the tenth of the seventh month, once a year for their sins; for they had grieved the affection of their father regarding Joseph his son. And this day has been ordained that they should grieve thereon for their sins, and for all their transgressions and for all their errors, so that they might cleanse themselves on that day once a year. (Jubilees 34:13–19)

According to this tradition, Yom Kippur is the anniversary of Joseph's sale, or at the very least, the day that Jacob was brought the devastating news of his beloved son's death. The dipping of the tunic in the blood of the slaughtered goat is atoned for through the scapegoat sent away on Yom Kippur. The Jerusalem Talmud (J. Yoma 38a) points out that the tunic of the High Priest was also a vehicle to atone for the tunic of Joseph. Consequently, this day was established as the day on which Israel must grieve for their sins and cleanse themselves of all of their iniquity. All of the elements connected with the sale of Joseph—sin, guilt, pain, fallout, and atonement—become the paradigm for Yom Kippur.

The Book of Jubilees supplies Yom Kippur with an early link to the story of Joseph. *Bereshit Rabbah* adds another important piece to this puzzle.

> "And Jacob rent his garments." R. Phinehas said in R. Hoshayah's name: The tribal ancestors caused their father to rend his garments; and where were they requited? In Egypt, "At this they rent their clothes" (Gen. 44:13). Joseph caused the tribal ancestors to rend their clothes and his grandson was requited. Therefore: "Joshua thereupon rent his clothes" (Josh. 7:6). . . . R. Aibu said: Because Jacob resorted to sackcloth, therefore it will not leave him or his descendants to the end of time, and it effects only the outstanding of his descendants. (*Bereshit Rabbah* 84:20)

Taking these two sources in tandem helps put *Eleh Ezkerah* into full focus. Yom Kippur, the day Jacob rent his clothing, set into motion bad news for the Jews in every generation. Although *Bereshit Rabbah* alights on a select few historic events, the concluding statement, "Because Jacob resorted to sackcloth, therefore, it will not leave him or his descendants to the end of time, and it effects only the outstanding of his descendants" could account for all tragedy that befalls the Children of Israel—including the death of the 10 Martyrs. The overarching message is that everything we do matters, and that all of our actions have far-reaching effects that extend beyond the farthest reaches of our imagination.

These texts may serve to explain the etiology of the perplexing *piyyut*. However, even if this scholarly detective work is convincing, the remaining theological question is still disconcerting. Why were innocent leaders of Israel killed for the crime of others? Our sensibilities are still offended by the distorted alignment between sin and retribution. However, perhaps we are intended to read both incidents—Joseph and his brothers and the 10 Martyrs—as having a common theme. The sale of Joseph is presented as the archetypical sin *bein adam le-havero*—between one another. In the Torah, the nadir in human relationships is exemplified by the story of one family of brothers, a story of the enemy within. In venting their hatred and jealousy, they resorted to murder, theft, coveting, and bearing false witness. They caused their father great loss and mourning. But this was not just any family; this was the foundational family of Israel. The list of their crimes included:

For the sin we committed before You by acting callously;
For the sin we committed before You, knowingly and deceptively;
For the sin we committed before You by oppressing a fellow man;
For the sin we committed before You through evil thoughts;
For the sin we committed before You through insincere confession;
For the sin we committed before You for contempt of parents or teachers;
For the sin we committed before You by violence;
For the sin we committed before You running to do evil;
For the sin we committed before You through tale bearing;
For the sin we committed before You swearing falsely;
For the sin we committed before You of groundless hatred;
For the sin we committed before You of breach of trust.

Seeking to explain the death of the innocent victims executed during the Roman period, the Rabbis came up with the following formula: The First Temple was destroyed on account of the cardinal sins of murder, idolatry, and illicit sexual relations. "But during the Second Temple period, the people engaged in Torah, mitzvoth and loving kindness. Why then was [the Temple] destroyed? Because there was unwarranted hatred (*sinat hinam*)" (B. Yoma 9b). The unwarranted hatred of which this text speaks describes the civil strife, factionalism, tale bearing, and backstabbing that characterized the social, political, and religious life of that dismal era. So, on the micro level, hatred and jealousy were the sources of discord between Joseph and his brothers. On the macro level, they typified all of Judean society at the end of the Second Temple period, and perhaps thereafter as well.

In *Shalshaelet ha-Kabbalah*, Ibn Yahya claims:

At that time, the great leaders fell into the trap of dissension and pride, just as the Tribes had done with Joseph, more than in previous generations . . . and God, who knows the inner workings of the hearts of man, knows how to measure the thoughts of man and his sins, to give each the proper punishment, both as befits them and for the edification of the people; these were the leading sages of the time, and their reputation was publicly known, so that the masses would see and consider for what crimes they had been punished. (Ibn Yahya, 14)

Even if we do not accept Ibn Yahya's contention that the martyred sages paid the price of their own moral failings, there is no doubt that even in their time, after the Second Temple had been destroyed, there was much to correct in the social realm. Continuing Roman domination, and the rabbis' ensuing martyrdom, may have been a consequence of the lack of national unity and commitment to mutual responsibility among the people.

In the Mishnah (Yoma 8:9), we are told that Yom Kippur is effective in atoning for transgressions between man and God. However, for the sins we perpetrate against others, Yom Kippur is of no effect, until restitution and forgiveness between people has been made. Every year we are taken aback by the actions of the brothers of Joseph and shocked by the martyrdom of Israel's most distinguished rabbis. Perhaps this dismay will catapult us into effecting change and reversing the sins that led to those tragedies, by achieving reconciliation among ourselves.

From yet another biblical perspective, the sale of Joseph was atoned for long before any rabbis were put to death. It was the Children of Israel, the immediate descendants of the brothers of Joseph, who actively harmonized their grandparents' discord and resolved their conflicts through a noble act of lovingkindness. The story is found in the Bible itself; not in Genesis, but in the final chapter of the book of Joshua. Joseph, you may recall, had embarked upon his role in covenantal history on his way to Shechem to visit his brothers. Coming full circle, we are told in Joshua 24 that it was there that he was buried.

The chapter opens with Joshua gathering all of Israel in Shechem to deliver his farewell address. Joshua begins by recapitulating Jewish history, starting with Terah, the idolatrous father of Abraham. His point is to emphasize the cultural challenge of living among pagans. The people of Israel left all that behind when Abraham left Terah's home in Mesopotamia. Joshua then reviews the Egyptian sojourn, once again stressing the liberation from the idolatrous lifestyle. In his farewell address, Joshua implores the people not to regress to times gone by, but to loyally adhere to their ancestral faith: "Then put away the alien gods that you have among you and direct your hearts to the LORD, the God of Israel" (Josh. 24:23).

The religious message of Joshua the son of Nun was clear. But why was it delivered at Shechem? Would it not have made more sense to gather the people at Shiloh, the main religious sanctuary at the time? The 13th-century biblical commentator Rabbi David Kimhi offers several ingenious literary explanations of Joshua's choice. He begins by noting that Shechem was Abraham's first stop in Canaan. Joshua, the first *oleh* (immigrant) in his generation, was continuing in the footsteps of the patriarch. Moreover, it was in Shechem that Jacob commanded his sons, "Rid yourselves of the alien gods in your midst" (Gen 35:2). It was this very message that Joshua impressed upon his constituency. What better place to do it than in Shechem? Kimhi also notes that the legal purchase of Shechem by Jacob (Gen. 33:19) served to validate the entry and possession of the land by his descendants.

But there seems to be another compelling reason that Joshua gathered the people at Shechem. Joshua, a scion of the tribe of Ephraim, a descendant of Joseph, returned the Children of Israel to the scene of the crime—to Shechem—where they devised to do their brother Joseph in. By gathering them at Shechem, Joshua implies that his final message to them is not just about the challenge of cultural assimilation and fidelity to the God of Israel. There is an additional challenge: the challenge of national unity. The tribes of Israel—*b'nai Yisra'el*—will now strike roots in the land they have conquered. In order to succeed, they must transcend jealousy and hatred, and make peace within their own territorial borders. The success or failure of the Zionist enterprise will depend on overcoming hate—the *sinat ahim* that later caused the destruction of the Second Temple—and achieving *ahavat ahim*, brotherly love. It is in Shechem that Joshua affords the people the opportunity to undo the past mistakes of tribal enmity and civil strife, and to commit to unity and brotherhood. It is therefore befitting that the book of Joshua ends with the interment of the bones of Joseph. This time, the pit into which he was cast is replaced by a grave into which he is laid in honor. This *hesed shel emet* provides a powerfully moving denouement to the story of Joseph and his brothers that dovetails with a key message of Yom Kippur.

Eleh Ezkerah—these I shall remember. Not only the martyred sages, but the reasons for their suffering, and the necessity of ensuring that they do not recur. Not only the sale of Joseph, but its lesson of the possibility of moving beyond hate to forgiveness and love. In the final analysis, taught R. Akiva, chief among the 10 Martyrs, the most important precept in the Torah is "Love your fellow as yourself."

Part Two

Waiting for Rain

Hoshana Rabbah

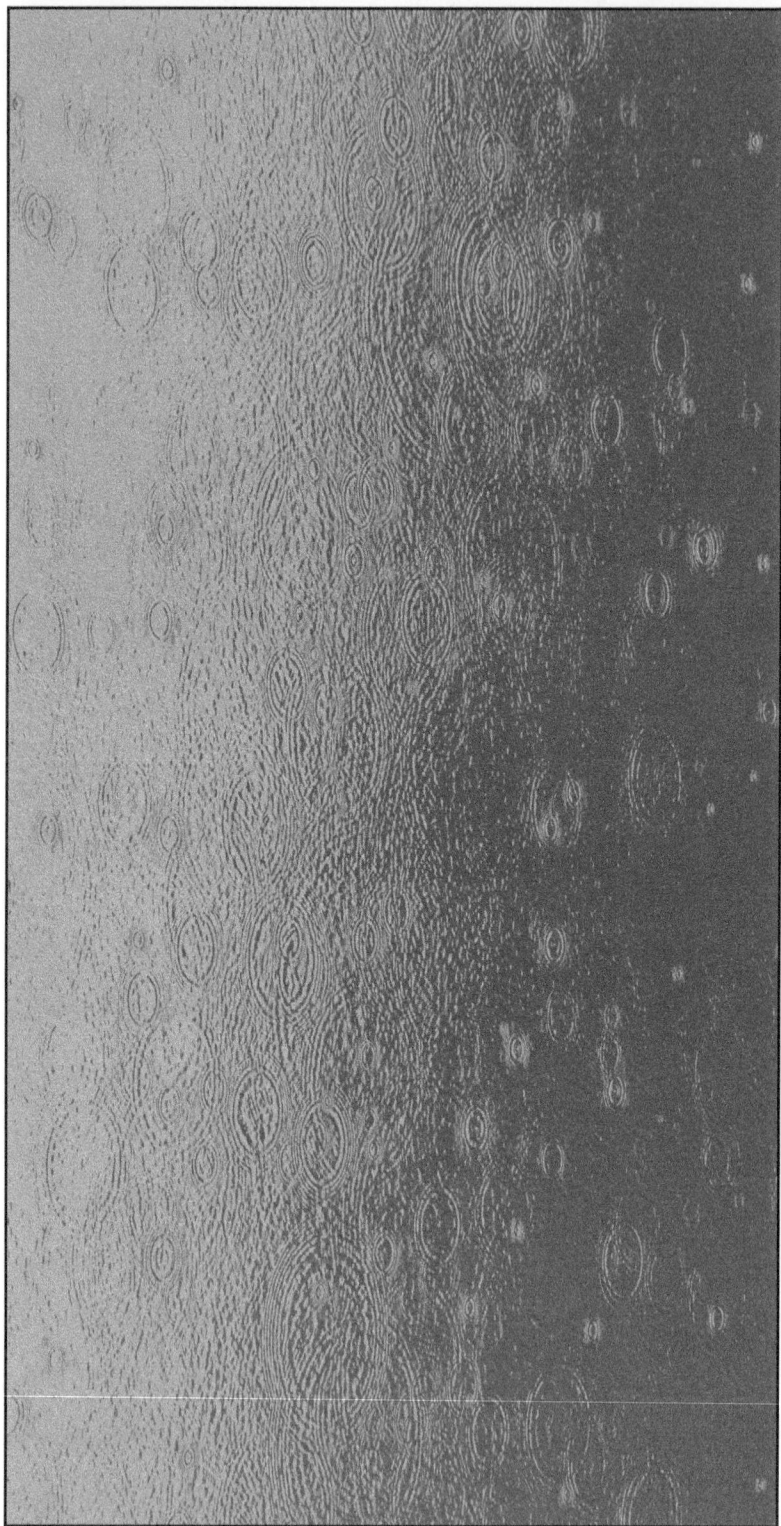

Waiting for Rain, photograph by Aharon Dov Mordechai Levy

Chapter Nine

⚬

Pouring Out
Our Hearts

⚬

The High Holy Days are a spiritual odyssey. We travel from Rosh
Hashanah to Yom Kippur, from Yom Kippur to Sukkot, and from
Sukkot, we arrive at Hoshana Rabbah. Liturgical texts and readings
from the Torah and the Prophets serve as signposts along the way.
They enable us to take stock of our relationship with God, with each
other, with our own selves.

In addition to texts and readings, we are escorted by people who
travel with us and steer our course. One of the most impressive figures
threaded throughout our holiday readings is Samuel. We follow
Samuel from his birth, recorded in the haftarah of Rosh Hashanah,
through his trailblazing campaign of repentance and atonement, commemorated in the penitential prayer we say on Yom Kippur (and, in
fact, throughout the *Selihot*), "He who answered Samuel at Mizpah—
Answer us!" It was Samuel who inspired the water libation on Sukkot,
and his call for salvation reverberates in our observance of Hoshana
Rabbah.

Samuel's inspiring victory at Mizpah (1 Sam. 7), commemorated in the *Hoshanot* prayers, was one of the noblest moments in the

spiritual history of the Jewish People. In this *Hoshana*, we implore God to deliver His nation by reenacting the salvation at Mizpah:

> For the sake of the good man whose reputation
> waxed and flourished (1 Sam 2:26).
> He who caused the assembly to desist from injustice.
> When the nation repented He commanded that they draw water (7:6).
> On behalf of those as beautiful as Jerusalem (Israel)
> Save us and deliver us, for You are our Father.
> (*Hoshana, "Le-ma'an tamim be-dorotav"*)

Samuel taught that recognition of the Kingship of Heaven, and concomitant acts of penitence and atonement, must precede our request for salvation. Only after we have fully internalized the lessons of Rosh Hashanah and Yom Kippur can we say with full hearts, "Please O Lord, deliver us." Only then can we pour out our hearts like water before God and hope for salvation.

To understand this idea, let us take a look at Samuel's assembly of penitence at Mizpah, focusing on the unusual and fascinating detail of the drawing and pouring of water, to which the author of this *Hoshana* refers. But first, let's examine two critical junctures in Samuel's military and religious leadership. They provide the framework for the seminal role he played in the history of Israel and the ongoing role he plays in our religious lives.

We begin with two important battles the Israelites waged against the Philistines (1 Sam. 13 and 1 Sam. 7):

The silence of the battlefield was deafening. It was the quiet after the storm. The ground was strewn with corpses of would-be invincible Philistine soldiers, felled by the wrath of God. The exhilarated but exhausted Israelites collected the spoils, while their victorious general Samuel combed the area looking for a particular stone. For others, it was an object of no consequence, but for Samuel, its stillness and power was an apt metaphor for the Rock and Deliverer of Israel. With the little strength left in him, he called his men to attention, approached the stone, and named it *Eben ha-Ezer*, declaring: "For up to now the Lord has helped us." Decades earlier, in the waning years of Eli the Priest, Samuel's predecessor, the same stone had witnessed a devastating defeat (1 Sam. 4). It was now transformed into a triumphal monument. The menace of the Philistines had been quelled, though not for long. They would return to threaten the people of Israel before Samuel's lifetime was over.

The Philistines are a nation about whom we know little. Despite extensive archaeological research, their language, culture, and religion remain a mystery. It seems they were related to the inhabitants of the Greek islands. They were an adventurous, pugnacious, and resourceful people, who fought tenaciously for their foothold in the Land. The Philistines were not one of the seven indigenous Canaanite nations or among the 31 local kings with whom the people of Israel fought for possession of the Land. At about the same time that the Israelites were entering the Land from the east at Jericho, the Philistines—the sea peoples—were entering the Land from the west. This group of late arrivals presented a serious challenge with which the Israelites were forced to contend.

A clear indication of the peril they posed is recorded in the Samson cycle from the book of Judges. The tribes of Dan and Judah of the Shefelah lowlands found themselves under the Philistine thumb, cowering before them, desperately afraid of confrontation. This bitter and long-standing conflict spanned the generations, as divergent religious and cultural orientations created an unbridgeable chasm between the adversaries. Despite the temporary setback of their defeat by Samuel, the Philistines worked relentlessly to assert their rule over the Israelites.

It comes as no surprise, therefore, that following the era of the Judges, when Saul, the first king of Israel, assumed the reins of leadership, the goal of liberation from the Philistine yoke loomed large in his mind. It is also understandable that the Philistines, who had gotten wind of the new monarchy, were anxious to nip it in the bud before

the Israelites could consolidate their incipient power under the direction of their new king.

And so the battle was joined, as we read in 1 Samuel 13. As the
story unfolds, we find Saul gathering his troops. The text tells us that
he had 3,000 soldiers (2,000 with him and another 1,000 under the command of his son Jonathan). In sharp contrast, we are told that the
Philistines had encamped in Michmash—the very heartland of the
territory of the tribe of Benjamin, from whence Saul hailed:

> The Philistines, in turn, gathered to attack Israel: 30,000 char-
> iots and 6,000 horsemen, and troops as numerous as the sands
> of the seashore. (1 Sam. 13:5)

The people of Israel were justifiably terrified:

> When the men of Israel saw that they were in trouble—for the
> troops were hard pressed—the people hid in caves, among
> thorns, among rocks, in tunnels and in cisterns. Some
> Hebrews crossed the Jordan, [to] the territory of Gad and
> Gilead. (1 Sam. 13:6)

As time passed, they rapidly scattered, so that when the battle began
there were a mere 600 foot soldiers left. Not the kind of odds with
which a king likes to start his career.

The Israelites were not only at a numerical disadvantage. Scripture also informs us that:

> No smith was found in all the Land of Israel, for the Philis-
> tines were afraid that the Hebrews would make swords or
> spears. So all the Israelites had to go down to the Philistines to
> have their plowshares, their mattocks, axes, and colters sharp-
> ened. The charge for sharpening was a *pim* for plowshares,
> mattocks, three-pronged forks, and axes, and for setting the

goads. Thus, on the day of the battle, no sword or spear was to be found in the possession of any of the troops with Saul and Jonathan; only Saul and Jonathan had them. (1 Sam. 13:19–22)

The Philistines had entered the Iron Age. They were the sole possessors of iron armaments in the region. The Israelites were still in the Bronze Age, and although weapons of bronze are a considerable advancement over stone, they cannot compare to iron. In order to prevent technological espionage, the Philistines even made the Israelites come to their territory to sharpen their tools. Arms were scarce. The Philistines presumably imported these weapons from their countries of origin and thereby cornered the market.

Furthermore, there was an additional problem: Saul had his hands tied. He had been explicitly instructed not to begin the battle until Samuel arrived:

After that, you are to go down to Gilgal ahead of me, and I will come down to you to present burnt offerings and offer sacrifices of well-being. Wait seven days until I come to you and instruct you what you are to do next. (1 Sam. 10:8)

The Philistines were positioned on the mountain ridges of Judea and Samaria while Saul had retreated to the hinterland in the Jordan valley to collect his troops. Samuel was nowhere to be found. Reaching a point of utter desperation, Saul could wait no longer:

He waited seven days, the time that Samuel [had set]. But when Samuel failed to come to Gilgal, and the people began to scatter, Saul said, "Bring me the burnt offering and the sacrifice of well-being." (1 Sam. 13:8)

Just as Saul finished the sacrifice, the prophet Samuel arrived on the scene. Rather than offering an explanation for his tarriance and encouraging words for the king and his disconcerted soldiers, Samuel expressed outrage at what the king had done:

> You acted foolishly in not keeping the commandments that the LORD your God laid upon you! Otherwise the LORD would have established your dynasty over Israel forever. But now your dynasty will not endure. (1 Sam. 13:13–14)

Saul responded reasonably with three relevant points: (a) the people were dispersing; (b) Samuel had not arrived at the appointed time; and (c) the Philistines were gaining ground. To which Samuel adamantly declared that Saul's hastiness and foolishness had cost him the kingship. The monarchy would pass to another.

The exchange at first glance is incomprehensible. Saul had waited for Samuel as instructed. Bereft of his spiritual guide, he took what appeared to be a responsible step of able religious leadership, by offering a sacrifice to God before plunging into what would no doubt be a crucial battle against a cruel and powerful foe.

Moreover, if we compare this incident to the second unforgivable transgression, which led to the termination of Saul's royal office (1 Samuel 15), again we find ourselves perplexed. There, Saul was commanded to wipe out the Amalekites, man and beast. In flagrant violation of his charge, he left their choice cattle and their king, Agag, alive. In that encounter Samuel's disapproval was understandable. But how do we explain his extreme response in chapter 13?

To know the mind of the prophet, some background is required. There are two previous battles with the Philistines recorded in the book of Samuel. The first is described in 1 Samuel 4 and the other in 1 Samuel 7. Both take place at a location called *Eben ha-Ezer*, slightly north of Jerusalem. The first was the dreadful defeat mentioned above, in which 30,000 Israelite soldiers and the officiating priests Hofni and Phineas were killed, the Ark was captured by the

Philistines, and the glory of Israel lost. The second was the battle in which the prophet Samuel led the Israelites to decisive victory.

In both battles, the outcome was a function of leadership. In chapter 4, the defeat at the hands of the Philistines resulted from the faulty leadership of the House of Eli, whereas in chapter 7, the victory over the Philistines was directly attributable to the competent leadership of the prophet Samuel. He ably prepared his people for spiritual as well as military triumph. A blow-by-blow account of Samuel's victory at Mizpah in chapter 7 casts light on his exasperation in chapter 13.

The campaign at Mizpah began with Samuel directing the people to purge themselves of idolatry:

"If you mean to return to the LORD with all your heart, you must remove the alien gods and the Ashtaroth from your midst and direct your heart to the LORD and serve Him alone. Then He will deliver you from the hands of the Philistines." And the Israelites removed the Baalim and Ashtaroth and they served the LORD alone. (1 Sam. 7:3–4)

After they had taken these steps, Samuel informed the people that he would intercede on their behalf, and pray for them. But then, the people take the initiative to perform an unusual ritual:

They assembled at Mizpah, *and they drew water and poured it out before the* LORD [italics added]; they fasted that day, and there they confessed that they had sinned against the LORD. And Samuel judged the Israelites at Mizpah. (1 Sam. 7:6) [author's translation]

While all this was going on, the Philistines got wind of this assembly and converged on the Israelite upstarts, determined not to lose the strategic advantage, which they had won in their previous victory. At this point, the people of Israel were gripped by panic and begged

Samuel to pray and redeem them from the hands of the Philistines. It is then that Samuel came to the aid of his people; in the words of the Jerusalem Talmud: *Lavash Shmuel halukan shel kol Yisrael*—"Samuel donned the cloak of all of Israel" (J. Ta'an. 11a)—the cloak being Samuel's distinctive symbol of leadership. He prayed and made sacrifice for them, and lo and behold: "The Lord thundered mightily against the Philistines that day. He threw them into confusion and they were routed by Israel. With victory assured, the site was officially named *Eben ha-Ezer*: "For up to now . . . the LORD has helped us" (1 Sam. 7:12).

The Israelites regained control of their chief cities and were relieved of Philistine oppression. The Philistines don't completely disappear (after all, they are back on the scene, as savage as ever, in 1 Samuel, chapter 13), but for 20 years there was a respite—and twenty years is a long time in Middle Eastern history!

As for Samuel, he returned home to make his rounds as an itinerant prophet—an ancient circuit court judge. One is reminded of Cincinnatus, the legendary hero of early Rome who left his plow and saved Rome from her enemies—an astonishing victory that took one day. He then entered Rome triumphantly, collected the spoils, and returned to his farm, saying that he had no need to be a ruler; it was enough for him to have been a deliverer. Samuel, too, went back to Ramah as the Judge of Israel, as their redeemer and spiritual guide, both on the battlefield and in civilian life.

The story of 1 Samuel 7 is remarkable indeed, a story of eminent leadership, and I would like to propose that it is the key to understanding Saul's tragic downfall in chapter 13.

Samuel was both the last of the judges and the prophet chosen to anoint the first king of Israel. His understanding of his station is what made him so successful—and perhaps so unappreciated.

The cases of the other illustrious judges—Ehud, Deborah, Gideon, Jephthah, and Samson—follow a clear pattern. The Jewish people sin and are delivered into the hands of the enemy. They suffer for a number of years and finally wake up and realize that their troubles are the result of their transgressions. They then cry out to the Lord, who sends them a judge to rescue them. This recurrent configuration illustrates that the judges of Israel were not religious barristers, but military redeemers who saved the people from the hands of their enemies. Samuel is the exception to this rule. He did not lead the people to salvation until he had led them to repentance.

At Mizpah, he assembled the people as the spiritual congregation of Israel before sounding the clarion call of battle. Notice that Samuel acted in what appears to be a foolhardy and irresponsible manner, frittering away time that he might have employed to assume a defensive posture against the ascending Philistine forces. In verse 7, the people express awareness that the Philistines are gaining on them. At that point, it would have seemed reasonable to suspend their revival meeting and prepare for fight or flight. But no; Samuel—by the force of his personality, by the dint of his leadership—controlled the crowd and brought them to the point where they intuitively understood what the Children of Israel did not realize when standing in crisis on the shores of the Red Sea. At that auspicious moment, it was Moses who explicitly stated: "God will fight on your behalf and you shall remain silent." (Exod. 14:14) [author's translation]. In our story, Samuel brought the Children of Israel to a remarkable degree of intuitive spiritual self-awareness. It is *they* who initiated the request that he entreat God on their behalf.

Let me stress this point. It is Samuel's great achievement that he does not submit to the fears of the people or to the pressures of the situation; rather, he used the urgency of the hour to transform the nation's desperation into a sublime moment of spiritual rebirth. He held them in a position of prayer before God until the very last instant, forcing them to great heights of belief and trust in the Lord. That faith was rewarded. Thunder resounded from heaven as God dramatically smote the Philistines, manifesting the clearest recorded case of supernatural intervention on the part of the Almighty in any of the battles of the Judges. Samuel saved the nation's soul and, by so doing, also saved them from the tyranny of their enemies.

It is precisely this great achievement that led to Samuel's outrage in chapter 13. Saul was about to go to war against the Philistines, but rather than following Samuel's well-established precedent—laying the spiritual groundwork, leading the people to God through repentance, and from repentance to victory—he reverted to the old model of pro forma sacrifice. This perfunctory gesture, devoid of any spiritual authenticity, caused Samuel unmitigated anguish. The pathetic scenario constituted a tragedy of wasted opportunity.

Samuel castigates Saul:

> You acted foolishly in not keeping the commandments that the LORD your God laid upon you! Otherwise the LORD would have established your dynasty over Israel forever. But now your dynasty will not endure. The LORD will seek out a man after His own heart, and the LORD will appoint him ruler over His people, because you did not abide by what the LORD had commanded you. (1 Sam. 13:13–14)

The classical commentators struggled to make sense of the extreme indignation that Samuel expressed regarding Saul's sin. They asserted that he did not uphold the letter of the law, failing to wait the full seven days. But Saul's failure here was not simply a logistical one; it reflected an essential misapprehension concerning kingship. It was a dismal reflection of the standards he failed to achieve as a religious leader, as a man of faith. Samuel was not punishing Saul. He was saying, your entire institution of monarchy is fundamentally flawed. You are a king like those of all the other nations, not a king after God's own heart. Samuel's response was one of grave disappointment. Twenty years earlier he had spearheaded a religious revolution by creating an important precedent. Samuel knew that the royal road to victory was paved with *teshuvah* (repentance). Saul had strayed from that path. Saul's failure was indeed a tragic turning point in Jewish history.

In contrast, Samuel's inspiring victory at Mizpah was a spiritual triumph, as was the people's ritual of drawing and pouring the water.

They assembled at Mizpah, and they drew water and poured it out before the LORD; they fasted that day, and there they confessed that they had sinned against the LORD. And Samuel judged the Israelites at Mizpah. (7:6) [author's translation]

This enigmatic ritual has yielded a cascade of interpretations. Modern commentators have suggested that this was a cultic water libation. Its purpose was related to atonement, purification, and the renewal of the covenant. Having disposed of their idols, the people then cleansed themselves with water before the Lord.

The Rabbis, in contrast, explained the gesture metaphorically. The outpouring of water signified the tearful prayers or words of Torah with which the action was performed. Such interpretations afford new meaning to the scriptural verse "Pour out your heart like water in the presence of the LORD" (Lam. 2:19).

Alternatively, perhaps this action was a definitive statement by the people to Samuel, their judge, that they had once and for all resolved to live lives overflowing with justice and righteousness, as it is written, "Let justice well up like water, righteousness like an unfailing stream" (Amos 5:24).

Rashi interprets the act as symbolic of contrition and humility.

Its significance was as an act of submission before the Lord— We are nothing but water poured out before You. (Rashi, 1 Sam. 7:6)

Facing mortality on the battlefield, the people of Israel had arrived at a rare understanding of the fleeting nature of life and of their total dependence upon God. Rashi's words allude to another poignant verse in the book of Samuel:

We must all die; we are like water that is poured out on the ground and cannot be gathered up. (2 Sam. 14:14)

In the context of an attempted reconciliation between David and his banished son Absalom, the wise woman of Tekoa uses this metaphor to highlight the utter helplessness of mortal man. At Mizpah, in the valley of the shadow of death, the Israelites gave expression to this profound realization—pouring water as testimony to their own powerlessness.

Let us now see how this spiritual triumph at Mizpah is related to Sukkot and Hoshana Rabbah.

As perhaps the most important of the biblical pilgrim festivals, the observance of Sukkot was, in ancient times, centered upon the Temple. Though millennia have passed since its destruction, vestiges of practices that were carried out there are still with us today. Throughout the world, Jews carry the four species during all the days of the festival, a practice once exclusively limited to the Temple precincts, now generalized in commemoration of the Temple. The Rabbis (B. Ta'an. 2b) suggest that the underlying rationale for bringing all four species, and the willow branches in particular, is our petition for rain at the end of the dry summer. The seventh day of Sukkot, known for centuries as Hoshana Rabbah, was called in the Mishnah (M. Suk. 4:3) yom ha-shevi'i shel aravah—"the seventh day of the willow," recalling the willow branches specially cut and placed around the altar on that day. Striking the floor with a bunch of willow branches is symbolic of a similar act performed with palm fronds on Hoshana Rabbah in the days of the Temple. The seven hakafot around the bimah recall the seven circuits of the altar in days gone by. These customs were accompanied by the chanting of prayers (M. Suk. 4:5), which received the named Hoshanot. These mantras beseeching God: "Please, O Lord Redeem us, Please, O Lord, bring us success," reach a crescendo on Hoshana Rabbah, when we encircle the bimah seven times and recite a veritable fugue of prayers that interweave biblical sagas of redemption into our impassioned pleas for imminent salvation.

However, there was one additional custom practiced in the Temple for which no parallel custom was ever instituted—the water libation. During the seven days of the festival, there was a special ceremony of pouring water on the altar and rejoicing before the Lord, known as *simhat beit ha-sho'eva*—the rejoicing of the water-drawing house. Although today this celebration is commemorated in some communities in festive gatherings known by the same name, there are no water libations today. A detailed description of the libation itself is recorded in the Mishnah (M. Suk. 4:9), yet there is no scriptural reference to it. The practice was therefore rejected by the Sadducees and stirred much controversy. The Rabbis relate this particular ritual (B. RH 16a) to our request for rain.

Much Rabbinic debate (J. Shevi. 33b) revolves around the origin of the custom of the pouring of the water. Whereas the prevalent opinion is that this libation was transmitted in the verbal instructions received by Moses at Sinai (*halakhah le-Moshe mi-Sinai*), R. Abba bar Zavdi makes the claim that it "derives from the early prophets" (*mi-yisod ha-nivi'im ha-rishonim*).

Who are these "early prophets"? It is entirely possible that R. Abba bar Zavdi is alluding to Samuel and the story of Mizpah—"And they drew out water and poured it before the Lord." This casts the water libation as a supplication to God, imploring Him to draw from His wellsprings of deliverance and bring us not only rain, but salvation.

Perhaps we can now appreciate the contemporary relevance of Hoshana Rabbah. Three thousand years after Mizpah, as the reconstituted people of Israel in the commonwealth of Israel reborn, we find ourselves struggling for survival, surrounded by a sea of enemies. Our fate still hangs in the balance. And so we approach Hoshana Rabbah as an opportunity for meaningful religious reflection and fervently pray for redemption: "He who answered Samuel at Mizpeh—Answer us!"

The ancient Israelites merited a leader of Samuel's stature to guide and inspire them. What about today? The Rabbis (*Midrash Shmuel* 9:8) offer the following insight. There were four biblical leaders whom God commissioned by paging them twice: Abraham, Jacob, Moses, and Samuel. Classically, the double call is explained as reflecting either the urgency of the moment or the endearment expressed by God in gently calling His chosen ones, several times, by name. However, R. Eleazar suggests something else. The first call, he contends, is to the leader in question; the second call reverberates throughout the generations, beckoning a contemporary leader to step forward and lead us to salvation. In Rabbi Eleazar's opinion, every generation contains an Abraham, a Jacob, a Moses, and a Samuel—great leaders who can and will guide us even through the darkest night. While we wait for these leaders to heed their call, we direct our *Hoshanot* to the Master of the Universe, as we nostalgically recall both the noble leadership of the prophet Samuel and his immortal parting words: "For the sake of His great name, the LORD will never abandon His people" (1 Samuel 12:22).

Shemini Atzeret

Chapter Ten

⌘

Through Fire
and Rain

⌘

In the Bible, Sukkot is a time of celebration, a harvest festival when the people are instructed to rejoice before the Lord. When the word *hag*—festival—is used without further qualifiers, it refers specifically to Sukkot and not to the other holidays. The Rabbis, however, transformed Sukkot into a day of judgment.

> There are four periods during which the world is judged.
> On Pesach regarding grain; on Shavuot regarding the fruit of the trees; on Rosh Hashanah all of mankind passes before Him like a flock . . . *u'ba-hag*—and on the festival (Sukkot) the world is judged regarding water. (M. RH 1:2)

As Sukkot draws to a close, we approach the seventh day, Hoshana Rabbah, as one last opportunity for impassioned pleas for salvation and the Eighth Day of Solemn Assembly, Shemini Atzeret, as the day we pray for rain. The divine judgment to which the Mishnah alludes is said to reach its climax on that day. It is a day for us to contemplate the needs of the coming year, and to recognize that God's gift of rain will either be granted or withheld relative to our worthiness.

This is a time of sober realization that the tally of our past actions is about to be translated into the divine allocation of life-giving water for the coming year. If we are found wanting, the threat of drought, suffering, and death hangs over our heads. The chief annual prayer for rain is found in the liturgy for Shemini Atzeret, which is characterized in talmudic law by a single practice: the insertion into our prayers of the declaration, *Mashiv ha-ruah u-morid ha-geshem*—"He causes the wind to blow and the rain to fall."

Several weeks (or outside of Israel, several months) before we petition God for rain through the prayer, "and give us dew and rain with blessing," we unequivocally assert that it is God,

> Who performs great deeds which cannot be fathomed,
> Wondrous things without number;
> Who gives rain to the earth,
> And sends water over the fields. (Job 5:9–10)

God's great works in nature are independent of our petty merits or requests.

Have we then no role to play in the divine economy of the universe? The sages have consoled us that despite our unworthiness and many failings, God takes careful note of each act of righteousness that we perform in determining when He opens the windows of heaven and pours down His limitless blessings. The following vignette is a poignant example of this notion.

> Rav arrived at a certain place and called a public fast, but no rain came. A man began to pray for the community and as he said, "He makes the wind blow"—the wind blew. "He makes the rain fall"—and the rain fell. Rav approached him and asked, "What do you do?" He replied, "I am a teacher of young children. I teach Bible to the children of the poor along with the children of the rich. Whoever is unable to pay studies free of charge. I also have a fishpond and any delinquent child I

encourage and calm by letting him play at the fishpond until he is able to regain composure and study." (B. Ta'an. 24a)

Rav, the first and greatest of the *Amoraim*, calls a fast in the wake of a drought—and absolutely nothing happens. It is only when a local parishioner says the words *"mashiv ha-ruah u-morid ha-geshem"* that the winds begin to blow and the rains begin to fall. Rav assumes that the *shaliah tzibbur* must be a man of great stature to have brought the rain, but when Rav inquires, he discovers that the *shaliah tzibbur* is a simple schoolteacher. The man describes his work by focusing on his devotion to his students. His nondiscriminating educational philosophy allowed for the poor to study along with the rich, and his patience and creativity enabled him to reach children who were educationally challenged and socially incorrigible. It is this *melamed* (schoolteacher) with his fishpond who was able to open the storehouses of heaven and bring forth God's bounty, through acts of justice, lovingkindness, and humility.

The Bible is replete with descriptions of drought and the far-reaching effects it has on man and nature. The prophet Joel, for example, vividly describes the devastating effects of a drought that occurred in his day, offering us a glimpse into the helplessness of all living things and their desperate seeking for God.

How the beasts groan!
The herds of cattle are bewildered
Because they have no pasture,
And the flocks of sheep are dazed.
(Joel 1:18)

There are many additional biblical passages describing drought as punishment for the iniquities of the people. However, the locus classicus in biblical narrative of the clear and immediate connection between the positive actions of the people of Israel and God's gift of rain is the story of Elijah and Ahab in 1 Kings 17.

In his first public appearance, Elijah declared a drought that last-
ed for three unbearable years. Elijah's proclamation contains no
explicit reason for this decree, but from the biblical context, it appears
to have resulted from the idolatrous ways of King Ahab and the people of Israel. This explanation is implicit both in Elijah's statement of
his own unwavering dedication to the Lord God of Israel (contrasting
with the infidelity of others) and the dramatic proclamation "The
LORD alone is God, The LORD alone is God!" (1 Kings 18:39), with
which the drought was brought to a close.

This idea of drought as punishment for a king's idolatry is reinforced when we consider the description of Ahab's infamy that immediately precedes Elijah's declaration of drought. In the final passage of
1 Kings 16, Ahab is vividly portrayed as an idolatrous infidel. He is
charged with a long litany of crimes and misdemeanors that include
(inter)marrying the Phoenician princess Jezebel, traveling to
Phoenicia to worship Baal, building an altar and temple to Baal in
Samaria, and bringing the worship of the Sidonian goddess Asherah
to the Land of Israel. Although he is neither the first nor the only king
of Israel guilty of such crimes, the extent of his felonies and the degree
of contempt motivating them were unprecedented. Evidence for this
may be found in the concluding verse of that passage:

> During his reign, Hiel the Bethelite fortified Jericho. He laid
> its foundations at the cost of Abiram his first-born, and set its
> gates in place at the cost of Segub his youngest, in accordance
> with the words that the LORD had spoken through Joshua son
> of Nun. (1 Kings 16:34)

Until the time of Ahab, no one had dared defy the daunting curse
of Joshua son of Nun, who had declared a life-threatening taboo on
the children of the rebuilder of Jericho:

> At that time Joshua pronounced this oath: "Cursed of the
> LORD be the man who shall undertake to fortify this city of

Jericho: he shall lay its foundations at the cost of his first-born, and set up its gates at the cost of his youngest." (Josh. 6:26)

Leaving Jericho in ruins was intended to be an eternal monument to God's victory over the Canaanites. The 13th century biblical commentator Rabbi David Kimhi (Radak) suggests that setting aside Jericho was a form of a first-offering to the Lord. Rebuilding the city was therefore a brazen lack of gratitude—an act of hubris. Whether Ahab commissioned the rebuilding of Jericho through Hiel or whether he simply created the climate that allowed for such an insolent violation of tradition is a matter of debate. What is clear, though, is that the king on whose watch this could happen was disloyal to the God of his ancestors.

In his excavations at the biblical city of Gezer, the British archaeologist R. A. S. McAlister unearthed foundation sacrifices—remains of children who had been buried under the foundations of this Israelite city as offerings to assuage the angry gods and to ward off enemies from entering the gates. This custom is known to us from cities founded by the Phoenicians—notably the great city of Carthage. McAlister suggested that during Ahab's time, not only did Hiel rebuild the city of Jericho and thereby bring about the death of his children, but he also proactively engaged in foundation sacrifices, achieving an all-time low in Israelite assimilation into pagan culture. The curse of Joshua, which asserted that the builder of Jericho would forfeit his children, was ironically transformed by Hiel the Bethelite from a threat into a chosen rite. Such an abhorrent act could not go unpunished, and so the prophet Elijah stepped forward and uttered his scathing imprecation: causing, "The skies to become like iron and the earth like brass" (Deut. 28:23) [author's translation].

In this regard, the story is a clear illustration of the biblical axiom found in the *Shema:*

Take care not to be lured away to serve other gods and bow to them. For the LORD's anger will flare up against you, and He will shut up the skies so that there will be no rain and the ground will not yield its produce; and you will soon perish from the good land that the LORD is assigning to you. (Deut. 11:16–17)

Elijah's indignation at the appalling worship of Baal drove him, as the loyal vassal of God, to shut the skies from bringing life-giving rain. The course of nature would be restored only when Israel reaffirmed its devotion to God. For that to happen, however, required the reconstitution of a series of essential relationships by the people, the prophet, and the king.

The drought began with the dramatic declaration of the prophet Elijah to King Ahab: "As the Lord lives, the God of Israel whom I serve, there will be no dew or rain except at my bidding" (1 Kings 17:1). Notably, this proclamation was not preceded by an instruction from God, as is usually the biblical norm. This initiative, seemingly, was Elijah's, and in the days that ensued, he experienced its consequences no less often than the people. The Bible presents the events that followed as a drama in three acts.

The word of the LORD came to him: "Leave this place; turn eastward and go into hiding by the Wadi Cherith, which is east of the Jordan. You will drink from the wadi, and I have commanded the ravens to feed you there." (1 Kings 17:2–4)

This command is introduced with the phrase, "the word of the LORD came to him" in contradistinction to Elijah's declaration "by my word." It is a gentle reminder to the prophet that although his righteous indignation, which led to the proclamation of drought, was appropriate, it is the word of God, not the word of the prophet, that will determine what happens. Furthermore, Elijah's miraculous sustenance by way of the ravens bringing him bread and meat morning and evening is a lesson to him that "man does not live by bread alone,

rather man lives by the word of God" (Deut. 8:3) [author's transla-
tion]. The following episode reinforces this lesson:

> After some time, the wadi dried up, because there was no rain
> in the land. And the word of the LORD came to him: "Go at
> once to Zarephath of Sidon, and stay there; I have designated
> a widow there to feed you." (1 Kings 17:7–9)

Whereas in the first act, Elijah hid locally, in the second act he was
forced to leave the borders of the Land of Israel and flee to the Phoenician city of Zarephath of Sidon. Phoenicia was the home of the
Tyrian Baal whose worship was introduced in Israel by Jezebel, the
wife of King Ahab. The word of the prophet of Israel drastically affected the land of this Canaanite god of rain and fertility, demonstrating
that the omnipotence of the God of Israel knows no boundaries.

However, Elijah was sent to Zarephath not only to witness God's
far-reaching power, but also to undergo a personal transformation. In
Zarephath, in addition to obeying divine directives, Elijah would be
compelled to forge relationships with others. God instructed him to
travel to Phoenicia and find a destitute widow who would provide for
him. Elijah would now be in a position of having to rely on this
woman and to prevail upon her to rely on him. Immediately upon
entering the city, Elijah encounters the widow and requests that she
prepare him a cake with the little flour she has left. The exchange
between the two makes it clear that she is uneasy about feeding this
stranger at the cost of her own life and that of her orphan son. From
the perspective of the prophet, this action was intended to precipitate
the miracle that he would presently perform. From the perspective of
the widow, it would result in certain death. Elijah grappled with the
ultimate leadership challenge—to convince the people to put their
trust in him and in God, despite all logical considerations to the contrary. In this, he was successful: the widow offered him her meager
rations, and her faith was rewarded with a miraculous jar of flour and

a never-ending jug of oil. Yet far more important is the bridge of mutual trust and understanding that was built between Elijah and the
widow through this experience.

In the final act of this drama, the widow's son died and Elijah
revived him. The child's death was ascribed by his mother to the
numinous presence of the holy man in her household. Elijah was
shocked; he never intended the death of innocents. Yet what of the
countless innocents who suffered as a result of the drought he
declared? Confronting his responsibility for the death of the widow's
son, Elijah became painfully aware of his responsibility for all of the
ramifications of his prophetic actions. Elijah responded by mobilizing
his prophetic powers of prayer and sacred presence and restored the
boy to life; in doing so, he became prepared to actively confront the
source of evil that demanded the declaration of drought in the first
place, and to restore the fortunes of his people. Bringing the child
back to life powerfully symbolized Elijah's next challenge—the revival
of the people of Israel. In Phoenicia, he achieved the ability to inspire
trust and make others cognizant of his power as well as his compassion.
More important, Elijah, the unrelenting zealot, taught the widow and
himself that his powers were not his own: "Now I know that you are a
man of God and that the word of the LORD is truly in your mouth" (1
Kings 17:24). Once Elijah internalized this truism, he humbly
received and accepted God's next command:

> Much later, in the third year, the word of the LORD came to
> Elijah: "Go appear before Ahab; then I will send rain upon the
> earth." (1 Kings 18:1)

Elijah is now to appear before Ahab rather than hide from him.
Moreover, the emphasis is clear: it is God who will call a halt to
Elijah's drought; it is He who will bring the rain. The long-awaited
reunion between the desperate king and the vigilante prophet is
described as follows:

When Ahab caught sight of Elijah, Ahab said to him, "Is that you, you troubler of Israel?" He retorted, "It is not I who have brought trouble on Israel, but you and your father's House, by forsaking the commandments of the LORD and going after the Baalim." (1 Kings 18:17–18)

This exchange seems a rather petty case of name-calling between king and prophet. Had Ahab been waiting three years just to call Elijah a troublemaker? Was it worthy of the prophet of God to repay the royal insult with an insult? The answer, of course, is that this verbal jousting reflected a much deeper conflict. The king and the prophet were simply not on the same wavelength. Ahab saw himself as the victorious savior of Israel, who had accomplished great things for his people through his international exploits. He saw Elijah as a thorn in the side of national progress. Elijah, on his part, pointed an accusing finger at Ahab as the real troubler of Israel. He and his household abandoned their ancestral faith and shirked their religious responsibility. Elijah's contention was that for a leader of Israel, the only measure of success is unwavering devotion to God.

Soon after the meeting, Elijah challenged Ahab to a contest, to establish once and for all who was the true god—Baal or the God of Elijah:

"Now summon all Israel to join me at Mount Carmel, together with the four hundred and fifty prophets of Baal and the four hundred prophets of Asherah, who eat at Jezebel's table." Ahab sent orders to all the Israelites and gathered the prophets at Mount Carmel. (1 Kings 18:19–20)

It is instructive that Ahab willingly agreed to the contest on Mount Carmel. Although one might argue that his agenda was to defeat Elijah and prove the power and preeminence of the prophets of Baal, it is more likely that Ahab suffered from the same syndrome as the people—he too wavered between ideologies. This real confusion that characterized the entire nation's state of belief is poignantly expressed in Elijah's call to the assembled:

> "How long will you keep vacillating between two beliefs? If the LORD is God, follow Him; and if Baal, follow him!" But the people answered him not a word. (1 Kings 18:21) [author's translation]

Rashi offers a fascinating interpretation of this last verse. The people, he explains, could not answer because "they could not tell the difference." In other words: the people's religious ignorance was so profound they could not discern between the pagan Baal and the God of their Fathers. It was not out of malice that the people had left the fold. They were merely victims of ignorance and alienation. They had lost all contact with their own cultural heritage and had been enticed by the lure of paganism. Only Elijah's pyrotechnics could jolt them back to the fundamentals of belief. But the dramatic denoue-ment was preceded by a far more significant step in the spiritual reha-bilitation of Israel.

> Then Elijah said to all the people, "Come closer to me"; and all the people came closer to him. He repaired the damaged altar of the LORD. Then Elijah took twelve stones, corre-sponding to the number of the tribes of the sons of Jacob to whom the word of the LORD had come: "Israel shall be your name" and with the stones he built an altar in the name of the LORD. (1 Kings 18:30–32)

At that moment, Elijah the prophet laid aside his daunting man-tle of authority and supernatural powers and compassionately reached out to the people to draw them close. The people, lost and confused, willingly responded to his call. He actively involved them in the rebuilding of the altar of God with 12 symbolic stones. Importantly, they do not build a new altar, but restore the ancient one that had fallen into ruin. This powerful action of rejoining 12 stones, representing the 12 tribes of Israel, was intended to educate the people that they could all return to God with one heart, one altar, one Torah. By using the 12 stones, Elijah made it clear that unity of spirit can allow for blessed diversity. And so, after many long years of estrangement, the people and their prophet joined forces. In essence, at that moment the battle was decided; the fire that Elijah called down from heaven merely confirmed what the people had begun to find once again in their hearts.

> Then fire from the LORD descended and consumed the burnt offering. . . . When they saw this, all the people flung themselves on their faces and cried out: "The LORD alone is God, The LORD alone is God!"(1 Kings 18:38–39)

This restoration of religious harmony came about first and foremost through the rebuilding of the relationship between the nation and the prophet. Having worked together to bring down fire from heaven, Elijah and the people of Israel found themselves waiting for rain. On some level, Elijah no doubt wished for a cloudburst—a thunderous clap for all of his courage and loyal devotion; none came. The valleys were still waiting for their rivers and the browns and yellows were still waiting for their greens. Elijah's work was incomplete and he intuitively knew that the rains would require another effort on his part. An additional relationship would have to be set right before the skies would open. Elijah the prophet would have to turn directly to God.

> Elijah meanwhile climbed to the top of Mount Carmel, crouched on the ground and put his face between his knees. (1 Kings 18:42)

This passage is enigmatic. The commentators claim that Elijah's bodily gestures indicated that he engaged in prayer and meditation. The actions are reminiscent of Elijah's revival of the widow's son, over whom he crouched and prayed. If it is indeed a description of prayer, this would indicate that Elijah had learned his lesson, that his powers are delimited by the Almighty, that rain would not come at his beck and call. Elijah must pray, wait, and yield to a higher authority. The Rabbis graphically described the situation as follows:

> Elijah prayed that the keys of resurrection might be given him, but was answered: Three keys have not been entrusted to an agent: birth, rain and resurrection. Shall it be said two are in the hands of the disciple and only one in the hand of the Master? Bring me the other and take this one, as it is written, "Go show yourself unto Ahab and I will send rain upon the earth." (B. San. 113a)

This stage in the course of events represents the restoration of the proper balance of power between God and the prophet.

> And he said to his servant, "Go up and look toward the Sea." He went up and looked and reported, "There is nothing." Seven times [Elijah] said, "Go back," and the seventh time, [the servant] reported, "A cloud as small as a man's hand is rising in the west." (1 Kings 18:43–44)

Elijah sent his servant again and again until finally God sent a tiny cloud, described as being in the shape of a man's hand—*ki-kaf ish*. This expression would seem to imply a diminution of Elijah—the smallness of his hand. This phrase seems to be placed in stark contrast with that which happens when the hand of the Lord rests upon Elijah, as we shall presently see.

And what about Ahab? What impact did the confrontation at Carmel have on him? When our story began, a vast ideological fissure existed between Elijah and Ahab. After Elijah miraculously impressed the people with God's omnipotence, the king followed his constituency and moved over to Elijah's side. Now that all recognized God's triumph over Baal, Elijah willingly brought the rain. However, he first instructed Ahab to eat. This command is curious; Elijah had just executed 450 prophets of Baal. Ahab perhaps wondered whether he would be next. Elijah required of the king to dissociate himself from the prophets of Baal by eating. This action would imply that Ahab was unmoved by their deaths, making it quite clear where his loyalties lay. Having acceded to that instruction of the prophet, Ahab is accorded legitimate royal status.

> Then [Elijah] said, "Go say to Ahab, 'Hitch up [your chariot] and go down before the rain stops you.' " Meanwhile the sky grew black with clouds; there was wind, and a heavy downpour fell; Ahab mounted his chariot and drove off to Jezreel. The hand of the LORD had come upon Elijah. He tied up his skirts and ran in front of Ahab all the way to Jezreel. (1 Kings 18: 44–46)

The rain was falling steadily; Ahab's chariot was on the way back to the royal palace in Jezreel. It had been a long day, leaving him with much to contemplate. He had been bested by the prophet, but the spirit of the nation of Israel had triumphed and their king was once again among them. From his royal chariot, his eyes caught sight of a runner, drenched by the downpour yet sprinting joyfully in front of his horses. He rubbed his weary eyes, certain that they deceived him. Who was that man whose cape was blowing wildly in the wind? Could it be? Indeed, there was no mistaking Elijah, the prophet who had been answered through fire and now through rain. It was Elijah, Ahab's prophet, paying him the respect due the king of Israel who walked in the ways of God. Another relationship was now restored.

Whereas the story of Elijah and the drought is a magnificent demonstration of rain resulting from altars rebuilt and bonds re-forged, the reverse is also the case—when relationships between man and God and between man and man go awry, rain is withheld. Anticipation turns into desperation, prayers go unanswered, and parched bodies shrivel and die along with desiccated souls.

Jeremiah 14 presents the dark side of the equation. In that chapter, we find the most detailed and painful description of drought in biblical literature. Jeremiah's goal in recounting the drought in a prophetic context is to negate the popular opinion that the catastrophe simply resulted from random vicissitudes of nature. Rather, natural calamities are problems whose origins as well as solutions lie in the religious realm. What is most unusual about this particular prophecy is that it does not contain within it a long roster of sins committed by the people. It places the emphasis on a larger issue—relationships that have come undone.

Jeremiah's prophecy begins with the impact of the drought on man and nature:

Judah is in mourning
Her settlements languish.
Men are bowed to the ground,
And the outcry of Jerusalem rises.
Their nobles sent their servants for water;
They came to the cisterns, they found no water.
They returned, their vessels empty.
They are shamed and humiliated,
They cover their heads.
Because of the ground there is dismay,
For there has been no rain on the earth.
The plowmen are shamed,
They cover their heads.
Even the hind in the field
Forsakes her new-born fawn,

Because there is no grass.
And the wild asses stand on the bare heights,
Snuffing the air like jackals;
Their eyes pine,
Because there is no herbage. (Jer. 14:2–6)

The far-reaching effects of the rainless skies are felt intensely throughout society; nobles, townsfolk, and farmers are desperate for water. Even animals abandon their young and fruitlessly seek pasturage. Jeremiah turns to God and passionately prays:

Though our iniquities testify against us,
Act, O LORD, for the sake of Your name;
Though our rebellions are many
And we have sinned against You.
Mikveh Yisra'el [author's addition]—O Hope of Israel,
Its deliverer in time of trouble,
Why are You like a stranger in the land,
Like a traveler who stops only for the night?
Why are You like a man who is stunned,
Like a warrior who cannot give victory?
Yet You are in our midst, O LORD,
And Your name is attached to us—
Do not forsake us! (Jer. 14:7–9)

Jeremiah addresses God as Mikveh Yisra'el. The double entendre of mikveh, meaning a body of water as well as hope, aptly sums up his heartfelt supplication that the source of all waters will become the source of all hope. However, the appellation is explained by Rabbi Akiva as possessing a third dimension, that of purity:

How fortunate are you O Israel that you are purified before your father in Heaven as it says . . . Mikveh Yisra'el—just as a *mikveh* purifies the impure, so too the Holy One, Blessed Be He, purifies Israel. (B. Yoma 85a)

While the Almighty has become a stranger to His people, a traveler in the night, a warrior helpless to fight for their causes, the people are in crisis. They implore Him not to forsake them, knowing full well that only He can offer them purity and forgiveness, life-giving waters and hope. Shockingly, the sincerity of the prophet and the people not only falls upon deaf ears, the Lord actually commands the prophet to cease and desist:

Do not pray for the benefit of this people. When they fast, I will not listen to their outcry; and when they present burnt offering and meal offering, I will not accept them. I will exterminate them by war, famine and disease. (Jer. 14:11–12)

Twice before, God commanded Jeremiah not to pray for the nation (Jer. 7:16 and 11:14) and he sadly complied with the divine decree. This time, he does not. He boldly continued to beseech God on behalf of his people.

For Your name's sake, do not disown us;
Do not dishonor Your glorious throne.
Remember, do not annul Your covenant with us. (Jer. 14:21)

In order to understand the nature of this dialogue, we would do well to compare the intimate prophetic exchange the prophet has with God with his public leadership role. Jeremiah allows us, his audience, to hear, behind the scenes, the unmediated dialogue of revelation, with the hope that the direct communication will impact in a way that formal exhortations would not. The rhetorical power of this approach is felt strongly in Jeremiah's report of God preventing him from praying. In this manner, he informs the people of Israel that their sins are so grave that God is no longer listening. What then is the point of announcing this to the people? There are two possible answers, one optimistic and one pessimistic. The former contends that Jeremiah intended to tell the people that their empty words and rituals had come to an end. The gates of prayer—be they the prayer of the people or even the prayer of the prophet, not to mention the gates of sacrifice, are locked forever. There exists only one avenue of salvation—and it runs through the gates of repentance. Only a true change in Israel's behavior could ward off disaster. However, the prophet does not express this notion directly, hoping to elicit this conclusion from the people themselves. Hearing that God has forbidden Jeremiah to pray, they should then turn to Jeremiah and desperately inquire what to do. The prophet would then lead them on the path of *teshuvah*.

The pessimistic approach explains the scenario differently. The prophecy is a reflection of the nation's current reality, of bridges they have burned. No more hope exists—no prayer will avert the evil decree. The prophet can simply attest to his people's evil ways and enumerate all of the impending disasters. Perhaps the intent of this prophetic rhetoric is that future generations draw the requisite conclusions. This explanation would clarify why Jeremiah continues to publicly prophesy even post-destruction, until he himself exits the stage of Jewish history—he is speaking to all eternity. Additionally, perhaps the prophet reports God's prohibition for him to pray in order to defend himself from those people who would claim that he could have prevented the destruction through his prayers. Jeremiah explains that this option was not available to him.

As a staunch defender of his people Israel, Jeremiah tries yet another technique in an effort to come to the defense of the nation. He suggests that it is not they who are at fault, but their wayward leaders—the false prophets.

I said, "Ah, LORD God! The prophets are saying to them, 'You shall not see the sword, famine shall not come upon you, but I will give you unfailing security in this place.' " (Jer. 14:13)

Yochanan Muffs makes the following observation:

> If God will not listen to the confession which contains within it supplication and audacity (verse 7) perhaps he will heed the logical contention. Here the argument takes on a more philosophical direction. "Ah, Lord God! The prophets are saying to them, 'You shall not see the sword, famine shall not come upon you, but I will give you unfailing security in this place.'" In order to absolve the nation from sin and punishment he transfers the guilt from the nation to God—"You are responsible for their sins, since you encouraged them on this path by allowing the false prophets to speak—how could You have allowed such a thing—and how could You hold them accountable, if You Yourself tempted them to sin. (Muffs, 62)

God is not convinced. Rather than relate to Jeremiah's claim that the people deserve clemency since they have been corrupted by false prophets, He blasts the prophets as being men of lies and falsehood; the people will now suffer miserably for having bought into their lies. There is nothing left to do other than lament their bitter fate. Again Jeremiah has reached a dead end. What is the purpose of this dispute in the context of his prophecy?

The same two rhetorical possibilities outlined above apply here as well. The pessimistic one would see this passage as testimony intended for the survivors of the destruction and their progeny as an explanation of what brought about the end. They had been lured by false prophets and self-serving prophecies; perhaps future generations will take heed. Conversely, the optimistic approach would claim that the prophet includes his listeners in the dialogue to intensify the litany of charges against the prophets. His hope is that by quoting God, he will cause the people to gird themselves and banish all of these soothsayers from the public domain—nullifying their worldview and taking decided strides toward repentance.

Jeremiah's skillful rhetoric is evidenced by his use of the term "prophets" rather than "false prophets." He leaves it up to God to determine the truth or falsehood of these seers, which He does, in no uncertain terms. In this fashion, it becomes clear that it is not a personal vendetta that Jeremiah has with these people, but a matter of principle. Israel's seduction by the false prophets is a symptom of the breakdown of their relationship with God. It has replaced a true spiritual bond and I-Thou connection with the Almighty that required commitment and dedication. It was far easier for Israel to cast their lot with false prophets who promised them everything and demanded nothing. The price that they paid for this faithlessness was the cessation of God's providence, resulting in the terrible drought. However, from our literary perspective, we can see that this chapter attests to another relationship that has unraveled.

Jeremiah unwittingly casts himself as a figure of ultimate pathos. His words, which began as a powerful moral imperative, have been neutralized and farcically undermined by the guile of his adversaries. God's anger reflects not only his disappointment with the people's disloyalty to Him, but His moral outrage at the contempt of Israel for the prophet who had devoted himself for so many years, with all his heart and soul, to their welfare. The breakdown in communication between the people and their prophet is yet another reason that the skies will remain rainless.

Jeremiah does not give up. He continues to pray. His hope is, no doubt, a function of his projective identification with the people of Israel. He championed their cause and interceded on their behalf. But this prophetic dialogue is ended with the harsh words of God:

Even if Moses and Samuel were to intercede with Me, I would not be won over to that people. Dismiss them from My presence, and let them go forth! And if they ask you, "To what shall we go forth?" answer them, "Thus said the LORD: Those destined for the plague, to the plague;

> Those destined for the sword, to the sword;
> Those destined for famine, to famine;
> Those destined for captivity, to captivity." (Jer. 15:1–2)

Although the prophet knew well how to transform a description of an agricultural crisis into a call for introspection and repentance, his generation had become inured to his warnings. Drought and famine, disaster and devastation will now scourge the land, a function not of Jeremiah's lack of competence, but rather of the tattered fabric of interactions among God, Israel, and the prophet.

Whereas the Bible connected the bounty of rain with loyalty and devotion to God and drought with alienation and indifference, in the world of the Rabbis, rain was viewed as being linked to man's actions toward his fellow man. *Bereshit Rabbah* 33 provides a masterful illustration of the connection between *caritas* and rainfall:

In the days of Rabbi Tanhuma, the people were in need of a fast. They came to him and said, "Rabbi, declare a fast!" One day, two days, three days passed, but no rain fell. He came and taught them: "My sons, fill yourselves with compassion for one another and God will be filled with compassion for you." While they were out distributing charity among the poor, they noticed a man giving money to his divorcée. They came to Rabbi Tanhuma and declared, "Rabbi, why are we sitting here when sin is out there!" He inquired, "What was it that you saw?" They replied, "We saw so-and-so giving money to his divorcée." He summoned the couple and placed them before the crowd. He asked, "What is she to you?" He replied, "She is my divorcée." He said, "Then why did you give her money?" He said, "Rabbi, I saw that she was in dire straits and I was filled with compassion for her." At that point Rabbi Tanhuma turned his face heavenward and said, "Master of the Universe! If this man who is not obliged to provide alimony for his divor-cée saw that she was in distress and was filled with compassion—You, about whom it is written that You are merciful and compassionate, (and moreover) we are the children of your beloved Abraham, Isaac, and Jacob—how much more so should You have mercy upon us!" Immediately, the rains began to fall and the world became saturated (*nitraveh ha-olam*). (*Bereshit Rabbah* 33)

Rabbi Tanhuma was accosted by the people, who came to tell their spiritual leader how to contend with the drought. "Declare a fast!" they demanded. He played along and did as they requested, in an effort to accentuate the inefficacy of ritual devoid of meaning and sincerity. He called a fast but no rain fell.

Rabbi Tanhuma then suggested a different approach. He told the people to fill their hearts with compassion for one another. It is noteworthy that he presented the challenge in a general fashion, leaving his constituency room for their own interpretation. They proceeded to go out and distribute alms to the poor. One senses that they took the alms box from the local synagogue and perfunctorily went about their business.

When they happened upon the divorced couple, they were delighted. The fact that the husband was giving his ex-wife funds clearly indicated that something was amiss. He must have disgracefully taken up with her again. This act of impropriety no doubt served to explain why the rains had ceased.

When Rabbi Tanhuma heard the report he seized the opportunity to teach his next valuable lesson—the lesson of personal responsibility. With startling ingenuity, Rabbi Tanhuma called the couple in for an interrogation. The audience congregated, gloating with pride over their important discovery. Rabbi Tanhuma placed the couple under the bright lights, only to ultimately turn the lights onto the sneering audience.

He listened patiently to the explanation of the husband. "Rabbi, I saw she was in dire straits and I was filled with compassion for her." Rabbi Tanhuma well understood the challenges the man had faced in helping his divorcée. He was forced to transcend self, to overcome turbulent feelings of resentment, guilt, anger, and embarrassment. Justifiably, he worried about what people would say. However, he was able to rise above all this and fill his heart with compassion, exactly as Rabbi Tanhuma had ordered. Rabbi Tanhuma used this man's admirable example as an object lesson for the community. In addition, Rabbi Tanhuma brought him as a character witness in his appeal before God to bring the rain.

It is noteworthy that the great prophets of Israel depicted the relationship between God and the Jewish people as one between a husband and an unfaithful wife whom he has divorced and expelled. Jeremiah 3:1 provides one such example:

If a man divorces his wife, and she leaves him and marries another man, can he ever go back to her? Would not such a land be defiled? Now you have whored with many lovers: can you return to Me?—says the LORD. (Jer. 3:1)

R. Tanhuma's appeal contains within it an allusion to this prophetic metaphor. He questions the Master of the Universe: "If this man's heart can be filled with compassion for his divorcée, how can You, with Your infinite mercy, do any less for Yours?" Notice that in this case as well, a relationship is the fulcrum of the problem and its solution. Consider the relationship of the community to one another, illustrated by the accusing finger they point at the compassionate husband. Could their patronizing attitude in this story be symptomatic of the larger malady and serve to explain the drought? Far less speculative is that a resolution is indeed brought about through a relationship. It is of great significance that here the relationship is not one that is simply resumed, but one that is built in place of that which had failed. The man and his ex-wife once again connected, not through romance but by way of true lovingkindness. Through their interaction they have touched the souls of others and opened the heavens to the needs of humanity.

And as the rain began to fall, the midrash tells us, *nitraveh ha-olam*—the world was saturated. However, an alternate reading found in some versions is *ve-nitrave'ah ha-olam*—the world became more expansive. Through kindness, the world became a better, more comfortable place to live.

All of the above-cited texts share the common theme of relationships. At the close of Yom Kippur, we—like the people of Israel on Mount Carmel—exclaim in dramatic crescendo: *Adonai Hu ha-Elohim,* "The Lord is God." We declare our sole allegiance to Him. Arriving refreshed at Shemini Atzeret, we prepare to renew our relationship with our Maker, hoping to enjoy His blessings in the year to come. Yet this midrash makes it clear that only when our interpersonal relationships are exemplary will our world be revitalized. If we use the transformational opportunity afforded by the Days of Awe to mend our interaction with man and God, then in response, the Master of the Universe will relate to us by opening the gates of Heaven and bringing forth gentle rain.

Simchat Torah

Chapter Eleven

❧

Standing on Holy Ground

❧

Simchat Torah marks the conclusion of the annual Torah reading cycle. As the final verses of Deuteronomy are read, a feeling of accomplishment and fulfillment spreads over the congregation. All rise and joyously sing: *Hazak, hazak, ve-nit'hazek!*—"May we be strong, mighty, and reinforced!" The Torah scroll is lifted high so that all may see it, and again the congregation proclaims: *Ve-zot ha-Torah asher sam Moshe!* "This is the Torah that Moses placed before all of Israel!" The service continues with an encore, as a second Torah is opened, dramatically demonstrating that our engagement with the Torah has not ended—it has just begun. Having come full circle, the reader continues with the first verse of Genesis: *Bereshit bara Elohim*—"In the beginning God created." Thus, we initiate a year of new beginnings, new opportunities for spiritual growth, and new hopes. Surely, to add any other readings to such inspiring selections could only be anticlimactic. However, the final Scriptural reading of the holiday season is neither the end of Deuteronomy nor the beginning of Genesis. It is the opening passage of the Prophets, Joshua, chapter 1: the haftarah of Simchat Torah.

After the death of Moses the servant of the LORD, the LORD said to Joshua son of Nun, Moses' attendant: "My servant Moses is dead. Prepare to cross the Jordan, together with all this people, into the land that I am giving to the Israelites. Every spot on which your foot treads I give to you, as I promised Moses. . . . Be strong and resolute, for you shall apportion to this people the land that I swore to their fathers to assign to them . . . observe faithfully all the Teaching that My servant Moses enjoined upon you. Do not deviate from it to the right or to the left, that you may be successful wherever you go. Let not this Book of the Teaching cease from your lips, but recite it day and night, so that you may observe faithfully all that is written in it. Only then will you prosper in your undertakings and only then will you be successful. (Josh. 1:1–8)

This chapter marks a pivotal transition from the death of Moses, with which the Torah ends, to the leadership of Joshua, which is about to commence. Michael Fishbane explains the thrust of the haftarah is that:

Joshua is thus enjoined to combine two ideals: that of action and that of study. He is asked to be at once a man of power and of piety—learning for the sake of actions and acting in accordance with God's will. Becoming in effect a "new Moses" through study makes Joshua also the first "man of tradition." The divine revelations received by Moses "face to face" (Deut. 34:10) must be learned and recited by his successor. Significantly Joshua is not called a "prophet"—but one "filled with the spirit of wisdom" (Deut. 34:9). Revelation sets the task that tradition tries to realize. (Fishbane, 415)

The book of Joshua begins on a sad note. Moses our teacher, the master of the prophets, who ably stood by his people for 40 years, is no more. We sorrowfully recall how Moses walked the Israelites to the Promised Land, step by step, only to be painfully compelled to take leave of his people at the border of the land for which he longed. His departure marked a significant turning point in the life of the nation. Joshua would now take over, both as the commander in chief of the Israelite army and as the religious leader in place of Moses.

However, Moses did not go down without a fight. In the book of Deuteronomy, he is described as having pleaded dramatically for a temporary reprieve, to "cross over and see the good land on the other side of the Jordan" (Deut. 3:25). This appeal is artfully embroidered in *Midrash Tanhuma*. In the Rabbis' version of the affair, Moses presents many different remonstrations against the verdict. He who is described by God as "the humblest of men" makes a poignant case for his worthiness above all others. The Master of the Universe counters Moses' claim by explaining to him that his time has simply come, and that Joshua's term of office must begin:

Thus it was in My mind even before I created the world, and this is the way of the world. Every generation has its own guides. Up to now it was your share to minister before Me, and now you have lost your share. The time is ripe for your disciple Joshua to minister to Me. (*Midrash Tanhuma, Va'ethannan* 6)

In the following midrashic rendition, Moses desperately proposes a compromise position. He appeals to God to allow him to continue not as a leader, but as an apprentice to Joshua. God consents, with the hope that the experience will force Moses to resign himself to death. What ensues is a heartrending episode:

So Moses rose early and stationed himself at the entrance of Joshua's tent. Joshua was seated expounding the Law, and Moses remained standing before him in stooped position with his hand on his mouth, without being noticed by Joshua. . . .

Meanwhile, the Israelites had gone to the entrance of Moses' tent of Torah study and they asked: "Moses our master—where is he?" They were told: He had risen up early and gone to the entrance of Joshua's tent. They followed and found Moses at the entrance of Joshua's tent. Joshua was seated while Moses was standing. "Joshua," they said to him, "what happened to you that you are seated while Moses our master is standing?" When Joshua raised his eyes and saw Moses standing, he rent his clothes and burst into tears crying out, "My teacher, my teacher, my father, my father, and my lord!" Thereupon the Israelites said to Moses: "Moses our master, teach us Torah!" But he replied: "I have no permission to do so." They insisted, however: "We will not leave you alone." But a heavenly voice came forth, saying to them: "Learn from Joshua, and accept upon yourselves to sit before him and hear his teachings." Joshua sat at the head, Moses at his right, and the sons of Aaron at his left, and Joshua expounded the Torah in the presence of Moses. Said R. Samuel bar Nahmani in the name of R. Jonathan: Hardly had Joshua uttered the words "Praised be He who has chosen the righteous," when the chain of authority and wisdom was taken from Moses and given to Joshua, so that Moses was not able to follow Joshua's discourse. When Joshua spoke no more, Israel requested of Moses: "Explain to us the Torah [bring the learning to a close]." But he said: "I know not how to reply to you," and he faltered in his speech. At that moment he cried: "Master of the Universe, until now I sought life but now I am ready to surrender my soul to You!" (*Tanhuma, Va'ethanan* 6)

The reversal of roles was not an effective solution for Moses. At this juncture Joshua had become the master, and Moses was unable to play apprentice to him nor even understand his words. During their lifetime together, a particular dynamic had been established between them. The Torah presents a series of significant encounters between the two that clearly delineates their roles: Moses the master and Joshua the attendant.

Joshua is first referred to as Moses' attendant when he accompanied Moses halfway up Mount Sinai to receive the tablets of the Law. "So Moses and his attendant Joshua arose, and Moses ascended the mountain of God" (Exod. 24:13). Moses proceeded to the summit by himself. However, on his way down, he again joined Joshua, who presumably waited for him to arrive. As they approached the camp, they were accosted by an unfamiliar noise.

> When Joshua heard the sound of the people in its boisterousness, he said to Moses, "There is a cry of war in the camp." But he answered, "It is not the sound of the tune of triumph,
> Or the sound of the tune of defeat;
> It is the sound of song that I hear!" (Exod. 32:17–18)

This exchange highlights the dissonance between what Joshua thought he heard and the actual source of the uproar at the foot of the mountain. Furthermore, there was significant disparity between what Joshua heard and what Moses knew. On the mountain, Moses had spoken directly with God and had been informed of the nation's sudden fall. It is likely that Moses chose not to share his knowledge with Joshua so as not to crush his young servant, or perhaps Moses was simply rendered speechless. Joshua, on the other hand, was oblivious. At this stage, Joshua was still Moses' apprentice, falling short of him in insight and foresight. He did not pick up the dismal signals of the nation's crashing religious downfall. The Rabbis note Moses' displeasure at Joshua's lack of comprehension:

> Rabbi Ahwa b. Rabbi Zera said: Joshua made two remarks in the presence of Moses which failed to find favor in his sight. One was in connection with the appointment of the elders, as it is written, "My lord Moses restrain them . . ." Moses replied to him, "Art thou jealous for my sake?" by which he really

meant, "Joshua, am I jealous of you? Would that my sons were like you! Would that all of the Lord's people were prophets!" The other was in connection with the Golden Calf, as it says, "And when Joshua heard the noise of the people as they shouted." Moses said to him: "A man who is destined to exercise authority over sixty myriads is unable to distinguish between one sound and another!" (*Kohelet Rabbah* 9:11)

Joshua's misreading of the situation was a function of his professional bias. He was a military man, and had only his military instincts upon which to rely. In fact, the first time we meet Joshua is in his role as a general. The story appears in Exodus, chapter 17.

Amalek came and fought with Israel at Rephidim. Moses said to Joshua, "Pick some men for us and go out and do battle with Amalek. Tomorrow I will station myself on the top of the hill, with the rod of God in my hand." Joshua did as Moses told him and fought with Amalek, while Moses, Aaron, and Hur went up to the top of the hill. Then whenever Moses held up his hand, Israel prevailed; but whenever he let down his hand, Amalek prevailed. . . . And Joshua overwhelmed the people of Amalek with the sword. (Exod. 17:8–13)

The lines of demarcation between Moses and Joshua are here clearly drawn. Joshua's role was to fight against the archenemy Amalek with troops and weapons. Moses, though, used alternative methods to wage this war. Scripture notes that he took with him not a sword but his staff, his divine instrument: "And take with you this rod, with which you shall perform the signs" (Exod. 4:17). Some commentators suggest that the staff was a standard, bearing a conspicuous symbol that signified the presence of God in the Israelite camp. What is of particular interest is that Moses tells Joshua: *U-matteh Elohim be-yadi*—"with the staff of God in my hand." The Rabbis add: "In my hand—and not in the hand of Joshua," *be-yadi ve-lo be-yad Yehoshua*. The staff, according to the Rabbis, was the exclusive provenance of Moses. With it, he was given the power to perform miracles, during the Exodus and throughout the desert sojourn. However, the staff did not cross the Jordan. The staff was not used by Joshua to part the waters of the Jordan; as we shall see, it was the collective action of the priests carrying the ark into their new land that brought about that miracle. The staff was not raised by Joshua the warrior to vanquish the people of Ai. Instead, Joshua raised a spear (Josh. 8:26), and together with his troops waged a battle that led the nation to victory.

But Moses used not only his staff in the battle at Rephidim, he used his hand: "Joshua did as Moses told him and fought with Amalek. . . . Then, whenever Moses held up his hand, Israel prevailed; but whenever he let down his hand, Amalek prevailed" (Exod. 17:10–11). The exact significance of this gesture is unclear. The Mishnah emphatically asks: "Did the hands of Moshe, then, control the course of the war?" The Mishnah answers: certainly not, "But rather, as long as the Israelites set their sights on High and subjected themselves to their Father in Heaven, they prevailed. Otherwise, they failed" (M. RH 3:8).

The hands of Moses appear to be the symbol of his God-given power. The final verse of the Torah would seem to corroborate this: "And for all the mighty hand (*u-le-khol ha-yad ha-hazakah*) and awesome power that Moses displayed before all Israel" (Deut. 34:12). The *yad ha-hazakah* is an allusion to the power of God with which Moses had been endowed, a power Joshua did not possess.

The story of the battle at Rephidim ends with an important addendum: "And Joshua overwhelmed the people of Amalek with the sword. Then the LORD said to Moses, 'Inscribe this in a document as a reminder, and read it aloud to Joshua: I will utterly blot out the memory of Amalek from under heaven!' " (Exod. 17:13–14). The defeat of Amalek was Joshua's first reported public appearance and his first interaction with Moses, and he is clearly portrayed as playing a leadership role. Notably, he is not called Moses' attendant in this episode. The final note of the narrative implies that he was appointed by God Himself to continue in his capacity as the military leader of Israel. It is little wonder, then, that thereafter Joshua was attuned to the winds of war.

In contrast, Joshua is cast not as a leader but as Moses' attendant or aide-de-camp in a most unusual story found in Numbers 11. There Moses complains that the people are too great a burden for him to carry. God reacted by commanding Moses to gather 70 of the elders at the tent of meeting, where God promises, "I will come down and talk with you there; and I will take some of the spirit that is on you and put it on them, and they shall bear the burden of the people along with you, so that you will not bear it all by yourself" (Num. 11:17). We are then informed that these men were imbued with the spirit of Moses, which enabled them to prophesy at that stage but never again. However, there were two other individuals, Eldad and Medad, who spontaneously began to prophesy in the camp.

> Two men, one named Eldad and the other Medad, had remained in camp; yet the spirit rested upon them—they were among those recorded, but they had not gone out to the Tent—and they prophesied in the camp. (Num. 11:26)

The ecstatic prophecy of Eldad and Medad solicited opposite reactions from Joshua and Moses, with Scripture again painting Joshua as guilty of a serious *malentendu*.

> A youth ran out and told Moses, saying, "Eldad and Medad are acting the prophet in the camp!" And Joshua son of Nun, Moses' attendant from his youth, spoke up and said, "My lord, Moses, restrain them!" But Moses said to him, "Are you wrought up on my account? Would that all the LORD's people were prophets, that the LORD put His spirit upon them!" Moses then reentered the camp together with the elders of Israel. (Num. 11:27–30)

What was the nature of the dispute between Joshua the attendant and Moses the master in the matter of the prophecy of Eldad and Medad? Joshua saw such unregimented prophecy as a breach that could undermine the establishment. Eldad and Medad were seemingly among those men approved by Moses as worthy of sharing in the delegation of leadership responsibility, and they were in fact filled with the divine spirit. However, they did not follow the operative guidelines; rather than going out with the others to the Tent of Meeting, they remained in the camp. Did that mean they intended to set themselves up as independent authorities, forging a direct relationship with the people that bypassed Moses? Joshua was concerned with maintaining the national hierarchy. As a military leader, he knew the importance of structure and rank. His tendency was to contain threats to national stability, and so his reaction: "My lord Moses, restrain them." However, this statement was also fueled by his jealous solicitude for the honor of Moses. Only those who acknowledged his primacy by coming out to the Tent—symbolically apprenticing themselves to Moses, much as did Joshua himself who "would not stir out of the Tent" (Exod. 33:11)—should merit revelation.

Moses, a man of true humility, did not interpret this occurrence as a threat. He responded with equanimity and magnanimity: "Would that all the LORD's people were prophets, that the LORD put His spirit upon them!" (Num. 11:29). From Moses' point of view, God was an equal opportunity employer. All Israel had the potential to achieve revelation. Moses had seen it happen fleetingly at Mount Sinai, and he hadn't completely despaired of the possibility of it happening again. With an eye toward the future spiritual redemption of the nation, Moses himself was delighted to share not only the privilege of leadership, but the sublimity of spiritual attainment. Nehama Leibowitz points out that this is a magnificent demonstration of Joel's soul-stirring vision of the end of days.

After that,
I will pour out My spirit on all flesh;

Your sons and daughters shall prophesy;
Your old men shall dream dreams,
And your young men shall see visions.
I will even pour out My spirit
Upon male and female slaves in those days. (Joel 3:1–2)

Moses reacted in precisely this tone. Joshua's outburst highlights his degree of devotion to Moses; Moses' words point to his extraordinary closeness to God.

Scripture does not inform us of the content of Eldad and Medad's prophecy, but the Rabbis fill in what Joshua heard and, in so doing, supply additional food for thought regarding why Joshua reacted as he did. In B. Sanhedrin 17a, the Rabbis suggest that the prophetic message of Eldad and Medad was "Moses will die and Joshua will take them into the land." By claiming that this blunt and shocking prediction was what Joshua heard, the Talmud reveals not only the message of the rogue prophets, but even more about the psyche of Joshua, the son of Nun. Contextually, Joshua's distress emanated from his fear that Moses was being undermined. The midrashic hypothesis takes this to the extreme; what Joshua heard was that Moses' transience was not only as a leader but as a person: "Moses will die." Joshua was suddenly gripped by the actuality that Moses was mortal. For Joshua, his loyal vassal and spiritual son, the thought of life without Moses was more than he could bear.

But was Joshua reacting to the death of Moses, or to the news that he himself would lead Israel into the land? His fear that Moses would be replaced by those two upstarts, Eldad and Medad, was now supplanted by his fear that *he* would be the upstart who replaced him—"and Joshua will take them into the land." For years, he may have harbored hope that he would succeed his role model, and perhaps was taken aback by hearing those hopes voiced aloud. Moreover, whereas at first glance the text describes Joshua's outrage that someone might usurp Moses' role, the Rabbis may be implying that Joshua psychologically engaged in transference. He feared that *he* could be upstaged by

Eldad and Medad. At present they threatened Moses, but in time they could threaten him and his coveted position as the heir of Moses. Could it be that he therefore heard them saying what he wanted to hear and have heard? Let it be made clear and unequivocal—Joshua will bring them into the land! Thus, Joshua's fears reflect the fine line between taking over from Moses and overtaking him.

Alternatively, the midrash allows us to consider the possibility that Joshua intuitively knew the proclamation to be true. He, not Moses, would indeed accompany the people into the land. It was this that caused him great trepidation. Knowing full well that he was far from worthy, he feared taking on the role of his Master. The Talmud additionally alludes to other insecurities that lay in Joshua's subconscious. It ironically embellishes Joshua's declaration: "My master Moses restrain them!" as follows: "What is the meaning of 'restrain them'? Place them in a position of leading the nation and they will cease prophesying!" This homily addresses Joshua's concern that the day-to-day involvement in mundane aspects of public life prevents one from achieving spiritual heights. Indeed, throughout the Torah, accounts of Moses' prophetic grandeur are interwoven with tales of his dealing with the demands of the nation for red meat. The Rabbis unquestionably also knew such conflicts in their own lives and give voice to their frustrations by attributing these concerns to Joshua. These comments accentuate the insecurity of Joshua the apprentice regarding the role he was to assume. Movingly, Joshua's anxieties are later allayed when Moses' spirit was indeed decanted directly to his successor. The resolution comes when Moses himself asks for a replacement.

Moses spoke to the LORD, saying, "Let the LORD, source of the breath of all flesh, appoint someone over the community who shall go out before them and come in before them, and who shall take them out and bring them in, so that the LORD's community may not be like sheep that have no shepherd." (Num. 27:15–17)

Moses appeals to the Almighty as *Elohei ha-ruhot le-khol basar*, "the LORD, source of the spirits of all flesh." Addressing God in that fashion, he implicitly expressed his wish for a perfect leader. This epithet is midrashically explained to mean "He who knows the spirit of each and every person." Moses' appeal was answered with God's selection of Joshua, *ish asher ruah bo* ("an inspired man"):

> And the LORD answered Moses, "Single out Joshua son of Nun, an inspired man, and lay your hand upon him. Have him stand before Eleazar the priest and before the whole community, and commission him in their sight. Invest him with some of your authority, so that the whole Israelite community may obey." (Num. 27:18–20)

The two earlier exchanges between Joshua and Moses—that of the Golden Calf incident and that of the Eldad and Medad affair—were both connected to *ruah*. They occurred early on, and in both cases Joshua misconstrued the course of events. Perhaps these preliminary experiences were intended to humble Joshua the warrior, to better serve his future role as the leader of the nation. In that regard, he would become more like Moses, "the humblest of all men on the face of the earth." In each of those episodes, the perspective of Moses superseded Joshua's. In both, he was called the attendant and was in need of spiritual correction. And in both cases, Moses' hands and his majestic spirit gave Joshua the assurance he needed. Moreover, Joshua's intense loyalty and devotion toward Moses served as his anchor.

It is noteworthy that we meet Joshua again in a starring role in another biblical narrative—as a key player in the story of the spies that Moses sent to Canaan. His sterling example of leadership in that incident may explain why, in the final analysis, he was chosen to fill in for Moses. Unlike the 10 dissenting spies, he was not daunted by the military challenges of the land and its oversized inhabitants. The Amalekites who caused terror to seize the hearts of the nation were not unfamiliar to him. He (and Caleb) focused in their report on matters of theological importance, transcending fear and demonstrating faith. Belief that God, not man, was the center of their universe was an essential premise for the brave warrior:

> The land that we traversed and scouted is an exceedingly good land. If the LORD is pleased with us, He will bring us into that land, a land that flows with milk and honey, and give it to us; only you must not rebel against the LORD. Have no fear then of the people of the country, for they are our prey: their protection has departed from them, but the LORD is with us. Have no fear of them! (Num. 14:7–9).

Significantly, Joshua is not called Moses' attendant at that juncture. On the contrary, he is given a new name. "And Moses called Hosea b. Nun—Yehoshua" (Num. 13:16). The 19th-century Italian biblical commentator Samuel David Luzzatto comments: "Now that he was sent with the eminent men, Moses changed his name so as not to call him a name reflecting the status of attendant, as with Joseph and Daniel the changing of the name was done when they rose to greatness."

Note that Joshua's new name is not given by God but by Moses, just prior to Joshua's entry into the land. Through this symbolic gesture, Moses hands over the task of taking the people into Israel. By adding to his name the letter yod, symbolic of the name of God, Moses' message is, "Go with God, Joshua," not as an attendant, but as a leader who can buck the tide, resist pressure, and bring the nation to its homeland.

Considering these accounts about Joshua, we notice an instructive dichotomy: in the public-religious milieu, Joshua is referred to as Moses' assistant, but in the military sphere he is very much his own person, renowned as a man of courage and conviction. We would therefore think that having taken the reigns of leadership after Moses' death, poised on the verge of the military adventure that will fulfill the long-awaited destiny of the nation, he would be portrayed as an independent agent. But that is not the case.

> After the death of Moses the servant of the LORD, the LORD said to Joshua son of Nun, Moses' attendant: "My servant Moses is dead. Prepare to cross the Jordan . . ." (Josh. 1:1–2)

One can imagine how Joshua felt, addressed by God at that propitious moment, not as Moses' heir, or even as his disciple, but as his *attendant*. However, God did not intend in any way to disparage Joshua by identifying him as Moses' attendant. Rather, He did so in the spirit of the dichotomy we have noted. God was hinting to Joshua that his greatest challenge and most important mission in the coming years would be not the military conquest of the land, but a far more difficult task.

> But you must be very strong and resolute to observe faithfully all the Teaching that My servant Moses enjoined upon you. Do not deviate from it to the right or to the left, that you may be successful wherever you go. Let not this Book of the Teaching cease from your lips, but recite it day and night so that you may observe faithfully all that is written in it. (Josh. 1:7–8)

Great valor was indeed imperative for the project of bringing the people of Israel into their land. What would be chiefly required, though, would be not martial bravery but having the courage to uphold Torah.

While God's central directive for him at that critical juncture was to adhere unwaveringly to the words of his master, slavish imitation of Moses' actions would not be enough to achieve Joshua's mission. The entry into the land required him to discover how to instruct and apply the Torah to the new generation who would now possess it. Joshua would find the wisdom necessary to do so not in the intellectual knowledge he had amassed as Moses' student, but in the procedural know-how he had absorbed as his attendant, seeing Moses in his inter-actions with individuals and the general public over 40 years of travel and travail. The Rabbis, themselves students, teachers, and leaders, were well aware of Joshua's challenge, and pointed out the termino-logical connection between his former and future roles:

> The Holy One, Blessed Be He, saw that the words of Torah were so dear to Joshua, as it says, "But his attendant Joshua son of Nun, a youth, would not stir (lo yamish) out of the Tent," He said to him, "Joshua, since the words of Torah are so dear to you, let not the book of Torah leave (lo yamush) your mouth; let you recite them day and night." (B. Menahot 99b)

As they crossed the Jordan, Joshua and the nation embarked on a rite of passage. Being an Israelite—and especially a leader—in the Land was essentially different from in the desert. Walter Brueggemann outlines the challenge the people faced upon entering the land:

> The moment drastically redefines who Israel will be. Land entry requires of Israel that it cease to be what it had been in the wilderness and become what it had never been before. Land makes that demand. At this moment Israel does indeed become a new creation, a slave becomes an heir, a helpless child becomes a mature inheritor; all tasks of self-identity need to be addressed again. . . . The Jordan is entry not into safe space but into a context of covenant. (Brueggemann, 45)

The requisite transition was made by way of a series of events that re-played scenes from the Exodus. Although seemingly familiar, they were carefully modified to adapt to the new reality. For example, the physical entry into the land required that the people cross the Jordan. The waters, like those of the Red Sea, miraculously split. "For the LORD your God dried up the waters of the Jordan before you until you crossed, just as the LORD your God did to the Sea of Reeds, which He dried up before us until we crossed" (Josh. 4:23). Through this action, Joshua ostensibly took the place of Moses: "On that day the LORD exalted Joshua in the sight of all Israel, so that they revered him all his days as they had revered Moses" (4:14).

The similarity of these events, however, is overshadowed by their differences. The splitting of the Jordan was not accomplished by Joshua taking his staff and waving it over the currents. Rather, the priests bearing the Ark of the Covenant into the river stopped the waters until the nation had crossed. This reflected a sea change in the type of leadership the people could expect. Joshua's style of command was strategic rather than charismatic. Having led the army in many battles, he understood how to let others be in the limelight while he coordinated the national effort. Joshua made the decision to operate in that fashion to prepare the nation for a new era. From now on, they would be settled throughout the land, rather than being concentrated in one camp, as they had been in the desert, with centralized authority close at hand in the person of Moses. Joshua could not hope to be everywhere at once. Instead, the assembly would now all become active partners with the Almighty in conquering, settling, and spiritually governing the Land of Israel. The Children of Israel would need to create the "context of covenant."

This process began with a sequence of events described in Joshua, chapter 5. In a remarkable undertaking, Joshua circumcised the entire nation, at God's command. If the breaking of the waters of the Jordan symbolized parturition, the nation's emergence into new life in the land, this rebirth was to be followed by circumcision. This rite confirmed their identity as the descendants of Abraham in the covenantal terrain (Gen 17:8–9). The text tells us that Joshua used *harvot tzurim*—literally, "flint swords," implements of war—to perform this deed. In a beautiful passage in the Septuagint, the ancient Greek translation of the Bible (on Josh. 24:30), we are told that these knives were later buried alongside Joshua. In so many legends of heroes and warriors, we find accounts of how their arms, with which they performed their feats of bravery, were buried with them. In contrast, after a lifetime of military victories, Joshua was laid to rest not with his sword and shield, but rather with the instruments with which he established the identity of the nation and renewed their covenant with God.

There is a pragmatic explanation for the timing of the mass circumcision. "The people came up from the Jordan on the tenth day of the first month" (Josh. 4:19). On that very date, every Hebrew family in Egypt had been commanded to prepare the Passover sacrifice, four days before the festival. In the days of Joshua, the process also began then, and "the Israelites offered the Passover sacrifice on the fourteenth day of the first month, toward evening" (Josh. 5:10). As we know, "Only those circumcised could participate in the paschal offering" (Exod. 12:48), and therefore whoever had not previously been circumcised (for whatever reason) now had that fault corrected, so they could participate in the paschal rite as a full-fledged member of the nation. With circumcision reaffirming the link with Abrahamic covenant, and Passover refreshing Israel's collective memory about God's acts of deliverance in the Exodus, the nation was now ready to take hold of their Promised Land.

The transition from Israel's surreal desert existence to the new realities of conquest and settlement was clear-cut:

> On the day after the Passover offering, on that very day, they ate of the produce of the country, unleavened bread and parched grain. On that same day, when they ate of the produce of the land, the manna ceased. The Israelites got no more manna; that year they ate of the yield of the land of Canaan. (Josh. 5:11–12)

The ephemeral food of the wilderness was suddenly a thing of the past. "And the Israelites ate manna 40 years, until they came to a settled land; they ate the manna until they came to the border of the land of Canaan" (Exod. 16:35). From hereon in, they would eat produce cultivated and harvested by their own hands. Passover, the holiday of liberation, would now take on the rhythms of nature as the spring festival. More important, Israel was now afforded an additional avenue of interaction with God, revolving around man's eternal struggle to bring forth bread from the earth.

The Rabbis' sensitivity to this transition is seen in their explanation of the development of the text of *Birkat ha-Mazon* (Grace after Meals). The Talmud (B. Ber. 48b) asserts that Moses composed the first blessing of this prayer when he gave the people the manna: "Blessed art Thou . . . who sustains the whole world in His goodness, with favor, grace, and mercy. He gives bread to all flesh." Joshua, though, is credited with the second chapter of grace: "We thank you, O Lord our God, that you gave our fathers the land of desire, goodness, and vastness and that you took us out of Egypt, the house of slavery, and for the covenant that You have sealed in our flesh, and that You taught us Torah and gave us Your commandments." *Birkat ha-Mazon* is such a ubiquitous part of our ceremonial lives that we rarely stop to consider why it contains multiple benedictions, and why the land is given such prominence in a prayer thanking God for our daily bread. In attributing the two aforementioned passages to Moses and Joshua, respectively, the Rabbis implied that while our basic gratitude to God for simple sustenance (symbolized by Moses' prayer of thankfulness for the manna) is foundational, we must go beyond that first stage to relate to God's multifaceted bounty as reflected in his granting us not only food but covenant, freedom, Torah, and land. It was Joshua's responsibility and privilege to have synthesized all those elements for the generation that took possession of Canaan.

What were the new challenges for Joshua as the leader of those who worked the land? One answer may be found in a talmudic debate between R. Ishmael and R. Simeon bar Yohai that grapples with the problem of striking a balance between material and spiritual activities.

Our Rabbis taught: "And you shall gather in your corn" (Deut. 11:14). What is to be learned from these words? Since it says,

"This book of the Torah shall not depart from out of your mouth" (Josh. 1:8), I might think this injunction is to be taken literally. Therefore it says, "And you shall gather your corn," follow the way of the world; this is the view of R. Ishmael. R. Simeon b. Yohai says: Is it possible that a man will plow in the plowing season, and sow in the sowing season, and reap in the reaping season, and thresh in the threshing season, and winnow with the winds—what is to become of Torah? Rather, when Israel perform the will of the Omnipresent, their work is performed by others. (B. Ber. 35b)

Moses' generation had received the Torah, and had the time to consider its message. The enforced leisure afforded them by their sojourn in the desert was wistfully portrayed by Rabbis of later generations as the ideal condition for Torah learning: "The Torah was given to be studied only by the manna-eaters" (Mekhilta Vayassa 2). The Israelites under Joshua's leadership had the opportunity to put the commandments into practice, but they certainly did not have the same opportunities for spiritual reflection as did their predecessors. Keeping his busy flock inspired was no doubt hard work for Joshua.

It seems, though, that Joshua's most difficult challenge came from a different quarter. Just prior to the conquest of Jericho we are told:

Once, when Joshua was near Jericho, he looked up and saw a man standing before him, drawn sword in hand. Joshua went up to him and asked him, "Are you one of us or of our enemies?" He replied, "No, I am captain of the LORD's host. Now I have come!" Joshua threw himself face down to the ground and, prostrating himself, said to him, "What does my lord command his servant?" The captain of the LORD's host answered Joshua, "Remove your sandals from your feet, for the place where you stand is holy." And Joshua did so. (Josh. 5:13–15)

Who was this "captain of the Lord's host"? On one level, he may be seen as the embodiment of an idea: "The LORD, the Warrior—LORD is His name!" (Exod. 15:3). He was a divine image reminding Joshua that "the LORD will battle for you; you hold your peace!" (14:14), a reflection of God's initial promise to Joshua, "The LORD your God is with you wherever you go" (Josh. 1:9). In the quiet before the storm, Joshua was reassured that God would support him and wage war for him. However, when Joshua utters the sentry's cry: "Are you friend or foe?" his question is not answered. The apparition is evasive, leaving the issue of his allegiance in animated suspension. He simply identifies himself—"No, I am captain of the LORD's host. Now I have come." The implication of this statement is, though I might not have appeared in the past, now I have indeed arrived. *Midrash Tanhuma* uses this hint to identify the angelic messenger.

"Behold I am sending an angel before you" (Exod. 23:20). . . . Moses replied: "If You intend to send an angel before me, I am not interested—rather, 'May the LORD travel in our midst!' " (Exod. 34:9). Consider the difference between earlier and later (generations). God said to Moses, "Behold I am sending an angel before you," and he replied, "I only want You." When Joshua the son of Nun saw the angel, he fell on his face, as it says, "Joshua threw himself on the ground and bowed." And he asked, "Are you one of us or of our enemies?" Rabbi Isaac asked, "What did the angel do when he heard [Joshua say] 'Are you one of us or of our enemies?' He started to shout . . . and said, 'NO! I am captain of the Lord's host. Now I have come! In fact, I came twice to (help) Israel settle the land. I am he, who came in the time of Moses your master, and he shunned me, and did not want me to accompany him, and now I have come.' " Joshua immediately fell down to the ground, and, prostrating himself, said to him, who Moses had shunned, "What does my lord command his servant?" (*Midrash Tanhuma, Mishpatim* 18)

Joshua was sent the angel that Moses had turned down. Moses demanded direct divine revelation and guidance, and God had conceded to his requests. However, while God compromised on His initial demand that an angel be appointed to lead Israel through the desert during Moses' lifetime, now that the moment had arrived for Joshua to bring them into the land, His will would be done. It was time for pragmatism, and the reasons that God had given Moses for the need for angelic intermediacy were compelling. "You are a stiff-necked people. If I were to go in your midst for one moment, I would destroy you" (Exod. 33:5). Joshua, who had come to master the art of the possible, recognized and accepted this reality. The Rabbinic assertion, "The face of Moses is like the sun, while the face of Joshua is like the moon" (B. BB 75a), is generally taken to mean that Joshua, the student, was merely a pale reflection of Moses the luminary. Perhaps this metaphor is not a quantitative judgment, but a qualitative appreciation of their respective leadership styles. Joshua did not need to be a blindingly bright star outshining all others. Just as he accommodated the priests leading the nation over the Jordan, he could accept the involvement of the angel in the conquest of the land.

Previously, the identity of this accompanying angel was left unspecified. We now learn that it was none other than an angelic version of Joshua. For who is the captain of the Lord's host if not Joshua himself? This comparison is certainly complimentary to Joshua: you are the terrestrial analogue of a holy angel. Don the mantle of holiness along with the accoutrements of war! However, the comparison is also a summons. It is as if God had held up a celestial mirror and asked Joshua to gaze within and respond to what he saw.

We now come to a critical point of connection between Moses and Joshua—who represent the past and future of the Israelites in their journey from slavery, through desert wandering, to conquest and settlement of land. Many images and messages might have occurred to Joshua as he stood before that nebulous figure. Indeed, Joshua asks: "What does my lord command his servant?"—in essence, asking himself what God expects from him at that fateful moment in the history

of Israel. In response, Joshua hears the angelic captain give him a curious directive: "Remove your shoes from your feet, for the place where
you stand is holy." It is not lost on the reader that what Joshua heard
was an echo of what his master Moses had heard many years before,
when standing before the burning bush. In his moment of uncertain-
ty on the eve of battle, Joshua was no doubt comforted to feel himself
following in the footsteps of Moses. We are taken aback, though, at
the abrupt end of the Joshua episode marked by that statement: Joshua
was told to remove his shoes, and he did so, obediently.

But was that all? L. Daniel Hawk has pointed out that the Joshua-
Moses parallelism raises expectations in the reader. When we read of
Joshua being told to remove his shoes, we expect what we experienced
with Moses: the divine charge coupled with strong assurances pointing to the imminent fulfillment of ancestral promises. After Moses
removed his shoes, he was then told of God's identity and His course
of action. The Almighty described what He had seen and heard of the
suffering of the slaves and of His intention to set them free and to
bring them to the "land of milk and honey." He appointed Moses and
continually reassured him that He would be with him. The Almighty
spared no details, informing Moses of the intransigence of Pharaoh,
the mighty wonders that He planned to use to force his hand, and the
abundant wealth with which the Children of Israel would leave Egypt.
And yet, in Joshua's case, we are simply told that he removed his shoes
as he had been commanded, and the story ends. This lacuna is startling. If the commander was sent to offer assurance, why didn't he do
for Joshua what the Lord had done for Moses? Surely, he and the
nation were in need of such moral support at that critical hour.

It is possible that the reason the exchange ended with Joshua
removing his shoes is simply that no more needed to be said. When
God appeared to Moses and told him that he was standing on sacred
ground, Moses was puzzled. What was holy about a pasture in the Sinai
Desert? The answer was that it was sanctified by the revelatory
appearance of God, by the fact that it was the site of Moses' initiation

into leadership, and by its later distinction as the place of the giving of the Torah. All this needed to be said, explained, and proclaimed. However, when Joshua was told that he was standing on holy ground, there was no question in his mind about the meaning of that statement. He stood, finally, on the soil of the Promised Land; its holiness was inherent and incontrovertible. "Remove your shoes from your feet, for the place where you stand is holy." Through these words, God assured him that he was walking on the path of Jewish heritage; and step by step he would lead the nation to destiny.

Standing on holy ground had yet an additional valence for Joshua, perhaps the most important of all. Joshua was about to engage in a war that would require painful moral and leadership choices. Lives would be lost, morale would wane, and the people would at times lose heart. It was not enough for Joshua to be the military leader of his people; he also had to be their inspiration, their anchor. He would need to stand his ground: And so he placed his feet on sacred soil, the cornerstone of national destiny, and thus was he prepared for war.

Indeed, for those living in the land, struggling to achieve their covenantal destiny in the face of mighty enemies, at every fateful crossroad the ultimate question—Who shall live and who shall die?—sends tremors through them and shakes the ground beneath their feet. This biblical episode filled my mind one Yom ha-Zikaron, Israel's memorial day for fallen soldiers. Every year at 11 o'clock, the bereaved families and friends gather in military cemeteries to commune with their departed ones. The rest of the nation participates in commemoration as well, as sirens throughout the land call all to observe two minutes of silence.

It was 10 minutes to 11 and I rushed outside to find my place among people before the siren went off; this contemplative moment is best appreciated in the community of others. The blast of the siren began, and a blanket of quiet fell over the land. In a country where words fly without respite, such silence is all the more resounding.

During that moment of inner reflection, I felt a strange and urgent need to take off my shoes. There I stood, between stone and sky, my bare feet touching earth soaked with the blood and tears of so many soldiers, wondering when the pain and suffering of our land would end. The direct contact with the contours of our historic terrain provided me with a modicum of consolation. It strengthened my commitment to continue to bear the legacy of the fallen and to sanctify their lives through building, planting, and growing.

> After the death of Moses the servant of the LORD, the LORD said to Joshua son of Nun, Moses' attendant . . . "Every spot on which your foot treads I give to you. . . . Be strong and resolute; do not be terrified or dismayed, for the LORD your God is with you wherever you go." (Josh. 1:1–9)

A version of the medieval composition *Midrash Petirat Moshe Rabbenu* (*Midrash Petirat Moshe Rabbenu* 1:115ff.) casts us back to the moment of the changing of the guard. This midrash describes how Moses took his last steps, accompanied by Joshua and an impressive entourage. As he ascended the mountain, Moses slowly divested himself of all others who had come along. Joshua, his last companion, clung to him like a shadow. Moses' final act illustrates how, despite the differences between them, when all was said and done, Joshua was the worthy successor who indeed filled Moses' shoes:

> All the people of Israel followed Moses until they reached Mount Abarim. He began to appease them, saying, "My sons, wait for me and I and the elders will go up. Perhaps it is not yet time for me to depart from the world." He went up the mountain, and when he was halfway to the top, he said to the elders, "You, too, wait for me here." He said to Eleazar, "Stay with the elders and Joshua will ascend with me." Moses and Joshua ascended. At length they reached the top of the mountain. Moses entrusted Joshua with Israel and with the study

and application of the Torah. And he said to Joshua, "Wait for me here." But Joshua did not accept this. When Moses saw that Joshua would not accept this, he dropped his shoes; while Joshua lingered to don them, Moses stole away.

Works Cited

Abrams, Judith Z. "Incorporating Christian Symbols into Judaism: The Case of *Midrash Eleh Ezkerah*." *CCAR Journal* 40 (1993): 11–20.

Auerbach, Erich. *Mimesis: The Representation of Reality in Western Literature*. Translated by Willard R. Trask. Princeton, NJ: Princeton University Press, 1969.

Ben-Noun, Louba. "Drinking Wine to Inebriation in Biblical Times." *Israel Journal of Psychiatry and Related Sciences* 39 (2002): 61–66.

Birnbaum, Philip. *Mahzor Ha-Shalem, High Holiday Prayer Book, Yom Kippur*. New York: Hebrew Publishing Company, 1988.

Bright, John. *A History of Israel*. Philadelphia: The Westminster Press, 1976.

Brueggemann, Walter. *The Land: Place as Gift, Promise and Challenge in Biblical Faith*. Philadelphia: Fortress Press, 1974.

Carmy, Shalom. "Destiny, Freedom, and the Logic of Petition." *Tradition* 24 (winter 1989): 17–37.

Des Pres, Terrence. *The Survivor: An Anatomy of Life in the Death Camps*. New York: Oxford University Press, 1976.

Elbaum, Dov. "Isaac: The Forgotten Patriarch." *Akdamot* 9 (2000): 131–141.

Fishbane, Michael. *The JPS Bible Commentary: Haftarot*. Philadelphia: Jewish Publication Society, 2002.

Fokkelman, J. P. *Narrative Art and Poetry in the Books of Samuel*. Assen, Netherlands: Van Gorcum, 1981, 1986, 1990.

Gellman, Yehudah. "Teshuva and Authenticity." *Tradition* 20 (fall 1982): 249–253.

ha-Cohen, Rabbi Zadok, of Lublin. *Peri Zaddik*. Jerusalem: Machon Misamchei Lev, 1999.

Halivni, David Weiss. *Revelation Restored: Divine Writ and Critical Responses*. Boulder, CO: Westview Press, 1997.

Hawk, L. Daniel. *Berit Olam: Studies in Hebrew Narrative and Poetry*. Collegeville, MN: Liturgical Press, 2000.

Herzl, Theodor. *The Complete Diaries of Theodor Herzl*. Edited by Raphael Patai; translated by Harry Zohn. New York: Herzl Press, 1960.

Heschel, Abraham Joshua. *Man Is Not Alone*. Philadelphia: Jewish Publication Society, 1951.

Heschel. Suzanne. "Prayer," *Moral Grandeur and Spiritual Audacity*. New York, 1945, 167–168.

ibn Yahya, Gedaliah ben Joseph. *"Asarah Harugei Malkhut."* In *Shalshelet Ha-Kabbalah*. Warsaw, 1881.

Jaffe, Rabbi Mordechai. *Levush ha-Tekhelet*. Prague, 1701.

Jellinek, Aharon. *Bet Ha-Midrasch*. Jerusalem: Vahrman, 1967.

Johnstone, William. *Chronicles*. Sheffield, England: Sheffield Academic Press, 1997.

Kook, Rabbi Abraham Isaac. *Seder Tefillah im Perush Olat Re'iyah*. Jerusalem: Mossad Ha-Rav Kook, 1983.

Lauterbach, Jacob Z. "Tashlik: A Study in Jewish Ceremonies." *HUCA XI*, 1936, 207–339.

Leibowitz, Nechama. *Iyyunim be-Sefer BeMidbar: Be-Ikvot Parshanenu ha-Rishonim ve-ha-Aharonim*. Jerusalem: Sifriat Elinor, 1960.

Leiman, Sid Z. *"Asarah Harugei Malkhut,"* 2000. West Side Tape #3543.

Levinson, Joshua. "Dialogical Reading in the Rabbinic Exegetical Narrative." *Poetics Today* 25 (2004): 497–528.

Levy, Bryna Jocheved. "Scripture Envisioned: The Bible Through the Eyes of Rembrandt." Available at www.jewishhistory.org. Commissioned by George S. Blumenthal and the Center for Online Judaic Studies, 2003.

———. "Visions and Voices: Women Creating Jewish Life Through the Ages." Available at www.visonsvoices.org. Commissioned by George S. Blumenthal and the Center for Online Judaic Studies, 2007.

Luzzatto, Samuel David. *Perush Shadal al Hamishah Humeshei Torah.* Tel Aviv: Dvir, 1966.

Macalister, R. A. S. *Excavations of Gezer.* London: John Murry, 1912.

Medini, Rabbi Haim Hezkiah. *Sedei Hemed.* Jerusalem, 1979.

Menn, Esther. "Praying King and Sanctuary of Prayer. Part II: David's Deferment and the Temple's Dedication in Rabbinic Psalms Commentary (*Midrash Tehillim*)." *Journal of Jewish Stud*ies 53 (fall 2002): 298–323.

Midrash Asarah Harugei Malkhut. In Aharon Jellinek, ed., *Bet ha-Midrasch,* 6:19. Jerusalem: Vahrman, 1853; reprinted 1967.

Midrash Eleh Ezkerah. In Aharon Jellinek, ed., *Bet ha-Midrasch,* 2:64. Jerusalem: Vahrman, 1853; reprinted 1967.

Midrash Petirat Moshe Rabbenu. In Aharon Jellinek, ed., *Bet ha-Midrasch,* 1:115ff. Jerusalem: Vahrman, 1853; reprinted 1967.

Muffs, Yochanan. "Between Law and Mercy: The Prayer of Prophets." In *Torah Nidreshet,* edited by Avraham Shapira. Tel Aviv: Am Oved, 1984.

Och, Bernard. "Jacob at Bethel and Penuel: The Polarity of Divine Encounter." *Judaism* 42 (1993): 164–176.

Rosenfield, Abraham, trans. *Tisha B'Av Compendium: Including Kinot for the Ninth of Av.* New York: Judaic Press, 1965.

Sarna, Nahum M. *The JPS Torah Commentary: Genesis.* Philadelphia: Jewish Publication Society, 1989.

Seidman, Rabbi Aaron Bear. "In Search." *Numbered Days* (March 7, 1972): 39.

The Septuagint with Apocrypha: Greek and English. Edited by Lancelot C. Brenton. Peabody, MA: Hendrickson Publishers, Inc., 1986.

Soloveitchik, Rabbi Joseph B. "Exaltation of God and Redeeming the Aesthetic." In *Worship of the Heart,* edited by Shalom Carmy. Hoboken, NJ: KTAV, 2003.

Steinmetz, Devora. "Vineyard, Farm, and Garden: The Drunkenness of Noah in the Context of Primeval History." *Journal of Biblical Literature* 113 (summer 1994): 193–207.

Stökl Ben Ezra, Daniel. *The Impact of Yom Kippur on Early Christianity: The Day of Atonement from the Second Temple to the Fifth Century.* Tübingen, Germany: Mohr Siebeck, 2003.

Wyschograd, Edith. "Memory, History, Revelation: Writing the Dead Other." In *Memory and History in Christianity and Judaism,* edited by Michael A. Signer, 19–34. Notre Dame, IN: University of Notre Dame Press, 2001.

Zakovitch, Yair. *David: MiRoeh le-Mashiah.* Jerusalem: Yad Ben Zvi, 1995.

www.ingramcontent.com/pod-product-compliance
Lightning Source LLC
Chambersburg PA
CBHW030939150426
42812CB00064B/3071/J